Lusofonia and Its Futures

Tagus Press
Center for Portuguese Studies and Culture
University of Massachusetts Dartmouth
Portuguese Literary & Cultural Studies (PLCS) 25

PREVIOUS ISSUES

Fronteiras/Borders (PLCS 1)
Edited by Victor J. Mendes, Paulo de Medeiros, and José N. Ornelas

Lídia Jorge in other words / por outras palavras (PLCS 2)
Edited by Cláudia Pazos Alonso

Pessoa's Alberto Caeiro (PLCS 3)
Edited by Victor J. Mendes

2001 Brazil: A Revisionary History of Brazilian Literature and Culture (PLCS 4/5)
Edited by João Cezar de Castro Rocha

On Saramago (PLCS 6)
Edited by Anna Klobucka

A Repertoire of Contemporary Portuguese Poetry (PLCS 7)
Edited by Victor J. Mendes

Cape Verde: Language, Literature & Music (PLCS 8)
Edited by Ana Mafalda Leite

Post-Imperial Camões (PLCS 9)
Edited by João R. Figueiredo

Reevaluating Mozambique (PLCS 10)
Edited by Phillip Rothwell

Vitorino Nemésio and the Azores (PLCS 11)
Edited by Francisco Cota Fagundes

The Other Nineteenth Century (PLCS 12)
Edited by Kathryn M. Sanchez

The Author as Plagiarist—The Case of Machado de Assis (PLCS 13/14)
Edited by João Cezar de Castro Rocha

Remembering Angola (PLCS 15/16)
Edited by Phillip Rothwell

Parts of Asia (PLCS 17/18)
Edited by Cristiana Bastos

Facts and Fictions of António Lobo Antunes (PLCS 19/20)
Edited by Victor K. Mendes

Garrett's Travels *Revisited* (PLCS 21/22)
Edited by Victor K. Mendes and Valéria M. Souza

Economies of Relation: Money and Personalism in the Lusophone World (PLCS 23/24)
Edited by Roger Sansi

Portuguese Literary & Cultural Studies is a multilingual interdisciplinary peer-reviewed journal published semi-annually by Tagus Press in the Center for Portuguese Studies and Culture at the University of Massachusetts Dartmouth. The journal addresses the literatures and cultures of the diverse communities of the Portuguese-speaking world in terms of critical and theoretical approaches.

Manuscript Policy

Portuguese Literary & Cultural Studies welcomes submission of original and unpublished manuscripts in English, Portuguese, or Spanish appropriate to the goals of the journal. Manuscripts should be in accordance with the MLA *Style Manual and Guide to Scholarly Publishing* (latest version) with parenthetical documentation and a list of Works Cited. The author is responsible for the accuracy of all quotations, titles, names, and dates. Font and sizes as close as possible to the style of the previous issue of PLCS should be used throughout the text. All of the information must be in the same language (e.g., abstract, body of the article, bio-blurb). Updated guidelines are available at http://www.portstudies.umassd.edu/plcs/editor.htm. PLCS encourages submission of manuscripts in the form of a single attached MS Word document. Please send submissions to João Cezar de Castro Rocha, Editor in Chief, at jccr123@yahoo.com.br.

PORTUGUESE LITERARY & CULTURAL STUDIES 25

Lusofonia and Its Futures

Edited by JOÃO CEZAR DE CASTRO ROCHA

Tagus Press UMASS DARTMOUTH / DARTMOUTH, MASSACHUSETTS

Portuguese Literary & Cultural Studies 25
Tagus Press at UMass Dartmouth
www.portstudies.umassd.edu

Manufactured in the United States of America
Managing Editor: Mario Pereira
Copyedited by Peter Fong
Designed by Richard Hendel
Typeset in Quadraat and The Sans by Integrated Publishing Solutions

Tagus Press books are produced and distributed for Tagus Press
by University Press of New England, which is a member of the Green Press Initiative.
The paper used in this book meets their minimum requirement for recycled paper.

For all inquiries, please contact:
Tagus Press at UMass Dartmouth
Center for Portuguese Studies and Culture
285 Old Westport Road
North Dartmouth MA 02747-2300
Tel. 508-999-8255
Fax 508-999-9272
www.portstudies.umassd.edu

Library of Congress Cataloging-in-Publication Data
Lusofonia and its futures / edited by João Cezar de Castro Rocha.
pages cm.—(Portuguese literary & cultural studies; 25)
ISBN 978-1-933227-43-6 (pbk.: alk. paper)
1. Portuguese-speaking countries—Civilization. 2. Portuguese-speaking countries—Intellectual life. 3. Portuguese language—Social aspects—Portuguese-speaking countries. 4. Portuguese language—Political aspects— Portuguese-speaking countries. 5. Language policy— Portuguese-speaking countries. 6. Portuguese literature—History and criticism. 7. Portugal—Colonies. I. Rocha, João Cezar de Castro.
DP534.5L88 2013
909′.097569—dc23

2013008854

5 4 3 2 1

Contents

JOÃO CEZAR DE CASTRO ROCHA

Introduction
Lusofonia—A Concept and Its Discontents

A Concept Is a Concept Is a Concept

A short introduction is not the proper place for a thorough theoretical discussion on the concept of Lusofonia. It is a complex multilayered concept—with linguistic, political, historical, and multi-secular cultural implications—and the dossier of articles under *Lusofonia and Its Futures* deals specifically with its history and theorization. I therefore refer the reader interested in grasping the current debates on the issue to the groundbreaking collection of essays gathered here, as they present an up-to-date rewriting of the boundaries of the lusophone universe.[1]

Moreover, it is important to remember that several other issues of *Portuguese Literary & Cultural Studies* have already discussed specific aspects of Lusofonia, including substantial case studies of particular contexts. I have in mind volumes 8 (*Cape Verde: Language, Literature & Music*), 10 (*Reevaluating Mozambique*), 11 (*Vitorino Nemésio and the Azores*), 15/16 (*Remembering Angola*), and 17/18 (*Parts of Asia*).[2] As a matter of fact, the editorial guidelines of *Portuguese Literary & Cultural Studies* have always been committed to rendering visible the plurality underlying the notion of Lusofonia. In this sense, the present issue provides a unique opportunity to propose a theoretical gaze at the work accomplished by the journal over the past fifteen years.

A wave of publications in English has been devoted to the topic, constituting a refreshing look at the field itself.[3] Two dominant tendencies can already be discerned, namely, deliberate efforts to revise the history as well as the concept of Lusofonia within the broader context of the world-system, as conceptualized by Immanuel Wallerstein,[4] and within the contemporary debates over globalization and its political and cultural consequences. These are relevant theoretical moves. Instead of being understood in isolation, as an autonomous historical force, Lusofonia is being read as an outcome of a historical and ideological movement that encompasses and at the same time surpasses the linguistic boundaries of any given linguistic territory. This vantage point prompts the overcoming of any essentialist concern, once what is privileged is the relational nature of the lusophone world, which can be better seized within a comparative framework. If in José Saramago's novel, *The Stone Raft*,[5] Portugal is literally set adrift from Europe, Lusofonia is a concept metaphorically adrift, and if any anchorage is to be found, it will have to be through a complex triangular structure, always implying a circuit (and sometimes a short circuit) of uncertain exchanges and reciprocal gazes. The insularity that fostered the search for "authentic" forms of Lusofonia is replaced by a dialogical model, in which the very notion of authenticity loses its former significance.

A telling example of the first approach—understanding the lusophone world within the dynamics of the world-system—is Boaventura de Sousa Santos's thought-provoking essay "Between Prospero and Caliban: Colonialism, Postcolonialism, and Inter-identity." As the author states, "The aim of this essay is to further ongoing research on identity processes in the time-space of the Portuguese language. A vast, multi-secular contact zone is implied involving the Portuguese people and other peoples of America, Asia, and Africa." His innovative viewpoint can only be unfolded within the acknowledgment of the semiperipheral position occupied by the Portuguese empire in the world-system, which brought forth "an intermediate economic development and a position of intermediation between the center and the periphery of the world economy."[6] It is, so to speak, a truth universally acknowledged that triangular inter-relations of all sorts are the leitmotif of Lusofonia.

Fernando Arenas's *Lusophone Africa: Beyond Independence* is the most recent and compelling example of the second tendency, underscoring the potential relationships between lusophone issues and contemporary approaches developed in the fields of literary, cultural, and anthropological studies. The author provides a lucid summary of his project: "One of the primary objectives of *Lusophone Africa: Beyond Independence* is to stress the importance of carefully situating discussions on globalization and postcolonialism within the specific historical, geopolitical and cultural contexts of given nation-states, regions, and/or linguistic communities."[7] One of the main concepts of the theoretical framework proposed by Arenas is the notion of "Lusophone transatlantic matrix,"[8] which allows him to establish a groundbreaking dialogue among Portugal, Brazil, and African nations based on a dialectical oscillation between the global and the local, the self and the other. Luiz Felipe de Alencastro had already shown how these triangular connections were crucial to the economic and cultural development of Brazil;[9] Arenas enlarges the scope of the reflection, providing analyses of case studies that shall become important references in the field. As far as the history of the diplomatic and cultural relationship of Brazil with the independent African lusophone countries is concerned, Jerry Dávila has produced a lucid account in *Hotel Trópico: Brazil and the Challenge of African Decolonization, 1950–1980*. Once more, his research relies on the seemingly inescapable triangularity that determines the strength as well as the dilemmas of the lusophone worldview.[10]

In light of recent publications and innovative approaches, *Lusofonia and its Futures* aims at contributing to this increase in dialogue. A succinct reflection on its contents is necessary in order to encompass the diversity of viewpoints conveyed by its contributors.

Discontent and Necessity

Traditionally, Lusofonia has been conceived as the historical outcome of the cultural identity forged among speakers of Portuguese. In a different context, and with a different objective, Oswald de Andrade dreamed of an anthropophagic civilization in which the common denominator would be a strategic gesture rather than an essential feature: "Cannibalism alone unites us. Socially. Economically. Philosophically."[11] By the same token, according to this traditional perspective, Lusofonia would refer to the act of speaking the "same" language across various countries and cultures. Thus understood, the concept seems to describe an objective circumstance; after all, Portuguese is the official language of eight countries: Angola, Brazil, Cape Verde, Guinea-Bissau, Mozambique, Portugal, São Tomé and Príncipe, and East Timor. And this list, for instance, does not include Macau, regions in Africa, and areas in India where the idiom of Camões is also present. It is no surprise then that Portuguese ranks fifth among spoken languages and among those used on the Internet: approximately 270 million persons employ the language daily. Finally, the creation of the Comunidade dos Países de Língua Portuguesa (CPLP) in 1996 was aimed precisely at fostering this alleged cultural unity, grounded upon the usage of Portuguese.[12]

This neutral description, however, does not allow for much-needed understandings of the plurality and, above all, the contradictions that underlie the concept. This issue of *Portuguese Literary & Cultural Studies* emphasizes a critical reappraisal of the history of Lusofonia, stressing its polemical meanings and its ideological resonances. The contributors to *Lusofonia and Its Futures* have assumed the task of turning the concept literally upside down. Their essays evoke

Reinhart Koselleck's reflection on the perception of time in moments of epistemological crisis, when it is not granted that the experiences of past and present can be aligned, much less properly interpreted. In hermeneutic terms, the "horizon of expectation" concerning Lusofonia does not look particularly promising nowadays, for it has become an overcharged word, with a long and sometimes distressing history. Indeed, the title of this issue could easily have been rewritten as "Lusofonia and Its Futures Past."[13]

In a nutshell, if we are to rescue a potential commonality promised by the usage of Portuguese, the common ground cannot be determined by a neutral image of a "natural" speech act; rather, it must be established by a collective effort toward a new understanding of the political and epistemological implications of sharing a language initially imposed as an intrinsic part of a colonial enterprise. We are not referring to an Adamic experience of naming a brave new world, but to a historical process that goes hand in hand with the suppression of alternative languages and worldviews. Antonio de Nebrija, in the preface to his *Gramática de la lengua española*, printed in 1492, rendered this dimension with unmistakable clarity. In his plain words, "siempre la lengua fue compañera del imperio" (language has always been the companion of Empire).

Miguel Tamen has voiced this misapprehension with great eloquence. According to his remarks, the very idea of Lusofonia has to be called into question because it "corresponds historically to a kind of liberal colonialism, the idea that with the disappearance of the Portuguese Empire, it might be possible to maintain its spiritual substitute." This notion would have enabled the postulation of a "Portuguese exceptionalism, the idea that Portuguese are different from anyone else."[14] The recent scholarship on Lusofonia precisely rejects any sort of exceptionalism, which cannot but reiterate outmoded essentialist assumptions. An emphasis on comparative approaches may then be considered an academic as well as a political statement.

This is the main contribution of the essays assembled in this issue of *Portuguese Literary & Cultural Studies*. Lusofonia can only become an important conceptual tool if, first and foremost, we fully acknowledge that, as in the case of Sigmund Freud's analysis of the civilizing process, it is paired with a corresponding notion. In other words, "Lusofonia and Its Discontents" should be the proper motto for our reflections on the topic.

However, in order to develop the analogy, Freud's notion of the necessary discontent produced by the civilizing process should be grasped in its complexity.

It is not simply a nuisance that in better circumstances could be circumvented toward a happier way of life. The discontent is intrinsically associated with the fact that, by merely living in society, one is obliged to measure the fruition of his desires according to their consequences upon others: measure for measure seems to be the Freudian law of desire. It is not a matter of either/or, but rather a question of simultaneously embracing and not embracing Lusofonia; above all, it is a matter of learning to turn this paradox into a productive machine for thinking and creating.

There is a double bind that constitutes the lusophone worldview. As a result, in order to renew our understanding of the concept of Lusofonia, a reading of Gregory Bateson's work may be as relevant as a discussion of the latest theoretical trends.[15] Or we may think of Paul Gilroy's usage of the notion of "double consciousness."[16] In both cases, the only way to deal with the difficulties created by the inextricable ambiguity of the predicament implied by the notion of Lusofonia is precisely to talk about it, to translate it into a theoretical discourse.

After all, it is not the language, alone, that unites us, but a critical gaze towards its complex history, plural presents, and plural possibilities.

About This Volume

The essays gathered in this issue systematically bring to the fore the diversity of the usages of Portuguese language, along with the different appropriations of its heritage in various cultural contexts.

Benjamin Abdala proposes a keen reflection on the limits as well as the possibilities of cultural flows and exchanges—trademarks of globalization. However, he keeps one eye open for the political implications of these movements; after all, they keep on being asymmetrical, faithfully obeying the current political hegemony. Abdala's article, therefore, critically unveils the foundations of contemporary lusophone connections: "Supranational community relations today are ties of a society that tends to organize itself into networks. In relation to Portuguese-speaking countries, these linguistic and cultural ties were formed through a common historical experience associated with the colonial system."

Bethania Mariani's essay vigorously relies on the case study of Mozambique in order to scrutinize the unavoidable exclusions that ground the formation of nation-states. In a famous lecture, Ernst Renan recalled that the establishment of modern nations was only possible through a methodic act of forgetting the conflicts of the national past, always tainted by "deeds of violence."[17] Mariani focuses on a paradox typical of Lusofonia: "Portuguese, like all languages, exists in relation to other languages, and it is precisely this aspect that the term 'Lusofonia' insists on silencing in multilingual countries, especially when it involves the long historical route that ranges from colonization to independence movements." Mariani's article, on the contrary, gives voice to the contentious encounters underlying the idealized notion of Lusofonia.

Christopher Larkosh is concerned with the Portuguese-American experience, although his essay also touches upon other aspects of Lusofonia as well. Larkosh offers the reader a multilayered text, fusing academic reflection with personal memoir. He wishes "to reexamine the dynamics of literary resonance, not only in the works of two contemporary Portuguese-American authors, Katherine Vaz and Frank X. Gaspar, but also across the sites and common places of lived experience in southeastern Massachusetts, the place from which I reconstitute my own encounter with the Portuguese language."

Luís Madureira's contribution has a perfectly descriptive title: "Lusofonia: From Infancy to Necrology." Indeed, he manages to establish a complex link between his personal experience and the vicissitudes of the lusophone worldview, mediated by a solid knowledge of its history. Moreover, Madureira produces a disquieting mapping out of Lusofonia, stressing the ambiguity of its predicament, grounded, as we now know, on a double-bind structure. As he states: "the history of the Portuguese language in Africa has been ambivalent. Its violent inception notwithstanding, Portuguese played a significant role in the liberation movements, not only in mobilizing and politicizing, [but also in] building a 'national culture' across ethnolinguistic lines."

Michelly Carvalho and Rosa Cabecinhas have conducted research on the high-voltage controversies concerning the orthographic agreement signed on 12 October 1990[18] and currently being implemented, although not without resistance. Their article provides evidence that, more than ever in its multifaceted history, the traditional concept of Lusofonia demands a radical rethinking of its assumptions. An assertion of the supposed commonality of language is no longer a necessary cause to sustain its claims.

Vincent Barletta's essay performs a keen deconstruction of the connection between Portuguese language and Portuguese empire. He does so by returning to the empire's origins in order to denounce even more poignantly the illusions drawn in the ideological promise of an alleged "Mapa Rosa." As Barletta clarifies, it "was a nineteenth-century document that represented Portugal's claim to sovereignty over Angola, Mozambique, and the wide strip of land between the two (modern-day Malawi, Zambia, and Zimbabwe). The Portuguese government discarded the Pink Map in 1890, in the wake of a British ultimatum that laid claim to the territory between Angola and Mozambique." This ultimatum renders explicit the semiperipheral status of the Portuguese colonial empire, even when it was at its peak. Its decline, therefore, does not represent an adverse historical moment, but the very "fado" of this predicament, properly recalling the simultaneity of both "chaos and splendor," as has been suggested by the uncompromising Eduardo Lourenço.[19]

This notion is particularly relevant to the set of articles dedicated to a complex and fascinating case study, "Inside/Outside Lusofonia: The Case of Goa." Joana Passos, Sandra Ataíde Lobo, Constantino Xavier, and Duarte Drumond Braga raise a disquieting albeit indispensable question: If, in spite of its impressive numbers, Portuguese has never been a hegemonic language, then how should one think of a peripheral experience within a semiperipheral circumstance? The double-bind structure of the lusophone worldview comes to a paroxysm: this is exactly the case of Goa within the world of Lusofonia. In terms rendered well known by Gilles Deleuze and Felix Guattari, how to theorize on a minority expression when it takes place within an already minor language?[20] The theoretical potential of these article-manifestoes deserves to be further developed.

For instance, a current cinematographic and literary project seems to take full advantage of this possibility. In *Nada tenho de meu* (I Have Nothing of My Own), a title inspired by a sentence extracted from one of Camilo Pessanha's letters, Miguel Gonçalves Mendes, a Portuguese moviemaker, Tatiana Salem Levy, a writer born in Portugal and raised in Brazil, and João Paulo Cuenca, a contemporary Brazilian author, travel together to the Far East.[21] One of their destinations is Macau, and some of the best moments of the project are derived from the surprise of finding oneself immersed in the repetition of the "same" language and yet surrounded by radical differences in historical and cultural environment.[22]

As the reader may now appreciate, *Lusofonia and Its Futures* provides sufficient food for thought concerning recent discussions of the concept. At the same time, however, *Portuguese Literary & Cultural Studies* is also composed of three other permanent sections—Essays, Reviews, and Fiction.

In the Essays section, Sandra Guardini Teixeira Vasconcelos, the foremost Latin American specialist on the phenomenon of the rise of the novel, studies the presence of the British novel in nineteenth-century Brazilian literature; her essay represents the most accurate research yet carried out on the topic. Walnice Nogueira Galvão offers a refined and comprehensive analysis of the reception of Fernando Pessoa in Brazil.

In Reviews, Greg Mullins provides an insightful reading of *The Book of Emotions*, a novel by one of the most important Brazilian contemporary authors, João Almino, whose growing international accolades have stimulated the translation of his work into several languages. Pedro Meira Monteiro, a leading scholar of Brazilian and contemporary literature, dissects with great acumen the work of José Miguel Wisnik, a renowned musician and powerful thinker. As part of a promising work-in-progress, Richard Simas initiates a careful interpretation of the fictional universe of Gonçalo M. Tavares, one of the most celebrated writers of the new Portuguese generation. Sandra Guerreiro Dias puts forward a well-informed and original discussion of Lídia Jorge's *A noite das mulheres cantoras*. Tania Martuscelli clarifies the importance of Márcia Valéria Zamboni Gobbi's critical work on the presence of myth and parody in the shaping of contemporary Portuguese literature.

Last but not least, we introduce a new section—Fiction and Interview—as part of our endeavor to create a venue for the translation of fictional works originally written in Portuguese. This initiative should energize *Portuguese Literary & Cultural Studies* by bringing its readers a sense of the different ways in which the language is currently being experienced across the lusophone world. Repetition *and* difference will be our compass in this enterprise. We welcome submissions from writers as well as from translators and scholars interested in promoting contemporary authors. It goes without saying that we also encourage the submission of new translations of classical texts. Ideally, this section should become an open forum for the development of linguistic experiences, including authorial comments on their specific literary craftsmanship.

The new section is inaugurated by the witty reflections of Brazilian author Evando Nascimento, in which literature engages actively with the memories of a personal and imaginary library. Millicent Borges Accardi contributes with an enlightening interview with the Portuguese author Jacinto Lucas Pires, whose story "L" is also included here. Finally, we present the first of Brazilian writer

Mario Araujo's short stories to be translated into English, "The Extreme Hour," an award-winning narrative by a new voice.

Portuguese Literary & Cultural Studies owes its existence and continuity over the past fifteen years to the indefatigable work of Victor K. Mendes. Thanks to his commitment, vision, and leadership, the journal now arrives at issue number 25. Both Frank F. Sousa, director and publisher of the Center for Portuguese Studies at the University of Massachusetts Dartmouth, and myself, the current editor in chief of *Portuguese Literary & Cultural Studies*, wish to acknowledge Victor's achievements. *Lusofonia and Its Futures* is the first volume to be published in this new phase. We hope to honor the tradition he initiated.

NOTES

1. In order to avoid unnecessary although predictable misunderstandings, I resort to a recent and straightforward definition: "The term 'Lusophone' is used analogously to the terms 'Anglophone' and 'Francophone' (i.e., the community of nations that share the same language, in this case, Portuguese). . . . [T]he prefix 'Luso' comes from Lusus, the mythical founder of the Roman province of Lusitania (the westernmost territory of the Iberian peninsula), where modern Portugal is situated. 'Luso' today indicates 'things' Portuguese or related to the Portuguese language. In spite of its possible neocolonial connotations, 'Lusophone' constitutes the most practical term available to refer to Portuguese-speaking nations." Fernando Arenas, *Lusophone Africa: Beyond Independence* (University of Minnesota Press, 2011), p. 205.

2. Ana Mafalda Leite was guest editor of *Cape Verde: Language, Literature & Music*; Phillip Rothwell of *Reevaluating Mozambique* and *Remembering Angola*; Francisco Cota Fagundes of *Vitorino Nemésio and the Azores*; and Cristiana Bastos of *Parts of Asia*.

3. As a matter of fact, the increasing number of publications, in English, renders any bibliographical list necessarily a tentative effort, which will always fall short even before it begins. Let me therefore only mention a few recent titles, with no intention to exhaust the field or to establish an artificial hierarchy among them. *A History of Postcolonial Lusophone Africa* (Indiana University Press, 2002) edited by Patrick Chabal, David Birmingham, Joshua Forrest, and Malyn Newitt, offers a comprehensive historical account of the dilemmas that still haunt the world of Lusofonia. As early as 1996, Patrick Chabal had already edited *The Post-Colonial Literature of Lusophone Africa* (Northwestern University Press, 1996). Susan Canty Quinlan and Fernando Arenas edited *Lusosex: Gender and Sexuality in the Portuguese-Speaking World* (University of Minnesota Press, 2002), aiming at rendering lusophone studies properly contemporary to some of the most recent theoretical

approaches in literary and cultural studies. As the editors stress in their introduction: "Since the 1980s in the English speaking-world, particularly in the United States, there has been an explosion of studies in the humanities, most notably in the field of literary and cultural studies, that place sexuality at the center of their analyses of human subjectivity in ancient and modern societies, as well as within national cultures" (p. xiii). In *Mother Africa, Father Marx: Women's Writing of Mozambique, 1948–2002* (Bucknell University Press, 2007), Hilary Owen added a new layer to the discussion by bringing to the fore the gender issue in the building of new lusophone nations after independence, with a specific analysis of Mozambique's literary and cultural history. In the same year, Nancy Priscilla Naro, Roger Sansi-Roca, and David Treece edited *Cultures of the Lusophone Black Atlantic* (Palgrave Macmillan, 2007). This collection of essays proposed to establish an innovative and comparative approach with Paul Gilroy's already classical study *The Black Atlantic: Modernity and Double Consciousness* (Verso, 1993). The main goal of the editors was to "suspend for a moment our rigid and dogmatic dichotomies between nations, civilizations, Us and Them, Europe and Africa, the West and the Rest" (p. 1). Also in 2007, Paulo de Medeiros edited an insightful collection of essays, *Postcolonial Theory and Lusophone Literatures* (Portuguese Studies Center, Universiteit Utrecht, 2007). His introduction to that volume, "Turning Points: An Introduction to Postcolonial Theory and Lusophone Literatures" (pp. 1–7), attempts to put Lusofonia in dialogue with contemporary cultural critique. There is, finally, a tendency to underscore the comparative nature of literary and cultural studies; indeed, it is becoming common to bring together lusophone and Hispanic historical experiences as well as to broaden the scope of analysis through the incorporation of cultural artifacts not exclusively oriented to the reading of texts. For instance, see the volume edited by Patricia O'Byrne, Gabrielle Carty, and Niamh Thornton, *Transcultural Encounters Amongst Women: Redrawing Boundaries in Hispanic and Lusophone Art, Literature and Film* (Cambridge Scholars Publishing, 2010). It is also worth mentioning the book edited by Lisa Shaw, Rob Stone, and Ian Biddle: *Screening Songs in Hispanic and Lusophone Cinema* (Manchester University Press, 2012).

4. The best introduction to Immanuel Wallerstein's world-system approach was provided by himself in *World-Systems Analysis: An Introduction* (Duke University Press, 2004).

5. I am referring to José Saramago's novel *A Jangada de Pedra*, published in 1986. It was published in English in 1996 as *The Stone Raft*, translated by Giovanni Pontiero.

6. Boaventura de Sousa Santos, "Between Prospero and Caliban: Colonialism, Postcolonialism, and Inter-identity," *Luso-Brazilian Review* 39.2 (2002): 9. An engaging reading of Sousa Santos's perspective is provided by Ana Paula Ferreira, "Specificity without Exceptionalism: Towards a Critical Lusophone Postcoloniality," in Paulo de Medeiros (ed.), *Postcolonial Theory and Lusophone Literatures* (Portuguese Studies Center, Universiteit Utrecht, 2007), p. 21–40.

7. Fernando Arenas, *Lusophone Africa*, pp. xxxvii–xxxviii.

8. "The nations composing the 'Lusophone transatlantic matrix' have been interconnected for several centuries through the experience of Portuguese colonialism and the slave trade that simultaneously involved Portugal, various regions of West, Central and East Africa, and colonial as well as independent Brazil. These historical phenomena and actors were key to the rise of Western modernity during the early stages of globalization." Ibid., p. 2.

9. Luiz Felipe de Alencastro, *O Trato dos Viventes: Formação do Brasil no Atlântico Sul, Séculos XVI e XVII* (Companhia das Letras, 2000). This important book will soon be published by Duke University Press. There is an article already available in English on the topic: "The Economic Network of Portugal's Atlantic World," in Francisco Bethencourt and Diogo Ramada Curto (eds.), *Portuguese Oceanic Expansion, 1400–1800* (Cambridge University Press, 2007), pp. 109–37. Let me recall that Luiz Felipe de Alencastro will be the guest editor of issue 27 of *Portuguese Literary & Cultural Studies*, which is dedicated to "The South Atlantic, Past and Present."

10. "In the end Brazilian diplomats and policymakers saw Africa through what Dzidzienyo calls the 'triangular mirror.' These Brazilians saw their actions with regard to Africa as reflecting upon Brazil's economic development and its system of race relations." Jerry Dávila, *Hotel Trópico: Brazil and the Challenge of African Decolonization, 1950–1980* (Duke University Press, 2010), p. 8.

11. Oswald de Andrade, "Cannibalist Manifesto," translated by Leslie Bary, *Latin American Literary Review* 19.38 (1991): 38. The original reads: "Só a antropofagia nos une. Socialmente. Economicamente. Filosoficamente." Oswald de Andrade, "Manifesto Antropófago," *A utopia antropofágica / Oswald de Andrade—Obras Completas*, 2nd ed. (Globo, 1995), p. 47.

12. For a history of the CPLP see its official Web site at www.cplp.org/id-45.aspx.

13. I am referring to Reinhart Koselleck's classic book *Futures Past: On the Semantics of Historical Time*, translated by Keith Tribe (Columbia University Press, 2004).

14. Nelson Pereira, "Miguel Tamen: 'A lusofonia é uma espécie de colonialismo de esquerda,'" *iOnline*, 24 April 2012. Interview available online at www.ionline.pt/portugal/miguel-tamen-lusofonia-uma-especie-colonialismo-esquerda.

15. I refer specifically to Bateson's key concept of the double bind in "Toward a Theory of Schizophrenia," *Steps to an Ecology of Mind* (The University of Chicago Press, 2000), pp. 201–27.

16. "Striving to be both European and black requires some specific forms of double consciousness. By saying this I do not mean to suggest that taking on either or both of these unfinished identities necessarily exhausts the subjective resources of any particular identity." Paul Gilroy, *The Black Atlantic: Modernity and Double Consciousness* (Verso, 1993), p. 1.

17. The whole quote is as follows: "Forgetting, I would even go so far as to say historical error, is a crucial factor in the creation of a nation, which is why progress in histori-

cal studies often constitutes a danger for [the principle] of nationality. Indeed historical enquiry brings to light deeds of violence which took place at the origin of all political formations, even of those whose consequences have been altogether beneficial." Ernst Renan, "What is a Nation?" in Hommi Bhabha (ed.), *Nation and Narration* (Routledge, 1990), p. 11.

18. The "Acordo Ortográfico da Língua Portuguesa" was signed by the representatives of seven countries: Angola, Brazil, Cape Verde, Guinea-Bissau, Mozambique, Portugal, and São Tomé and Príncipe.

19. Eduardo Lourenço, "Chaos and Splendor," in *Chaos and Splendor & Other Essays*, edited by Carlos Veloso (Center for Portuguese Studies and Cultures, University of Massachusetts Dartmouth, 2002), pp. 25–29. It is important to note that, in this essay, the author is not characterizing Portuguese culture, but proposing a general reflection on the topic.

20. I am actually radicalizing the concept. In the authors' definition: "A minor literature doesn't come from a minor language; it is rather that which a minority constructs within a major language." Gilles Deleuze and Felix Guattari, *Kafka: Towards a Minor Literature*, translated by Dana Polan (University of Minnesota Press, 1986), p. 16.

21. It is worth noting the peculiarity of the creators of the project: on the one hand, a Portuguese; on the other, a Brazilian; in between, a Brazilian contemporary author, born in Portugal. The in-betweenness, as a matter of fact, is the main motive of *Nada tenho de meu*. The category of in-betweenness is inspired by the work of Silviano Santiago, an acclaimed Brazilian writer and literary critic. See Silviano Santiago, *The Space In-Between: Essays on Latin American Culture*, edited by Ana Lucia Gazzola, translated by Tom Burns and Gareth Williams (Duke University Press, 2002).

22. A Web site of the project is available at http://canalbrasil.globo.com/programas/nada-tenho-de-meu/materias/nada-tenho-de-meu.html.

Lusofonia and Its Futures

BENJAMIN ABDALA JUNIOR
Translated by Alexander R. Luz

Asymmetric Cultural Flows and Community Reflections

ABSTRACT: Analysis of the rise of cultural communitarianism, as it stands before the international political covenantal rearrangement that originated in the 2008 financial crash. At the Brazilian locus of enunciation, two main connections arise from the literary and cultural standpoint: with Portuguese-speaking countries and with Ibero-American ones. Such formulations do not restrict policies of cooperation and solidarity, because, according to the author, the world is increasingly configured as a place of multiple borders and plural identities.

KEYWORDS: management of difference, cultural communitarianism, cultural hybridity, Ibero-African-America.

Supranational community relations today are ties of a society that tends to organize itself into networks. In relation to Portuguese-speaking countries, these linguistic and cultural ties were formed through a common historical experience associated with the colonial system. The first settlers of Latin America came from the region that the Arabs called Al-Andalus. The name Algarve comes from *al-Gharb al-Andalus* (Andalusia West), which currently covers Algarve and low Alentejo. The greatest part of Lisbon's population in the age of discovery was of Moorish origin. These were culturally hybrid regions, where many cultures from the Mediterranean basin converged. Extending this observation, we could say that the Mediterranean basin, considered as a field organized as a network, is composed of a polysemic *node* with historical and cultural intersections among Europe, Africa, and Asia. In the process of the colonization of the Americas, its hybrid and polysemic repertoire became even more mixed owing to interactions between Amerindian and African peoples. We understand that these Ibero-American countries, and even Ibero-African-American countries, meet the conditions, at present, necessary for the establishment of a community bloc, which, along with others, more limited or more comprehensive, may be able to set limits to the imperial asymmetries of cultural flows.

I have argued that the world is increasingly configured as a place of multiple borders and identities that should be perceived as plural.[1] Cultural-linguistic rapprochements demand multilingual horizons and reciprocity in terms of symbolic power. In our case, besides the noteworthy connections with Spanish-speaking countries, there is the variety and breadth of community networks. In a world where English has become a kind of lingua franca, it is also necessary for us to speak in Portuguese and in other languages, even in the technological field. In linguistic terms, it is necessary to use Portuguese as a language not only of culture but also of science.

Many supranational community networks are being consolidated on a planetary scale, as for instance the movements related to gender issues, the protection and promotion of human rights, ecology, and so on. Thus fields for dialogue are established beyond the borders of the state, creating possible counterpoints to the monology of hegemonic flows. Such multiple fields of supranational community life are in a position to contribute to the democratic interference in social life, where the national idiosyncrasy tends to be articulated in a supranational network. It may be possible to continue to dream, as in the past and in view of a future not too distant, of a time when an American worker will be concerned about the salary of another worker from Latin America or Asia. It is true that the conditions necessary for this to occur will exist only when this worker becomes aware—the crisis is systemic, with globalizing effects—that how much another worker earns will have an impact on his own salary. In this way the possibility would arise of a desirable link between the community and the social.

A Mixed World: Reconfigurations

At this moment of crisis in global capitalism, a moment of strategic reconfiguration, it seems vital that criticism assume a more active attitude in order to create or promote cooperation and solidarity, and, if possible, to let the ground for political action in the form of blocs converge toward community dialogue. These blocs are politically more effective in the attempt to establish counterpoints to the monology of competition that has marked the globalizing process and that reached its climax, as the dominant global ideology, prior to the financial crash of 2008.

However, as stated by Riobaldo, one of the characters in Guimarães Rosa's novel *Grande Sertão: Veredas* (*The Devil to Pay in the Backlands*), "the world is very mixed." Riobaldo is tormented by the fact that he cannot identify sharply demarcated pastures. He searches for a binary rationality, as if reason did not involve limitless variations of a whole package of possibilities:

> I need the good to be good and the bad to be bad, that on one side there be black and on the other there be white, that ugliness stays far apart from beauty and joy far from sorrow! I want all pastures clearly demarcated. . . . What kind of world is this? Life is unpleasant in its own softness, but cross-brings [*transtraz*] hope even in the midst of the gall of despair. So, this world is very mixed.[2]

In a similar manner, from economics to the cultural arena, adverse effects were caused by the articulatory models of finance capital, which made borders less rigid so as to enforce a hegemonic order; on the other hand, the principle of contradiction gave rise to reactive attitudes, and this weakening favored the strengthening of community actions through the breaches of this policy. In this new post-neoliberal situation—we can allow ourselves this optimistic statement—community associations become even more urgently needed, and they involve the possibility of new articulations in addition to traditional ones. It is worth remembering the emergence of BRIC—Brazil, Russia, India, and China—among other possibilities.

Because of the expansion of communication between countries and blocs, there is now the possibility of a better dialogue, including in relation to the United States itself, in the possible reconfiguration of the politics of that country. At the state level, of course, the United States seek to establish new ways to preserve the asymmetries in the field of cultural circulation, and to promote the acceptance of discursive formulations that inculcate and naturalize particularistic and universal American assumptions. In the new international configuration born in the midst of the current crisis, the possibility of greater openness unfolds. It is time for a paradigm shift—that is to say, a shifting of the pigeonholes we have created in order to make sense of the world.

Cooperation, Reciprocity

Literary output increasingly requires an understanding of the supranational meaning of cultural flows, especially when it comes to literary comparisons. In comparative literary studies in Brazil, the consolidation of a kind of comparison that derived from impositions of our colonization process was due to historical facts. To verify this foundation has been a way to place ourselves before the flows inclined to colonize our imaginary. This is an important kind of comparison; it is even necessary for our own self-knowledge. In the attitudes of cultural actors of the past, one can identify lines that are essential to a better understanding of our current social and cultural environment. However, to limit ourselves to this comparison does not seem enough in political and cultural terms. We have proposed another form of comparison to stand next to this one, with which it may be integrated in practice: a prospective form of comparison, guided by community relations and based on solidarity and cooperation. We must undertake comparisons while facing problems that involve us all, in order to know ourselves in terms of what makes us unique and what we have in common, to explore the connections that tend to promote relations of reciprocity.

Clearly, any new approach that implies actions of a political nature can generate new forms of hegemony. Even when we get carried away by the establishment of bonds of cooperation, we must still pay attention to ingrained cultural habits that embody hegemonic gestures in the dealings between countries and regions, in situations of apparent reciprocity. To illustrate this point, we would do well to recall the comment of the Cuban critic Roberto Fernández Retamar[3] who claimed that he liked European critics who described the Caribbean as the American Mediterranean, but added that he would be much happier if they would also describe the Mediterranean as the European Caribbean.

The colonial process bred habits and literary and cultural repertoires that came from this historical experience as well as from cultural contacts between peoples who, until then, did not know one another. Although today there is an inclination in criticism for paradigm shifts, be they philosophical, aesthetic, or otherwise, I would argue that this trend cannot be naturalized under a generic label of "post"-something, which is only to reduce to obsolescence a whole experience that is embodied in the present. Something even worse may occur in the political arena, where the "post-," accustomed to the terms set by the media and fashion trends, seeks to reduce everything to a tabula rasa, with no past at all.

Postcolonialisms

We must take into account that postcolonial theorization has conveniently discussed issues related to globalization, the displacement of peoples, and the Americanization of the world under the rubric of media and consumer marketing. In relation to political and social issues, however, it may tend toward generic inclinations. The view that all societies marked by colonialism are equally postcolonial, without further consideration of their historical particulars, puts countries that emancipated themselves during the post–World War II period on the same plane with those that emancipated themselves in the nineteenth century. To speak about postcolonialism without regard to specifics implies equating a culture such as that of Canada or South Africa, for example, with the complex cultural situation in India, though all three countries are former British colonies. Only a sociocultural analysis may reveal to which postcolonialism it refers. This situation becomes even more complex if associated—as often happens—with the diasporic emphasis of postcolonial studies. Once again there is the need to consider the critic's orientation and the sociocultural ties that end up entangling his discursive formulations.

As noted in a good-tempered but ironic observation by Retamar, the construction lines of the imaginary, when coupled with an intellectual field, as a form, continue to operate beyond the original situation. They are updated many times as marks of the hegemonic symbolic power that comes from specific historical situations and cannot be concealed. Critical thinking cannot override, by adding the prefix "post-," five centuries of contact and cultural asymmetries, including the cultural repertoire that was built over that period. The big problem with the concept of postcolonialism is that it can mitigate what is fundamental to the critical act: a critical and active view, able to discuss historical and cultural facts that arise from specific historical experiences.

There are many postcolonialisms—for example, the postcolonialism of the former colonizer, which can be found in a novel like Lobo Antunes's *Os cus de Judas*,[4] and, that of the ex-colonized, as in Pepetela's *Mayombe*.[5] The first deconstructs myths and makes his memory a testimony that aims to be history. Pepetela, by contrast, is motivated by myths, while criticizing individuals who pretend to embody myths. This criticism highlights the past ethnocentric attitudes that are abundant in the present. In Lobo Antunes there is the deconstruction of myths and dystopia, whereas in Pepetela there is the construction and utopia that lie in the formation of a new nation-state. There is also the postcolonialism of the settlers who remained in the metropolis and that of the ex-colonized who migrated. The clear delineation of the so-called locus of enunciation and its historicity is therefore essential for a criticism that aims higher than generalization.

Cultural Mimetism and Cultural Power Relations

Reflecting on national characteristics implies situating them in a process of community assemblages that have a historical framework and relations of symbolic power. We have highlighted the political meaning of discussing literature under Ibero-African-American communitarianism, but community articulations can be of many different types, and politically it seems important to emphasize that the contemporary world is one of multiple boundaries and plural identities, from both an individual and a national perspective. Those are interactions that lead to the analysis of an interactive hybrid cultural complex in which Brazilian culture, for instance, is multifaceted and productively feeds itself with pieces of many cultures, while suffering the effects of the asymmetries of cultural flows. Such considerations, which go beyond national circumstances, make it necessary to account for the strongly hybrid repertoire of Brazilian cultural heritage. In the appropriation of this repertoire, the consciousness of such historicity and of the power relations to which it gave rise may contribute to the detachment from mimetic productions that have affinities with conventions or stereotypes. This critical sense contributes to the development of a propensity for creativity that sometimes turns to the question of ideological corsets and mythical identities. This is what happened, for example, with Carlos Drummond de Andrade's poem "Camões: história, coração" (Camões: history, heart, language), written in a post–Revolução dos Cravos context. Through the appropriation of Camonian images and poetic methods, Drummond established a dialogue with the historicity of the Portuguese poet's readings and with the new historical democratic situation in Portugal:

> Of the heroes sung by thou, what is left
> but the melody of thy song?
> The weapons crumble into rust,
> barons in tombstones say nothing.[6]

In this de-ideologization of conservative apprehensiveness, particularly in the era of Salazar, while still following Camonian images and rhythms, the Brazilian poet ends with these lines:

> Louis, strange man, who with the verb
> thou art more than an amateur, thou art love itself
> throbbing, forgetful, angry,

submissive, resurgent, reblooming
in a hundred thousand hearts multiplied.
Thou art language. Private pain
ceases to exist in order to become
pain of all men, musical,
in the voice with Orphic accent, pilgrim.

Identifying the common repertoire, therefore, does not lead necessarily to the mimetic. Critical distance comes from the perspective not only of a Brazilian but especially of someone who establishes his poetic grounding by persisting in a determined community language. Extending these observations, we can state that it is important from the critical standpoint to study these critical dialogues embedded, explicitly or not, in the literary repertoire that circulates among the Portuguese-speaking countries. On the other hand, highlighting the power relations involved in this movement can ward off the celebration of the mimesis, or of an alleged syncretism, or of a hybridity that ignores power relations and assumes assimilationist attitudes in favor of the culture of the colonizer, with all the implications this might have regarding political co-optation. One cannot, however, ignore the fact that the plasticity of Portuguese literary language has endured since medieval times and can be adequately studied only in the dynamics of the tendencies of supranational intellectual fields, in the globalization processes of European cultures.

Beyond Skin Color

It seems important to counter the flexibility of the circulation of cultural products, the nomadic pace of financial capital, which is articulated as a network, always decreasing distances by increasing speed, with counterhegemonic strategies associated with supranational communitarianism. This vertiginous process of standardizing cultural products in the market economy is not restricted to mass standardization. We should not forget that hegemony has broad foundations, which are nonetheless market-oriented, and seeks to incorporate into its networks even disagreement with the system itself. This is the perspective of managing the difference—the difference as administration policy and the opening of a niche market. In another sense, this co-optation can contribute to the dynamic survival of the system: promoting the appearance of change so that things will remain structurally the same. As Giuseppe Lampedusa put it in *The*

Leopard, "Some things must be changed so that everything remains the same." The partial emergence of the new, under the political and social control of pre-established structures, enforces their hegemony in order to control it, while benefiting from its apparent novelty to enforce their power in a new historical configuration.

There is no way, however, for engaged criticism to escape this situation; otherwise it risks isolation. The critic must get into these waters, being careful not to lose the direction of his or her project and be co-opted by the apparent nomadic flows that ultimately always shore up the hegemonic base. This is a political issue enmeshed in sociocultural network. To this end, in view of the need for a forward-looking attitude, the critic cannot be limited exclusively to negative critical attitudes, although this is always an essential counterpoint. From the political point of view, one should fundamentally be motivated by a kind of critical optimism that aims to give continuity, under new forms, to gestures that came from the past, with actors imbued with the hope that social life can always improve. It is worth noting the following excerpt from the poem "Coração em África" (Heart of Africa), by the São Toméan Francisco José Tenreiro, with its relevance to postwar intellectual culture, and particularly to the context of Ibero-African-American horizons and the cold war:

> with a heart in Africa with his hands and feet deformed encumbrance
> and deformed as the Portinari paintings of the sea dockers and the boys
> snotty addicts of the deep dark circles from the Orchard's gums
> I was considering the blackness of the world beyond skin color itself
> of yellow black white men[7]

Tenreiro is one of the intellectuals of the 1950s for whom "the blackness of the world" surpasses the skin color of "yellow black white men." His poem illustrates not only the cultural communitarianism of the Ibero-African-American but also, in other passages—it is a long poem—the libertarian attitudes of black personalities in Africa, the Caribbean, and the United States.

The actors of a supranational intellectual field, whether situated at the center or at the margins (though there are margins at the center and a center at the margins), who effectively consider themselves critics, cannot ignore the relations of belonging of these subjects. Those are ties that lead to sociocultural life and that cannot be usurped, owing to the very objectivity of criticism. Even if one acts as if they are in the same psychosocial situations as migrants, dialogue is performed abstractly, but with different cultures and historical experiences informed by particular political motivations. And being in the United States is not like being in Brazil or any other part of the planet, in spite of certain speeches aimed at neutralizing the difference. A critical lens may sharpen perception, but it cannot create an optical convergence that will preserve the colonization of the imaginary on the margins or outskirts of the capital.

Uncritical considerations, dissociated from the sociocultural situation and especially from historical specifics, are part of the process of colonizing the margins. In this sense, the critic cannot stick to the narcissistic performance that would be proper to those who are only passing by, as an apology for an apparent lack of commitment, with affinities for the hyperindividualism of the situation prior to the financial crash. By adopting postures related to a kind of nomadic relativism, it eventually confines itself to tripping over the obstacles, without maintaining any situational ties beyond the ephemeral speech of what is fashionable. Basically, it ties itself to circumscribed parameters with predetermined dimensions. To be limited to them means to be restricted to a monological course, even when it is erected as a temporary bridge. An effective and serious critical praxis will not remain restricted to these discursive frameworks, oblivious to other dialogic bonds, especially those that lead to a multidiscursive *node*, connected with discourses that take the world of culture to the cultural-political ground. Even the migrant—recall the paradigmatic case of Edward Said—connects him- or herself via networks, lives in certain areas, and bonds with defined social meshes.

NOTES

1. For an in-depth treatment of this subject, see Benjamin Abdala Junior, *Fronteiras múltiplas, identidades plurais: Um ensaio sobre mestiçagem e hibridismo cultural* (São Paulo: Editora SENAC São Paulo, 2002).

2. João Guimarães Rosa, *Grande Sertão: Veredas* 29. ed. (Rio de Janeiro: Nova Fronteira, 1986), 191–92. All translations are my own unless otherwise noted.

3. Roberto Fernández Retamar, *Para el perfil definitivo del hombre*, 2nd ed., rev. and exp. (Havana: Letras Cubanas, 1995).

4. *Os cus de judas*. Lisboa, Editorial Veja, 1979.

5. São Paulo: Ed. Ática, 1982.

6. Benjamin Abdala Junior, *Camões—épica e lírica* (São Paulo: Editora Scipione, 1993), 62.

7. "Coração em África," in Mario de Andrade and Francisco José Tenreiro, *Poesia negra de expressão portuguesa* (Linda-a-Velha: África Ed., 1982), 68.

WORKS CITED

Abdala, Benjamin Junior. *Camões—épica e lírica*. São Paulo: Editora Scipione, 1993.

———. *Fronteiras múltiplas, identidades plurais: Um ensaio sobre mestiçagem e hibridismo cultural*. São Paulo: Editora SENAC São Paulo, 2002.

Andrade, Mário de, and Francisco José Tenreiro. *Poesia negra de expressão portuguesa*. Ed. by Manuel Ferreira. Linda-a-Velha: África Ed., 1982.

Fernández Retamar, Roberto. *Para el perfil definitivo del hombre*. 2nd ed., revised and expanded. Havana: Letras Cubanas, 1995.

Lobo Antunes, António. *Os cus de judas*. Lisbon: Editorial Veja, 1979.

Pepetela. *Mayombe*. São Paulo: Ed. Ática, 1982.

Rosa, João Guimarães. *Grande sertão: Veredas*. 29. ed. Rio de Janeiro: Nova Fronteira, 1986.

BENJAMIN ABDALA JUNIOR is a full professor of Estudos Comparados de Literaturas de Língua Portuguesa at the Universidade de São Paulo. He is a leading specialist on issues related to Lusofonia. His current research project focuses on the interaction between literature and politics. He is the author of several books, including *Literatura, história e política*; *De vôos e ilhas: literatura e comunitarismos*; and *Literatura comparada & reflexões comunitárias*. He is a senior researcher at CNPq. He may be reached at benjamin@usp.br.

BETHANIA MARIANI

Translated by Beatriz Caldas

Lusofonia, Language Policies, and the Formation of Nation-States
Mozambique

ABSTRACT: The historicity of the Portuguese-language pathway as a symbolic object is not always visible. Portuguese, like all languages, exists in relation to other languages, and it is precisely this aspect that the term "Lusofonia" insists on silencing in multilingual countries, especially when it involves the long historical route that ranges from colonization to independence movements. The objective of this article is to present a set of linguistic and historical reflections on the Portuguese language in Mozambique.

KEYWORDS: multilingual countries, historicity, Mozambique.

Language as a Symbolic Object

My focus has been to develop a discussion of the political in the organization of language policies, and vice versa, in countries linguistically colonized by Portugal.[1] I seek to understand how the language-production movement affects the political, producing the "need" for regulation. It is worth remarking here that the political is in the order of conflict (Orlandi 1990), and "it is typical of the division that affects language materially" (Guimarães 2004). The exercise of politics, in turn, is the exercise of legal and administrative regulation of conflict. As an example, I would mention a *découpage* of possible discussions concerning politics in language: deliberations about the name of the national language, or about which language will be the official one; considerations directed to linguistic protectionism, or whether teaching materials should be produced in minority languages; debates on behalf of a "lusophone community" in order to make it stronger, and so on. What we want to show with these *découpages* are discussions related to contexts in which the linguistic and the political cannot be dissociated in social practice but remain under the ideological effect of a naturalization of senses carried out by a historically hegemonic political-ideological practice. The sociopolitical history of languages and linguistic ideas is also the history of the ever-confrontational route of national identities' sociopolitical construction.

Lusofonia: Past and Present

Several articles collected in the book *A língua portuguesa: Presente e futuro* (2005), which includes papers presented at the international conference (2004) of the same title—both book and conference organized by the Calouste Gulbenkian Foundation—bring up the issue of "Lusofonia." The expressions used, such as "lusophone space," "Lusitanian-descendent communities," "lusophone African countries," and "lusophone world," refer both to a geographical space and to a quality; therefore, they designate a territory not restricted to a specific geographical location since its unity is granted by the quality of being "lusophone."

As it is well known, one's linguistic and cultural place of origin has a determining impact on one's linguistic practices and what one says. It is therefore quite understandable that many Portuguese politicians and intellectuals consider the term Lusofonia intrinsic to the history of Portugal. As Cristóvão states, "*Lusofonia* is not an artificial construct; it has gone through 500 years of history, it has many commercial, religious, scientific, and other relations of human dialogue. This is the reason why its existence finds justification" (Cristóvão 1991). Ferreira (1996) argues that, although there is no consensus on its use, the term always implies that the linguistic unity of the Portuguese language is an inheritance that favors homogeneous communication. Thus to speak of "Lusofonia" is to speak for or against a transnational territory marked by a language in its imaginary unity and homogeneity. Mello (1991), for example, attributes to the concept of Lusofonia "the sense of unity of the language practiced by speakers who keep a radical cultural identity between one another, in this case, the Luso-Christian culture."

Here, the language issue is covered by a sociocultural policy, by a collection of ideas that adds to the term "Luso" a Christian value or a "symbolic return to the caravels," as Aguiar e Silva (2005) remarks ironically. More recently, especially in discussions about the role of Brazil in formulating a state policy toward the internationalization of the Portuguese language, the concept of Lusofonia has begun to lose steam in light of new geopolitical configurations that give Brazilian Portuguese the leading role.[2]

Linguistic Colonization: Mozambique

To discuss linguistic colonization (Mariani 2004) is to enter the core of the moments prior to the very idea of Lusofonia; that is, it is to seek to apprehend a complex and contradictory relationship between the homogeneity imposed by the colonizer and actual heterogeneity, between a desired imaginary unit and the fact of concrete diversity. In the discourses of colonization, the colonial Portuguese subject position, encumbered by six centuries of the Eurocentric gaze, guided by an ideology of *deficit*, and pointing to deficiencies in indigenous languages, affirms a completeness in the Portuguese language.

First, it should be noted that the Portuguese language as the language of colonization had a place of its own in sixteenth-century Europe, for it had gone through institutionalizing processes that granted it a symbolic value, specifically (a) a written form and (b) grammatization (cf. Auroux 1992 and Orlandi 2002); its standard norms were organized by the grammars of Fernão de Oliveira and João de Barros. The language had a legal-administrative function that legitimized royalty, a use in literature and translation, and was being taught with primers of its own. When I speak about "the Portuguese language," I refer not only to the different linguistic practices used in the Portuguese territory but also to the constitutive image of this language as an imaginary unit (in opposition to dialectal diversity, in opposition to Latin and other European languages).

In the early centuries of discovery, linguistic expansion was the result of an ideology of national legitimacy enacted in terms of both an internal language policy of the Portuguese nation and the whole range of other unknown tongues, yet to be grammatized, taught, and translated. Once established, this nation-language relationship became an emblem of the real Portuguese sociopolitical order that was taken to the colonies.

Mozambique: Linguistic Oppression and Resistance

Nowadays, among the ten most important sub-Saharan African languages, each with more than three million speakers, four are Bantu: "Kirwanda, Zulu, Xhosa and Emakhwa (Macua), the latter spoken only in Mozambique" (Rocha 2006, 14). According to many historians and linguists, as well as Mozambique's 1997 population census, around sixty languages in the Bantu family, with their dialectal variations, are spoken in Mozambique. More than six million Mozambicans (40 percent of the population) speak Makua-Lomwe (ibid., 19). In general, indigenous languages are used in the rural areas of the country (Firmino

2006). These languages are also used on the radio and on television talk shows, and in official statements, music, and the news. There are also cases of bilingualism in various regions of the country. The Protestant religious environment relies on the use of indigenous languages; in the Catholic Church, local languages are used less and, following the colonial ideology, Portuguese is more frequent (ibid., 63–65).

This complex linguistic situation in Mozambique is not a recent development. The Portuguese decolonization of Africa began at the end of the nineteenth century with the Berlin Conference (1885) and the Brussels Conference (1887), which determined Europe's partition of Africa on the basis of uniform international rules for the occupation of territory. Land possession no longer depended on the rights arising from the discovery of African lands but rather on their effective territorial occupation. As a result of that international political reorganization, Portugal began administrating its overseas territories with socio-educational measures that aimed at an effective subjugation and "civilization" of the African people by the introduction of Portuguese language and customs.

As I have written elsewhere (Mariani 2005 and 2007), decrees issued in 1845 and 1869 inaugurated a new educational system that "defined the different types of education to be provided to Africans and Europeans" (Ferreira 1996, 63). In the case of religious policy, the modus operandi was no different from what it had been in previous centuries: "Those in charge of the mission schools were mostly concerned with getting conversions. . . . The teaching was generally done in the local African language, and sometimes in Portuguese" (ibid., 65). Thus only in the late nineteenth century did Portugal begin to implement a policy of making Portuguese the hegemonic, civilizing language.

As Firmino puts it:

> Portuguese became the official language in which colonial policies were implemented. Portuguese was imposed as the symbol of the Portuguese cultural identity and became one of the most important instruments of the assimilationist policy promoted by the Portuguese authorities. In the context of colonial ideology, the natives could only become 'civilized' after demonstrating a mastery of the Portuguese language." (2006, 69)

Portuguese was imposed as the language of civilization with the aim of silencing indigenous African languages, which were not allowed at the institutional level. However, only a small part of the African population had access to schooling. Thus Portuguese became the language of the elite, the means of expression of the social class that occupied the most important positions in the colonial government in all urban centers.

Portugal's language policy in Africa had the dual purpose of enforcing domination and exclusion through the so-called democratization of access to school, and the imposition of one language to the exclusion of all others (as evidenced, for example, in Decree 6322, dated 24 December 1919, the Colonial Act of 1930, and Decree 31207, dated 4 May 1941). The legal discourse of these government decrees described the "primitive mentality" of the inhabitants of the African colonies and the need to bridge the gap between them and the Portuguese in terms of their degree of "civilization." Command of the Portuguese language, especially in its written form, as transmitted by the schools, could lead to prestigious social positions, though not, of course, for everyone.

During this period, the Portuguese colonizers invented the legal concept of assimilation. An African's status of being *assimilado* brought with it a "charter of citizenship" available to Africans who could successfully adopt Portuguese cultural, social, and linguistic practices. Mozambican society was thus divided into three categories: "White ('non-indigenous') Portuguese and their descendants, enjoying full rights of citizenship; '*assimilados*,' Negroes who could read and write Portuguese and enjoyed, at least theoretically, the same rights as whites; and Negroes ('indigenous') that had no rights of any kind under the Portuguese law" (Rocha 2006, 47).

But there can be no linguistic colonization without linguistic resistance. In Mozambique, this resistance took the form of revolts in rural areas, strikes in urban areas, and cultural activities such as the foundation of the Grêmio Africano de Lourenço Marques—all ways to oppose the civilizing political ideology, with its overt language policy; African languages were still spoken, sung, and transmitted from generation to generation in the form of oral narratives. The resistance was carried out through the effective use and appreciation of those unwritten languages, and also by "journalists, writers and clerks," and other African professionals (ibid.), who devoted themselves to preserving African identity in general and Mozambican identity in particular.

In the early decades of the twentieth century a linguistic development gradually began to modify Mozambican communication practices (Auroux 1992), when African languages spoken in Mozambique started gaining traction in written form, primarily in the African press, a direct act of resistance and an affront to the Portuguese colonizers. The press was run by a dissatisfied Mozambican elite "that used to circulate articles written in the local languages. . . . This presence of African references, however, was not enough to reduce the importance of the Portuguese language as an instrument of affirmation of the excluded" (Chaves 2005, 253, 236).

Thus resistance to the colonial oppressor materialized linguistically in two ways—in African languages, in both oral and written form, and in Portuguese. As a result, the communication practices of the Mozambican resistance, constitutively marked by linguistic heterogeneity, became contradictorily marked by more than one language of resistance in written form. When the struggle for decolonization began, the historicizing development of the Portuguese language gained another dimension: the language of independence began to compete with the colonizer's language. That is, two senses of the Portuguese language started circulating: on the one hand, the memory of the colonizer's language kept it as the language of oppression, while on the other hand, the (future) event of the revolution pointed to the Portuguese language as the language of revolution, a development made possible by the other local languages. Thus Portuguese linguistic colonization took place, as memory and oblivion did not lose their force but rather were absorbed and reframed by the elite and insurgents, causing a change in the uses of the Portuguese language as a symbolic object. This did not take place without tensions, as power relations work contradictorily and contradictions are inscribed in the language. This is what allows us to read the history of societies in the history of languages, and vice versa, as Orlandi (2002) has observed.

In Mozambique the ideology of the independence movement and the revolution was enshrined in armed struggle, in fighting for the dream of a socialist society, a revolutionary struggle that sought a political and ideological rupture with the previous political and social order. Beyond the separation from the colonial system, the revolution in Mozambique offers another alternative for the political system, based on another mode of production.

From a twenty-first-century perspective on the Mozambican revolution of the 1970s, the question of the colonizer's language is added to the linguistic fact that there is an actual presence of local or native languages used by most of the population. The linguistic colonization of Mozambique did not take place in the same way as the linguistic colonization of Brazil: there was no investment in the grammatization of the Bantu languages, nor was there any investment, until the twentieth century, in spreading Portuguese among the general population. During the revolutionary and postrevolutionary period, the question became how to speak to the rest of the modern world.

The revolution's leaders were in charge of making a difficult linguistic choice. Imposing Portuguese as the official language would allow external recognition—required for international relations—and lead to internal integration, as a single, unified language was fundamental for internal institutional balance. Although they chose the language of the former colonizer, it is worth posing the question: how could the language of a former colonizer, even as the official language, be considered the national language (Firmino 2006, 45)? After all, if a language is to be chosen for the sake of national integration, shouldn't it be familiar to all Mozambicans? Portuguese was a foreign language, spoken by a small elite, and it became a bargaining chip in the Portuguese assimilationist policy.

Frelimo and Political Discourse on Languages

To present an outline of the Mozambican revolutionary movement and the politics of language proposed by the Mozambican government after independence, let us turn to the third edition of Armando Pedro Muiuane's *Datas e documentos da história da* FRELIMO (Frente de Libertação de Moçambique, or the Liberation Front of Mozambique). This book (2006) is a compilation of documents of the First National Information Seminar, held in Maputo in 1977, two years after Mozambique's independence, and provides the basis for a discussion about language and political discourse in Mozambique. This political discourse was built on behalf of the collectivity and its future, and was produced by Mozambican leaders at two important historical moments: during the sixteen years of the revolutionary war and after the declaration of independence in 1975.

The effective demarcation, domination, and administration of the Mozambican territory took place between 1850 and 1930 and saw many wars. While these internal events were occurring, Mozambicans were exploited as a workforce in a system of forced labor in the South African mines (Rocha 2006, 45). With the end of World War II, the Portuguese government increased and promoted white immigration, even as workers seeking opportunities began to flow in. Meanwhile, a "small assimilated elite" with access to nationalist ideas put into action the project for independence and decolonization. Portuguese repression was organized by the PIDE (Polícia Internacional e de Defesa do Estado, or International and State Defense Police), which arrested, deported, and killed Mozambican rebels but was not able to stop the production and circulation of literary and journalistic manifestos by João Dias, Marcelino dos Santos, the writers Bertina Lopes and Malangatana Ngwenya, the poet Noemia de Sousa, the journalist and poet Jose Craveirinha, and the musician Fany Mpfumo (ibid., 50, 59)

In an effort to secure its overseas territory, Portugal changed its colonial policy in 1961—abolishing the Statute of Indigenato (Decree 43.983, which defined the difference between settler-citizens and native subjects in colonial Mozambique), forced labor, and the compulsory teaching of culture—and started promoting schooling, even creating an institution of higher education (ibid., 50). With the abolition of the Statute of Indigenato, the "indigenous population" and the *assimilados* became citizens overnight, but this did not mean that access to education and opportunities available to the white elite became available to all Mozambicans. Nor did it mean that the Portuguese language would become the mother tongue.

After the assassination of Eduardo Mondlane and Sebastian Mabote, Samora Machel—another revolutionary leader and the president of the National Liberation Front—commented on the fallacy of the assimilation policy in a 1968 interview with the historian Basil Davidson:

> I managed to get some education, and completed a technical course in nursing [one of the best job opportunities open to *assimilados* in Portuguese Africa]. During our practice, we socialized with white people, and only after receiving the diploma did we discover the different treatment, different attitudes toward us and them. We also found out that the level of wages was different. . . . Even so, they wanted me to accept the *assimilado* status. My father was against it and so was I. Why? Because I knew what the real situation of the assimilated was, it was the same as the indigenous. Later I had to become an *assimilado* in order to look for a better job, but I was never able to get it. (Quoted in Muiuane 2006, 93)

It is worth remarking here that the revolutionary leaders used both Portuguese and their own African mother tongues. Eduardo Mondlane, for example, at the request of a church minister, wrote his autobiography in the "Changane language" (ibid., 7). The language issue is addressed in Frelimo's political discourse, and linked to a broader debate between honoring and upholding the language and customs of Mozambique's many tribes and privileging the project of national unity.

At Frelimo's 1967 Congress, the party defined itself as a "nationalist political organization, composed of elements from all parts, from national tribes or ethnic groups" (ibid., 85). Frelimo sought to define the cultural traits in the Mozambican panorama that would allow a mapping of tribes and ethnic groups and an incorporation of their meaning in the struggle for national liberation. Examining the Mozambican population on the basis of linguistic criteria in 1967, the existence of seven ethnic or tribal groups can be inferred. Linguistic diversity, however, did "not mean 'that the *cultural manifestations* of a tribe are completely foreign to those of other tribes. . . . *We all belong to our Bantu linguistic family*, characterized by an identical grammatical form, words of the *same origin*, equal phrase and sentence structures'" (Muiuane 2006, 81, emphasis added). The designation of belonging was made in an inclusive and generalized way, marked by the use of the first-person-plural "we all" and "our Bantu linguistic family." The seven tribes or ethnic groups were all related by the "same origin" of "grammatical form," "words," and "phrase and sentence structures." The differences between ethnic groups were defined not as linguistic or cultural but as economic, based on material conditions, occupation, and region.

According to Muiuane, the main vector of difference between the various tribes was defined by colonialism, which "imposed a forced geographical separation." Without colonialism, Muiuane says, "it does not sound like an exaggeration to say" that a "natural process of social and cultural assimilation . . . would have taken place, and after a few centuries the different ethnic groups would have merged into a single one" (82) as a consequence of the historical process resulting from intertribal wars that produced an amalgamation of usages and customs. This story is told from the perspective of the African rebel Eduardo Mondlane, who conveys the sense of an unfulfilled past and implies that a different history might have unfolded in Mozambigue had Portugal not colonized the country: "Aware of the cultural and historical contradictions *between us*, the Portuguese used them, maneuvering one tribe against another. . . . *We still lack* a national consciousness" (quoted in ibid., 152, emphasis added).

Frelimo's political discourse builds links between the need to unite as a form of resistance, the struggle against the colonizer, and a suspended past. Mondlane's evocation of Mozambique's missed opportunity to transform tribal differences into a future of unity weaves a path between the struggle for independence—which might have failed owing to the quality of being Mozambican—and a potential future harmony. The construction of this political discourse was felt to be a necessary unifying factor in the political war for independence. Mondlane is saying that only "in the unity of various tribal groups would our people have been able to resist the European invaders," who "exploited all of us without any distinction" and "enslaved us all" (82). The past-subjunctive verb tense—"would have been able"—evokes the wistful hope of an unrealized potential. "The National Liberation Struggle," says Mondlane, "is itself a process that *creates a new* reality. While our past was characterized by linguistic, cultural and historical divisions, our *future* is being established on the basis of *unity*" (85, emphasis added).

In 1970, with the death of Eduardo Mondlane, Samora Machel was elected president of Frelimo. Salazar's government in Portugal fell in 1974, and on 7 September, after a twelve-year war, Frelimo and the Portuguese government signed a peace agreement. On 25 June 1975, the anniversary of Frelimo's founding, Mozambique proclaimed its independence and the project of national reconstruction began.

Postindependence Discourse

On 20 September 1974 the transitional government led by Frelimo published a long statement addressed to Mozambicans in which it enumerated the tasks ahead as well as the primary political and economic issues facing the nation, giving priority to education and culture. The statement put combating illiteracy on a par with the struggle against "ignorance, obscurantism, superstition, individualism, selfishness, elitism, greed, racial discrimination, [and] gender-based discrimination." These were the foundations of a revolutionary movement that aimed to "create a new man with a new mentality" (Muiuane 2006, 217).

At the Mocuba Congress, held in February 1975, these goals were reaffirmed and the theme of national unity was reasserted, with educational and language policies at its center. An explicit policy on literacy and language was aimed at the majority of the population, which did not speak Portuguese. If the Mozambican people were to assume power and gain access to worldwide communication, "the provincial-level study of Portuguese" had to become "mandatory, since it is the vehicle of communication that attends to actual conditions" (Muiuane 2006, 301).

> The Portuguese language is the medium of communication between all Mozambicans, and it can break the language barriers created by the mother

> languages. Through it, FRELIMO's party ideology, which embodies the interests of the working masses and expresses the revolutionary values, is widespread and studied to be applied, guiding our people in the struggle for the creation of a more just, prosperous and happy socialist society. The Portuguese language is also the language of communication for scientific and technical knowledge. . . . Also, by using the Portuguese language we can communicate with other people in the world, transmitting our people's rich experience and receiving the contribution of the world's cultural heritage. (speech by Frelimo's minister of education and culture's, quoted in Firmino 2006, 141)

With independence, then, the Mozambican state established a policy under which Portuguese became the official language and was expected to operate symbolically as an element of national unity. This institutionalization of Portuguese (formalized in the 1990 constitution), cemented the disjuncture between the national languages and the official language of Mozambique, which was still a foreign language for most of the population.

The revolutionary government had decided that the best way to accomplish its legal and linguistic ideal of homogenizing and unifying citizens was through the adoption of Portuguese as the official national language. Both a restatement and a disruption of the "ancient equivalence" of language and nation (Auroux 1992), this decision envisioned a unified future for Mozambique by denying and silencing the other languages in use in the Mozambican territory.

Let us remember that during the revolutionary war, language differences were both minimized and valued (considering "our common Bantu origin") and defended as part of the nation to be built. With the end of the revolution and the constitution of the Mozambican nation-state, language became both a tool that would promote national unity and a way to defend other tribal languages. Portuguese was already a "prestigious language . . . used institutionally, which would operate as a distinct mark of people's identity" (Firmino 2006, 164), whereas African languages had not yet been grammatized, and no single native language was common throughout the Mozambican territory. Firmino observes that the choice of Portuguese was related to "the fact that elites integrated in state institutions . . . did not know the native languages well enough to use them as working languages in official activities" (ibid.). In other words, African languages had never been employed in prestigious, official, institutional contexts.

The state, however, recognized the political need to use native languages as a means of addressing Mozambicans who did not speak Portuguese. At the First National Information Seminar, held in Maputo in 1977, "it was decided that the Mozambican languages would be used in the mass media, especially on radio broadcasting, . . . as an irreplaceable means to make their action effective among broad masses. Every trace of regionalist and tribal content must be removed. . . . The programs in Mozambican languages and dialects shall be concerned with encouraging the learning of Portuguese" (Proceedings of the First National Information Seminar 1977, 73).

In the early postindependence years, the official political discourse ran the decolonization process in Portuguese and, at the same time, kept the prestige of other indigenous languages alive: as the minister of education put it, they were a "rich depository"; "the main constituent elements of our cultural uniqueness live and are preserved" in them (quoted in Firmino 2006, 164). However, without promoting the study and grammatization of those languages—that is, without providing them with grammars and dictionaries, the language tools necessary for their dissemination and institutionalization, especially in the educational environment—the "rich depositary" was restricted to representing the roots of identity, the origins of the genuine native traditions, almost as in nineteenth-century romantic discourse.

For Firmino and other intellectuals, this is the locus of a strong contradiction in Mozambican official political discourse: on the one hand, the tribal languages were considered the expression of Mozambican identity,[3] symbolic objects of national identity, but nothing was done to give them the prestige of Portuguese; on the other hand, Portuguese could not play the symbolic unifying role that its proponents desired. As Firmino puts it, "The official discourse designates native languages as *Mozambican languages*, or *national languages*, but never as *ethnic languages*. In contrast, it refers to Portuguese as the *official language* or the language of *national unity*, but never as a *Mozambican language*, neither as a national language" (166, emphasis added).

Still, it is interesting that during those early years of decolonization nothing was said about the social differences produced by the use of Portuguese itself. Nothing was said, either, about the potential changes it would create in this African region. The Portuguese language was seen not as an inheritance but as an instrument intended to be neutral, an academic, educated, political tool for the use of politicians. Its use, however, delineated social position, drawing boundaries between those fluent in Portuguese and those illiterate in the language of the colonizers.[4]

In those early years, as José Luís Cabaço noted, not everyone shared the ideal of a "Portuguese language with a Mozambican personality." Thus, paradoxically, instead of promoting national unity, the Portuguese language excluded and divided people, promoting internal differences between rural and urban areas, between the educated and the uneducated, the literate and the illiterate. Traces of the ideological function of Portuguese as the language of colonization, however unwelcome and unintentional, tainted the choice of Portuguese as Mozambique's official language.

Only in the 1980s, after much resistance by intellectuals, writers, and members of the government, did a new phase in Mozambique's linguistic and cultural history begin, with the mapping of linguistic diversity in Mozambique and a decision to promote some languages to the status of national languages, seeking to encourage bilingualism in schools and cultural activities (Firmino 2006, 168). Debate about the place and meaning of the Portuguese language in the Mozambican state started taking place. For the first time discussion began to include the notion of "Mozambicanizing" the Portuguese language. A 1983 report from the Department of Culture noted that "the Portuguese spoken in Mozambique shall necessarily change and distance itself from the Portuguese from Portugal because the Mozambican reality, different from the one in Portugal, has its own course of development" (quoted in ibid., 169). This form of the language was given the derogatory name "pretoguês" (black Portuguese), which, according to Firmino, referred to "incorrect forms" of the language (146) traditionally associated with African speakers.

The opposition between Portuguese and pretoguês signifies a language with a stabilized writing system, on the one hand, and a form of the language that has been historicized and modified and has incorporated features of the native language and culture. One learned the aseptic language in school, but most of the Mozambican population, as we have seen, spoke the modified language, a function of the way in which linguistic colonization was carried out.

The Portuguese/pretoguês opposition ascribes ideological value to the institutional knowledge of those who learn European Portuguese. It marks the difference between the official language—organized and systematized in grammar books and taught in schools—and the fluid language of the streets and hamlets (Orlandi 2009, 18). Perhaps the expression "pretoguês" reflects the way in which the historicizing process of Portuguese developed in other places and times, something that the revolutionary government only began to appreciate and incorporate in the 1980s.

The process of acknowledging that the Portuguese language is not an asset to be preserved but a symbolic object, a language pervaded by a historical process in which other languages have interfered, is already under way in Mozambique. In its historical and ideological operation, the Portuguese language in Mozambique has been changing: phonetic-phonological alterations, lexical and morphosyntactic modifications, and neologisms have been observed and are beginning to be perceived as an indication of a truly Mozambican Portuguese (Firmino 2006, 146–50).

Final Considerations: The State and the Languages

A review of Mozambique's language policy is now under way, with several plans and proposals being debated. The likely outcome of this debate is the continuation of Portuguese as the official national language. In addition, however, some native languages will probably also be granted the status of national languages. Bilingualism is likely to be promoted, with schooling in those languages and their use in public administration virtually guaranteed.

I have observed elsewhere, in a discussion of the relationship between language and economics (Mariani 2008), that nowadays we must pay critical attention to political discourses that see language as an economic variable. Some linguists argue that politicians and economists must take into account the relationship between languages and the labor market—the cost-benefit calculus of an employee's acquisition of a second language, for example. Unless there is a government incentive, or the prospect of a wage increase, workers tend to speak only their native language. But is that really the best way to look at the question? Does it really make sense to frame the issue as an opposition between learning a new language and forsaking one's native language for the sake of financial gain?

I have also called attention to other discourses that claim the benefits and the inevitability of globalization and the formation of a single world market, with a common currency and a common language. Those discourses maintain that the multiplicity of languages is a barrier to trade and to the mobility of labor and technology. Linguistic boundaries are thus viewed as obstacles to economic integration, and the problem is particularly pronounced for the poorest countries, where multilingualism can slow modernization. From this perspective, an "ideal" economy implies a single language.

But is this really the point? Should we really be asking people to give up their native languages for the sake of national economic growth? I would pose the following question: given that the term "Lusofonia" originated (or, as some maintain, was appropriated) some forty years ago, in the era of the African movements for independence, perhaps it makes sense that there would have been an attempt to defend the hegemony of Portuguese at that time. But haven't things changed enough since then to make this term, and the ideology it embodies, obsolete?

NOTES

1. The archive I have built to write about Mozambique began with my trip to that country in 2010. I want to acknowledge here my deep gratitude to Brazilian researchers Rita Chaves (USP) and Laura Padilla (UFF). In Maputo, I thank the historian Antonio Sopa, director of the Historical Archives, and Matheus Ângelus, director of the library at the Portuguese embassy in Maputo. I also want to thank José Luiz Cabaço, who helped me understand how the history and economic and political direction of the Mozambican revolution is permeated by the language issue. I extend my thanks to Gregório Firmino, a Mozambican linguist whom I met in Brazil and whose book I quote countless times. I also want to acknowledge the importance of the intensive and extensive theoretical and analytical production of my fellow researchers involved in the History of Linguistic Ideas project, whose contribution is recorded in these pages. Finally, without the support of CNPq's productivity scholarship, the trip to Maputo would not have been possible. All translations are my own unless otherwise noted.

2. Cf. Zoppi-Fontana's edited volume (2009), especially Zoppi-Fontana's article "The Portuguese from Brazil as a Transnational Language."

3. It is worth quoting Firmino here: "In fact, I have already heard many people inquiring one's Mozambican identity by asking the following questions: 'What kind of Mozambican would not know a Mozambican language?'" (Firmino 2006, 66n64).

4. "Addressing a stranger in an autochthonous language in Maputo may be regarded as an offense or a sign of tribalism," Firmino observes (2006, 144). Firmino calls the Mozambicans' appropriation of Portuguese "nativization."

WORKS CITED

Aguiar e Silva, Vitor. "Contributos para uma política da língua portuguesa." In *A língua portuguesa: Presente e futuro*, ed. Adriano Moreira et al., 25–36. Lisbon: Fundação Calouste Gulbenkian, 2005.

Auroux, Sylvain. *A revolução tecnológica da gramatização*. Campinas: Ed. da Unicamp, 1992.

Balibar, R. *Le français fictif*. Paris: Hachette, 1974.

Bonvini, E., and Margarida M. T. Petter. *Portugais du Brésil et langues africaines*. Paris: Larousse, 1998.

Chaves, Rita. *Angola e Moçambique. Experiência colonial e territórios literários*. São Paulo, Ateliê Editorial, 2005.

Cristóvão, Fernando. "Hoje ninguém se acha dono da língua portuguesa—Todos nos entendemos como condôminos da língua." *Nortisul* 1 (July–September 1991): 16–34.

Ferreira, Maria José Simões de Brito Lopes. "A lusofonia e a política da língua e da cultura: A cooperação com os países africanos lusófonos." PhD diss., Universidade Aberta, Lisbon, 1996.

Firmino, Gregório. *A questão lingüística na África pós-colonial. O caso do Português e das línguas autóctones em Moçambique*. Maputo: Texto Editores, 2005.

Guimarães, Eduardo. *História da semântica: Sujeito, sentido e gramática no Brasil*. Campinas: Pontes, 2004.

Gonçalves, Perpétua. "A formação de variedades africanas do português: Argumentos para uma abordagem multidimensional." In Moreira, *A língua portuguesa: presente e futuro*, 223–42.

Mariani, Bethania. *Colonização lingüística: Língua, política e religião (Brasil e Estados Unidos da América, séculos XVI a XVIII)*. Campinas: Pontes, 2004.

———. "Da colonização lingüística portuguesa à economia neoliberal: nações plurilíngües." In *Gragoatá*, número 19. Niterói: EDUFF, 2005.

———. "A institucionalização da língua, história e cidadania no Brasil do século XVIII: O papel das academias literárias e da política do Marquês de Pombal." In *Construção do saber metalingüístico e constituição da língua nacional*, ed. Eni Orlandi, 99–124. Campinas: Pontes, 2001; Cáceres: Unemat Editora, 2001.

———. *Língua e conhecimento lingüístico: Para uma história das idéias no Brasil*. São Paulo: Cortez Editora, 2002.

———. "Quanto vale uma língua? Custo e benefício político nas relações econômicas e lingüísticas." In Ana Cristina dos Santos, Claudia Almeida, and Geraldo Pontes Jr. (orgs.), *Relações Literárias Internacionais II; Interseções e fricções entre fonias*. Niterói, Rio de Janeiro: Editora da Universidade Federal Fluminense & de Letras, 2008.

Mello, Gladstone Chaves de. "Lusofonia." *Nortisul* 1 (July–September 1991).

Moreira, Adriano, et al., eds. *A língua portuguesa: Presente e futuro*. Lisbon: Fundação Calouste Gulbenkian, 2005.

Muiuane, Armando Pedro. *Datas e documentos da história da FRELIMO*. 3rd ed. Maputo: Ciedima SARL, 2006.

Orlandi, E. *Terra à vista. Discurso do confronto: velho e novo mundo*. São Paulo: Cortez Editora, 1990.

———. *Língua brasileira e outrashistórias. Discurso sobre a língua e ensino no Brasil.* Campinas: RG Editora, 2009.

Proceedings of the First National Information Seminar. Maputo, 1977.

Rocha, Aurélio. *Moçambique: história e cultura.* Maputo: Texto Editores, 2006.

Zoppi-Fontana, Monica G. *Português do Brasi como língua transnacional.* Campinas: RG Editora, 2010.

BETHANIA MARIANI is professor of linguistics at the Universidade Federal Fluminense. She specializes in discourse analysis and the history of linguistic ideas. In 2006 she edited a book on discourse analysis and psychoanalysis. She has been a visiting scholar at Stanford University (2001–2002). Dr. Mariani is a senior researcher at CNPq. Her current research project focuses on "O brasileiro hoje: língua, cultura e novas relações sociais." She is the editor and author of several books, among them *Colonização linguística: linguas, política e religião no Brasil (séculos XVI a XVIII) e nos Estados Unidos da América (século XVIII)* and *O PCB e a imprensa: o imaginário sobre o PCB nos jornais (1922–1989)*. She may be reached at bmariani@terra.com.br.

CHRISTOPHER LARKOSH

"Ex-Centric" Lusofonias
On Remembered Language and Its Possible Futures in Portuguese-American Culture

ABSTRACT: I re-examine the dynamics of literary resonance, not only in the works of two contemporary Portuguese-American authors, Katherine Vaz and Frank X. Gaspar, but also across the sites and common places of lived experience in southeastern Massachusetts, the place from which I reconstitute my own encounter with the Portuguese language and a region that, while it may fall clearly outside the official boundaries of the Portuguese-speaking world, has been as much a home for Portuguese language and lusophone cultures over the past 150 to 200 years as many of the other spaces officialized by governmental institutions, whether as part of Portugal and its empire or as part of more recent authorities, such as the Community of Portuguese-Speaking Countries (in Portuguese, CPLP).

KEYWORDS: literary resonance, Portuguese-speaking world, Portuguese-American authors.

> Eu nunca guardei rebanhos,
> Mas é como os guardasse.
> —Alberto Caeiro, *Poemas*

> *I am not a keeper of sheep*, he says. The night
> will be long and soft with stars and the heat and the ticking
> of one heart or another. He leans back in his chair with that uncertain
> charisma, that narrow head. I can tell he is here to stay.
> —Frank X. Gaspar, "I Am Not a Keeper of Sheep" (21)

Remembering in Portuguese, from the "Outermost Azores"

In the poem "I Am Not a Keeper of Sheep," from his 2004 collection *Night of a Thousand Blossoms*, the Portuguese-American poet Frank X. Gaspar ponders the ineluctable presence in his life and work of one of Portugal's most omnipresent literary phantasms: the national poet of the twentieth century, Fernando Pessoa. In this poem, Pessoa has been around for so long that Gaspar can no longer pinpoint the exact moment of his arrival, cohabitating as he now does alongside the mundane presences of Gaspar's everyday life: the cat at the screen door, his papers and books, an August evening in California. And the particulars of Pessoa's arrival have for some time been overshadowed by the nagging possibility that this guest may never leave. Yes, believe it or not, Pessoa seems to have overstayed his welcome in this remote literary abode on the Pacific Coast. His genius, once seductive, has by now grown oppressive, and however fascinating he and his melancholy, poetic Lisbon may be, he must now, at this late hour, sip his little cup of coffee and puff on his cigarette all the more slowly to prolong his stay.

Gaspar is by no means alone among authors in this regard; in fact, he is in fine company. As many readers of Portuguese literature will recall, in the Portuguese novelist José Saramago's *O ano da morte de Ricardo Reis*, Pessoa appears as "o corpo apodrecido de um fazedor de versos que deixou a sua parte de loucura no mundo, é essa a grande diferença que há entre os poetas e os doidos, o destino da loucura que os tomou" (the rotting corpse of a maker of verses who left his share of madness in the world, and that is the great difference between poets and madmen: the destiny of that madness that overtakes them; 39).[1] Pessoa is nonetheless revisited by a remnant of his own literary invention after his death, namely, his literary alter ego, or, as he called it, his heteronym, Ricardo Reis.

But how does one measure the destiny of folly? Where does one's madness go when it leaves the mortal body? What is the future repository of our seemingly innocent quirks and idiosyncrasies, especially as expressed in Portuguese language, literature, and culture? If they are in fact left behind as a kind of residual energy in this world, as Saramago suggests, could it mean that "ex-centricity," especially in the unorthodox way I spell it here, is in fact the most durable part of the human spirit?

Admittedly, the word "eccentric" is already a euphemism, standing in politely for terms like crazy, insane, demented, or mad, but in the form of a neologism the term "ex-centric" can also suggest another meaning, referring to that off-center space, mental flight, or exploration of geographical horizons, diasporic cultures, or other presumably marginal spaces, all of them hospitable to poetic imagination and intellectual discourse, however unofficial their assigned spaces on a map, whether of the Portuguese-speaking world or any other global linguistic community. As Gaspar's contemporary Katherine Vaz writes, "everything audible in history, from an eyelash falling to Ovid's pen leaking, remains circulating in the airwaves" (1994, 101).[2] So how much of this poet's—or anyone else's—lingering madness really does pervade the here and now?

In the words of the Italian novelist Antonio Tabucchi, not even *Requiem* (1991), written in Pessoa's native Portuguese, is enough to shake him. In explaining how this work came to be written, Tabucchi even goes so far as to say, "acima de tudo, este livro é uma homenagem a um país que eu adoptei e que também me adoptou, a uma gente que gostou de mim de quem eu também gostei" (above all, this book is an homage to a country that I adopted and that also adopted me, to people who liked me and whom I liked as well; 7). What, then, is it about this story that demands that it be written in Portuguese, English, or any other language? Is it just that any truly devoted requiem must be articulated by way of that added sense of awareness that is only palpable in the language of another? Through the choice to write in Portuguese, this act of literary admiration at the moment of loss becomes an elegy not only for an obscure (though hardly forgotten) literary companion but for the relationship with language that that relationship brought into being. For all the foreignness that can be captured and conveyed in translation, there may well remain a part of any text that must appear in another language, or even more than one, if it is to convey adequately not only meaning but an irreplaceable sense of cultural identity and difference, perhaps one that even tests the very perceptions of such identity and difference on the fluctuating border between Portuguese and those inevitably recurring worlds in any number of other languages.

Needless to say, the potent lingering effects of this cross-cultural literary relationship upon Tabucchi's work are by no means diminished in subsequent writings, as Pessoa's presence is still perceptible in Tabucchi's subsequent novels, written in Italian, above all the one titled *Sostiene Pereira* (1994), in which Pereira, the editor of a Lisbon literary review, is reduced to writing successive drafts of an eternally insufficient necrology:

> Then he was reminded of his column "On This Day" and began to write. "It has been three years now since the great poet Fernando Pessoa passed away. He was culturally English but had decided to write in Portuguese, as he stressed that his homeland was the Portuguese language. He left us beautiful

> poems scattered in magazines, and one short poem, *Message*, which is the story of Portugal through the eyes of a great artist who loved his homeland." He then reread what he had written and found it repugnant, Pereira maintains. So he threw the sheet of paper in the trash and wrote: "Fernando Pessoa left us three years ago. Few had noticed him, almost no one. He lived in Portugal like a foreigner, perhaps because he was a foreigner everywhere. He lived alone, in modest guesthouses or rented rooms. He is remembered by his friends, his companions, and those who loved poetry." (36)[3]

All of these authors, regardless of national origin or language, appear to face the same challenge of confronting Pessoa's seemingly ineffaceable and hypnotic heteronymics: Gaspar might even wonder, when these voices arrive by way of his own poetic hallucination, how he can be sure that it is actually Pessoa and not the original *guardador de rebanhos* Alberto Caeiro who sits before him, that precursor of literary heteronyms par excellence and putative author of the lines in Portuguese that inspire Gaspar's poem. Or any of the others: Alexander Search, Álvaro de Campos, Ricardo Reis, or Bernardo Soares? One thing is for sure, if Gaspar, Vaz, and this faraway "flock" of disparate literary voices are any indication: it would take a major rewriting of the terms of Pessoa's passing at this late hour to ensure his permanent departure from this or any other literary scene (Martinho).

Back to the Ethnic Garden: Diasporic *Saudades* in Vaz and Gaspar

It is nonetheless in this context of continually recurring cultural references that I wish to reexamine the dynamics of literary resonance, not only in the works of two contemporary Portuguese-American authors, Katherine Vaz and Frank X. Gaspar, but also across the sites and common places of lived experience in southeastern Massachusetts, the place from which I reconstitute my own encounter with the Portuguese language, a region that, while it may fall clearly outside the official boundaries of the Portuguese-speaking world, has been as much a home for Portuguese language and lusophone cultures over the past 150 to 200 years as many of the other spaces officialized by governmental institutions over the years, whether as a part of Portugal and its empire or as a part of more recent authorities, such as the Community of Portuguese-Speaking Countries (in Portuguese, CPLP).

Moreover, the initial interventions of a nonnative author like Tabucchi raise an equally important question: why give primary importance in one's life to a language and culture that is presumably "not one's own"? And to what extent is it possible to "migrate" not only into a metropolitan Portuguese or other officially Portuguese-speaking culture, but also into any number of diasporic, immigrant, and/or bilingual communities, like those of southeastern Massachusetts?

This is by no means the first time and place in which these two authors have been discussed in tandem with writers from the Portuguese literary canon, as would be expected after even a superficial reading of each: their two best-known novels, Vaz's *Saudade* (1994) and Gaspar's *Leaving Pico* (1999), lend themselves to comparative study on the basis of thematic content alone, as each traces the connections of immigrants in the United States to the islands of the Azores and their popular and literary traditions. For instance, the Portuguese literary critic Reinaldo Silva's 2005 article "The Ethnic Garden in Portuguese-American Writing" points out the many common cultural elements for those unfamiliar with the everyday life in the Portuguese-American community, and highlights the representation of "ancestral culture" as emblematized in the "ethnic garden," one that is re-created on the basis of personal experience evoked in Vaz's and Gaspar's novels and poems: planting potatoes and kale, growing hydrangeas, lilacs, or blackberries, and raising chickens in the backyard.

Most with an emotional connection to such gardens would probably welcome an in-depth discussion of their cultural significance, especially in a collection such as this on the topic of Lusofonia and this region's possible place within it. On the island of Martha's Vineyard, Massachusetts, for example, Azorean gardens can still be found, especially off Vineyard Avenue in the town of Oak Bluffs. Even in cases where domestic agriculture has been erased by gentrification, its memory is still immortalized in place-names such as Chicken Alley, given to a stretch of Lagoon Pond Road near the post office in Vineyard Haven. A recent article in the *Vineyard Gazette* on a prize-winning rooster, soon to be evicted from his coop in a recently built residential neighborhood by the Tisbury zoning board, illustrates the current tensions between rural necessities and suburban aspirations:

> Mayflower Lane homeowners complained at the zoning board hearing last week that chickens were not appropriate for their neighborhood. They expressed concern that the [coop in question] would affect their property val-

ues, and said they were worried that fowl would attract rodents and other pests. The complaints reflect the changing character of a town that has a street known as Chicken Alley, where lifelong Vineyard Haven resident and current Mayflower Lane homeowner Eugene De Costa spent much of his life.

"I lived there 20 years, and everyone had chickens," Mr. De Costa told the zoning board last week. "But fowl bring rats. And I didn't build up there [on Mayflower Lane] to have rats." (*Vineyard Gazette*, 2 February 2007)

This local example, while perhaps not literary in its strictest sense, nonetheless illustrates the Portuguese ethnic character of Chicken Alley as represented in the memories of Mr. De Costa. Nonetheless, the Rhode Island Red in question here is a far cry from that of the emblematic "Galo de Barcelos" or any other proud symbol of Portuguese ethnic identity, for that matter—just the crowing of another unwelcome neighbor, and the newspaper stories show that such feathered neighbors continue to be unwelcome in certain corners of this island. As for the row of wooden two-story houses nicknamed Chicken Alley: although this place remains an important point of reference in oral accounts of Portuguese-American life on Martha's Vineyard, it is recalled here by one of its former residents with little or none of that emblematically Portuguese sentiment called *saudade*, at least not in the nostalgic and culturally exclusive sense in which it has too often been understood.

This raises the question: is the concept of *saudade* as important to Portuguese-American culture as it is to Portuguese culture? Is it, as Vaz maintains, truly "an untranslatable word" (186)? I imagine that this depends on what language you are attempting to translate it into (certainly not always English), and what you consider the range of acceptable equivalence. After all, one could just as easily make a similar case for the incommensurability of other words in Portuguese, words like *pelourinho*, *azulejo*, *porto*, *galo*, and *pão*, for the cultural specificity and symbolism they evoke.[4]

If the example of Chicken Alley seems to open up a series of anecdotal digressions, they may illustrate that, with or without translation, we are often left only with the startling realization that perhaps nothing is truly transmissible: that the meaning of all lived experience is bound to be lost, not only in translation between languages but in the attempt to express it in any language. I return to Vaz by way of an example from her novel *Saudade*: "Her father often took her to visit hydrangeas; she thought it was so that she would lose herself in some quality that purple had. (Now that she could speak, she wanted to scream, What did they mean to you, Papai? What did you mean for them to mean to me?) Hydrangeas more than anything else remind her of home. They are her father (94)." As this short garden passage illustrates, people may share and inherit cultural commonplaces, but they also transform, distort, or forget them, and the meaning of the simplest of things may well escape them. In this context of continual motion, forgetting, and new beginnings, what we might call *saudade* seems to have either an uncertain future or a future that can longer decide on a name for itself.

One more brief look at Chicken Alley before we allow Mr. De Costa to get on with his life: in this discussion of the limits of *saudade*, it seems all the more ironic that the name of De Costa's current place of residence—Mayflower Lane—might suggest a much more ominous definition for Portuguese-American culture than any sentiment for lost chickens ever could, for the vessel after which De Costa's lane is named still holds within it an entirely different story, one of a violent rerouting of cultural historiography itself, in which earlier arrivals are blown off course in the official story, so that it can culminate in an adoption of Yankee identity, iconography, attitudes, and values (perhaps of culture but, more important, of property). No fear: there are other vessels on the horizon in the works of Gaspar, and they will be salvageable as seaworthy competitors in a discussion of culture that transcends documented historical facts. Then again, this too is simply another way to say *saudade*, that is, the wish to reclaim an imaginary, heroic past as a promise for the present and future. Any attempt to answer seems insufficient, or perhaps the Portuguese poet Florbela Espanca, in her "Sóror saudade," was indeed able to give a voice to this interminable cycle of ambivalence when she wrote: "quem dera que fosse sempre assim: / Quanto menos quisesse recordar / mais a saudade andasse presa a mim" (That is how I wish it could always be / that the less I wanted to recall / the more my longing took hold of me; 246).

So perhaps it is best to set aside this discussion of *saudade* for a moment, or leave it to others for the time being (Lourenço 1978, Botelho 1990) in order to ask: is there another level of Portuguese (and more specifically, Azorean) consciousness in the works of Gaspar and Vaz outside "the ethnic garden," and other inherited cultural practices, of parents and grandparents and quickly receding childhoods? Is there a Portugal that emanates not only from the home but also from the cross-identifications of personal experience as readers and writers? Silva does allude to these other elements in his article by way of a list of literary readings or influences, yet we are left without a close reading of the texts that explores these intertextual references, whether with Portuguese or other cultures. I would submit that it is this literary experience that allows for a vision of Portuguese-American culture not fenced in by the dictates of cultural tradition but open to a number of other complex cultural references and divergent, contradictory, and, yes, "ex-centric" interpretations of a common history.

As both Vaz and Gaspar invoke the land- and seascapes of their ancestral Azores as a point of departure for other discoveries farther west, this common trajectory becomes a conduit for the transatlantic passage of a number of other Portuguese literary tropes and attendant ideological "messages." From the myths of lost explorers and the prophecies of forgotten Portuguese kings to their eventual reworking by way of Pessoa's poetry, let us explore how Portuguese-American literature thus combines literary myth and ethnic memory in a potent New World vision for reconfiguring the present terms of ethnic identity and of imagining one's "place in the world," both in the Americas and in the greater Portuguese-speaking diaspora, one that stretches across the world to this day.

A reading of Katherine Vaz's work reveals numerous references to Portuguese culture that extend far beyond the boundaries of everyday Portuguese-American experience, and she enriches her cultural landscape with a number of cultural references that might be considered obscure to many Portuguese-Americans today, most notably in her frequent return to Portuguese literature, in which she is similar to other authors in this context. This is by no means at the center of her literary imaginary: in her 1994 novel *Saudade*, the main character, Clara, lives in a world of fantasy stretching between the Azores and northern California, one that makes the reappearance of this literary connectivity between Portuguese tradition and U.S. lived experience conceivable. This world is experienced not only in and between Portuguese and English but also by way of an entire range of languages beyond them, languages that come to be equally essential in the narrative: languages of conch shells and telepathy, sugar and love (19–21), color and music (53). Questions of bilingualism are thus set aside in favor of other spontaneous and personal extralinguistic modes of expression, and it is primarily through these attempts to communicate sensory states beyond the reach and reason of spoken language that the foundations of reality are articulated and eventually transformed.

That said, a network of literary references does inform the novel, but more often in forms comic and transient than intentionally erudite: one character, Caliopia, even names her one-eyed puppy Luís, "after Luís Vaz de Camões, the epic poet who lost an eye during military service" (66). Those inclined toward more reverent invocations of this foundational Portuguese literary figure needn't worry; as important to the Portuguese as Shakespeare is to the English or Cervantes to the Spanish, the poetic giant Vaz de Camões (or, in this case, Vaz's Camões) reappears in a more recognizable form later in the novel, when Clara re-creates that part of the fifth book of Camões's *Os Lusíadas* in the form of a painted piano recital, in which the mythical giant Adamastor's love for Tétis is expressed through a mixture of color and music so complete that they are rendered indistinguishable (231). This is by no means the traditionally lamented "ditadura de Camões," in which the poet's style and vocabulary leave their indelible mark on both the Portuguese language and its literatures, but rather a reinterpretation in which language itself is once again placed off center, the registers of solipsism and migration eclipsing those of tyranny and tradition.

It is through the character Viriato das Chagas, however, that much of Portuguese literary tradition eventually finds a durable conduit into the novel's fictional world—above all, the aforementioned spectral presence and self-styled "Super-Camões," Fernando Pessoa. Though Viriato might evoke for some readers the second poem or "castle" of Pessoa's *Mensagem*, emblem of a foundational Iberian identity characterized by his resistance to the Roman invasion led by Scipio (Pessoa 1952, 26), for the purposes of this novel he is simply a "man of letters on the Island of São Miguel [who] frequented the library of Universidade dos Açores in Ponta Delgada" (Vaz 1994, 100), invents heteronyms for Clara's infant son and the town's residents, and reads Pessoa's *Oda marítima* over his teenage daughter's annoyance and indifference (219–20). When Clara eventually tears a page from the poem and puts it in her mouth, Viriato is actually pleased: "That was right, just right, thought Viriato. Pessoa had written the mournful heart that Viriato could not claim for himself, because it belonged to them all" (221).

The resonant point here is that there are many ways to consume and digest literature, whether Pessoa's or others,' a sentiment that also underscores the ex-centric dynamics of literary circulation, by which we need not read or listen in order to understand. To put it another way, one could easily read through a pocket edition of Pessoa's poem *Ode marítima* on the forty-five-minute boat ride between Woods Hole and Vineyard Haven, but one could also read, that is, live and contemplate, this short everyday ocean voyage, continually recurrent over the course of a lifetime of embarkations, in the spirit of the *Ode marítima* without ever having to actually take the book onboard: "Ah, quem sabe, quem sabe, se não parti outrora, antes de mim, dum cais: se não deixei, navio ao sol, oblíquo na madrugada, uma outra espécie de porto?" (Ah, who knows, who knows, if I didn't depart at some other time, before myself, from a dock: if I didn't leave behind, boat in the sun, oblique at dawn, another kind of port? [9]). Such questions on Pessoa's *Ode* could occupy us for a lifetime, but even a reading restricted by the space limitations of this essay would still affirm, and in no uncertain terms, that in Pessoa's poetic voice de Campos's view of Portuguese maritime tradition is by no means an unqualified glorification of exploration and empire, but rather one that balances the thrill of discovery with the misery, cruelty, and humiliation that accompanied it, one emphasized, by way of Campos's monologue, perhaps as sincerely penitent as self-sacrificial: "obrigai-me a ajoelhar diante de vos"; "fazei de mim vossas vítimas todas" (Force me to kneel before you; make me into all of your victims), etc., etc. (36–37). In this context, this *chiaroscuro* of maritime experience takes us back further than we ever imagined: past Camões's own ambivalence, expressed in his classic poem *Os Lusíadas* (10:5, 145), and even the words first uttered by the Roman general Pompey two thousand years ago—"navigare necesse est, vivere non nocesse"—that have worked their way back through Portuguese fado music to reappear both in *Saudade* (233) and in Vaz's subsequent collection, *Fado and Other Stories* (1997, 101–2): "navegar é preciso, viver não é preciso" (to sail is necessary, to live is not).

For most on dry land, however, these words no longer seem to hold, and probably never did. Is it really more necessary to sail than to live? Like Clara's lover Hélio, an Azorean immigrant who appears as an unconventional spectator at a major-league baseball game, such words seem strangely out of place in the life of the mainland: "By the seventh inning, the pyramid of beer cups was threatening to block his view. His mind wandered to how insular he and his fellow Azoreans remained, how weighted with fantasies and chary of well-organized ambitions, even when they moved into the larger world. He had left his house today hoping to change that, and yet here he was, an island on the bleachers, timidly clutching an empty cup (150)."

Is this encounter with the world of others also a form of *saudade*, that longing for contact with the larger, off-island world, one that nonetheless might never fulfill one's expectations? One can make an effort to translate the less commonly spoken languages of our own personal experience, and still that is no guarantee that the message will be understood, much less responded to. And yet Hélio cannot escape the gnawing feeling that the island is never the ultimate measure of one's worth, that he must also be understood *here and now*. In a discussion of insularity, it would no longer be enough to reconsider whether Hélio or any other man is truly an island, as not even islands are always islands; all need their lifelines, a working *lingua franca* in spite of inherent differences and variations. And even if it is true that we never really understand each other across these and other bodies of water, perhaps it is not the game in itself that makes communication possible but the practice, the admittedly imperfect effort over separation and distance, between islands, with no winners, no losers, and, like most fictional histories, blissfully inconclusive.

In contrast, Gaspar's 1999 novel *Leaving Pico* is set in Provincetown in the 1950s; its protagonist is a boy named Joaquim Carvalho, nicknamed Josie, who lives with his extended Azorean family. They call themselves "Picos," thus distinguishing themselves from the established continental "Lisbons" as being from another, more marginal Portugal. In the summer they rent their attic out to two men from New York, Lew and Roger. Lew is a history teacher and he brings boxes of books to Joaquim and his grandfather, John Joseph, every summer, mailing more to them each winter: "all stamped with the faint red-ink labels of the New York Public School System. We had atlases, histories, geographies, copies of *Kidnapped*, *Captains Courageous*, *Moby Dick*. On long winter nights, when John Joseph would stay home, he'd read to me and his pals from *Captain Blood* or *Treasure Island*, sometimes stopping in the book and going off into his own twists and explanations" (13).

These materials thus combine with the imagination of Joaquim's grandfather and begin to form a narrative of origin at the heart of Joaquim's search for meaning and identity. There is no Fernando Pessoa here, to say nothing of Camões, only a minor character named Freddy Pessoa, "a skinny man who always wore a Red Sox baseball cap and a mess of brass keys on his belt" (67), who hangs out with a guy nicknamed Manny Buckets. Aside from these colorfully named characters, there are only a grandfather's embellishments upon the English classics of boyhood literary adventure, a powerful canon in its own right, with which not even Camões himself can compete in this case. It is nonetheless interesting that the source of this narrative of origin is collaborative, anchored in the tales spun not only by male family elders but also by outsiders, the English authors passed on to them by the two confirmed bachelors who share their roof every summer. Gaspar thus presents a compound model of cultural identity, one that departs neither from mere genetic inheritance nor ethnic patrimony, that is, one that is just as dependent upon outsiders as it is upon his own family.

This narrative ultimately explains the discoveries of Joaquim's ancestor, who, his grandfather maintains, sailed from the Azores to Florida and up the coast to Provincetown a year before Columbus, stating: "we are the Princes of America. We descend from the great Carvalho, Navigator, Finder of the New World" (114). One cannot resist the comparison implicit in the parallel between the author's last name and the first name of that often-forgotten explorer of the early sixteenth century, Gaspar de Corte Real, who some maintain visited southeastern Massachusetts in the early 1500s, long before the English Pilgrims, leaving pictographs on rocks in nearby rivers that have been enshrined as a mythical part of local cultural consciousness (da Silva 1974). Regardless of the wealth of historical texts that either question or continue to build a case for the importance of Portuguese sailors in the initial phase of discovery of the New World, what is ultimately more compelling in this context of Portuguese-American cultural identity is the way in which historical narratives and chronicles are reappropriated and retold to formulate a more personal version of a common past, not only to bring a sense of adventure to a young boy and by extension an entire community, but to bring with it a sense of legitimacy, belonging, and meaning.

And yet, even this interconnected, deterritorialized poetic vision of past, present, and future—or perhaps in the rewritten words of Saramago, "o destino da loucura que *(n)os* tomou"—is not the sum total of our identity. We are indeed, at least in part, what we inherit, whether the primary school patriotism set to the tunes of John Philip Sousa or reconstituted by way of a literary canon of national heroes. We are also, nonetheless, what we live over the course of our lives, and what we choose for our futures to make better sense of it all. If the message of all this is in fact that we can invent our meanings as well as inherit them, then perhaps this ex-centric reading of time and space is possible after all.

Gaspar grapples with a similar task of pulling together vast expanses of space and time in his poem, called, appropriately enough, "The Standard Times," after the name of the newspaper delivered by every boy from the Cape and Islands who ever had a paper route. On this routine twilight itinerary, guided not only by familiar street names but also by the same moon, stars, and planets that accompanied the early navigators on more historically recognized excursions, the protagonist of the poem muses on "the sky in its ordained hieroglyphic, each pulsing star holding something just out of reach, each of my successive footsteps growing lighter and lighter as if I moved away from the earth, as if the wind would ever stop its whining and finally bear me up" (2002, 73). Poetry thus allows personal experience and the elusive order of the cosmos to collide; the mundane moments of remembered, lived experience become not merely facets of the celestial and the eternal but their very essence.

In a web of such complexity, it may seem all the more ironic that the banality of everyday life, whether of abandoned chicken coops or Azorean gardens, can hold any meaning at all. But perhaps I don't need to make a point of looking for an ex-centric Portugal in my own backyard, for here I am, still in the here and now, only now it is I who am haunted by Gaspar's words in that poem from *Night of a Thousand Blossoms*, titled "The Garden Will Come to You": "Don't despair. Don't lose yourself in all these daily vexations. You'll see, if you are still, if you are disciplined, that the garden will come to you" (43). And now, as his flowers sprout up around me, along with those of all the other dispersed inhabitants of this resilient English- and Portuguese-speaking archipelago, I recognize that he, too, "is here to stay."

One More Walk in the Park: On the Futures of Ex-Centric Lusofonias

> Como haviam de cuidar, nem lhes havia de vir ao pensamento, que os profetas falavam dos Americanos, se não sabiam que havia América?
> —António Vieira, *História do Futuro* (230)

In the presence of this recurrent question, which reappears in its original Portuguese to posit this present time and place as at least one possible, if not completely foreseeable, future of a certain history, I wish to pose another: where do the discursive ends of prophecy and futurity lie, and what would be the point of uncovering them with any degree of accuracy today? It was with these two questions in mind, one more than three hundred years old, the other presumably my own, that I continued this theoretical inquiry in a most unlikely place: a baseball field and adjacent grove of oak trees on the edge of my hometown of Oak Bluffs on Martha's Vineyard, its green space set within a traditionally Azorean-American neighborhood of small homes and backyard gardens. Older residents in my town who remember such things remind me that this place, Veira Park, was named after one Tony Vieira, the former owner of the neighborhood market and longtime supporter of the local Little League, but for most people in the town today it is just one more Portuguese surname on the local landscape, even its multiple spellings (Viera, Veira) the result of numerous attempts to make it fit into the norms of linguistic and cultural assimilation in the region.

After all, it would not be the first or the last time that the mythical and the real intersect in Portuguese(-American) literature and culture in places like Veira Park, the baseball field at the center of that Oak Bluffs neighborhood of Azorean gardens. As I continue to reinterpret this corner of my hometown, I cannot help but ask: what if this name, like Vaz's one-eyed dog, Luíz, or Gaspar's Freddy Pessoa, were placed into the more ex-centric context never explicitly mentioned in any of the Portuguese-American works considered here, and what if we were to take this message further out in its ring of ex-centric, concentric circles to other outlying points in this empire of letters?

That is to say, what if Vieira's prophecy, as channeled through Pessoa in the heteronymic guise of Bernardo Soares, concerned not only Portugal but also a more ex-centric dream, one fulfilled by the aspirations and lives of countless everyday Portuguese-American "Tony Veiras"—and not just *padres* but also parents, shop owners, fishermen, and schoolteachers? Are we perhaps not already part of this elusive "history of the future" by simply partaking of the here and now? And isn't that part of Pessoa's message? "Minha loucura, outros que me a tomem / com o que nela ia. Sem a loucura que é o homem mais que a besta sadia, cadáver adiado que procria?" (My madness: may others take it up, with everything that went with it. Without madness, what is man but a healthy beast, a procreating postponed cadaver? [42]).

How might we extend our perspective to imagine, especially when transposed into this space by way of a recent translation published here in lusophone New England, an even more complex vision of ourselves through an ex-centric vision of "Portugal and its destiny"? I refer here to an essay by the well-known contemporary Portuguese philosopher Eduardo Lourenço by the same title, "Portugal como destino":

> There is nothing more impassioned or sublime in Portuguese culture than António Vieira's discourse. It is the ecstatic but also the symbolically coherent synthesis of five centuries of collective life lived with the deep-rooted and

> culturally nurtured conviction that Portugal's very existence was of a miraculous and also prophetic nature. . . . Vieira creates a single prophecy out of the pronouncements of the cobbler Bandarra, an adept of Nostradamus, and hopes for the return of D. Sebastian, who would reestablish his lost kingdom and inaugurate a new empire, the utopian Fifth Empire that (according to Vieira) had been promised to the first King of Portugal and was part of Prince Henry's original, foundational discoveries. This utopian dream was taken over intact by Pessoa in his *Mensagem*. (Lourenço 2002, 119)

(Most readers are no doubt aware that this is in fact another António Vieira, a brilliant seventeenth-century priest and theologian who established himself as a foundational figure in the development of Sebastianism—the belief in the eventual return of a Portuguese empire as a global power—centuries before Pessoa discovered and repopularized him.)

As I continue to cut across and reinterpret this and other well-known corners of my hometown, however, I cannot help but notice that this common name invites at least one localized reinterpretation. After all, there would naturally be more than one António Vieira besides the seventeenth-century Portuguese Jesuit author and cultural mediator; he may be the best known from a purely historical perspective, but he cannot be said to have made any definitive reappearance in the present context of contemporary Portuguese-American culture, at least not by way of an extended and localized reading of his work. How, then, might an opening up of this apparent conjuncture of repeated proper names and commonplaces allow us to imagine an even more complex vision of both our own cultural identity and that of others, and perhaps even allow for a more ex-centric interpretation of both the name "Portugal" and Vieira's hopes for it?

In his reinterpretation of the prophecies of his own time, Vieira establishes himself, in my view, as a contradictory figure in the history of teleology. In his 1659 letter "Esperanças de Portugal," written in the Amazon and addressed to the Jesuit bishop of Japan, Alexandre da Silva, his reinterpretations of the dreams and visions of a man he deems an "idiota infelice" still form the basis of an entire futurology. While this vision does draw in part, as Lourenço affirms, upon the traditional narrative of Sebastianism—in which the lost king Sebastião is to return from the battlefield of Alcácer Quibir to reign over a Portugal restored to its former glory—by way of Vieira's stated goal of "conversão e paz universal em todo o Mundo" (36), the defunct yet eternally awaited D. Sebastião (Portugal's Godot?) would ultimately play no concrete role in its realization.

Far more troubling than Sebastião's absence, however, is the unavoidable fact that, in accordance with prevailing dogma, there is little or no room for anyone who does not conform, both in mind and in spirit, to the terms of its totalizing and singular vision. In his letter to Bishop da Silva, Vieira refers to such events as "a vitória dos Turcos, a redução dos Judeus se seguirá também a extirpação das heresias" (35), perhaps most succinctly expressed in the disturbing vocabulary continually repeated in *História do futuro*: "conversão," "extirpação," "extinção" (30–31). Given the terms of such a future, in which all diversity of belief and culture is miraculously translated and made one, it may seem all the more ironic, if not actually inevitable, that Vieira himself would eventually fall victim to the same inquisitional mechanisms of imprisonment and suppression that his own prophecies of a universalized spiritual and temporal empire attempt to call forth.

But what concerns me most as I traverse this space of reflection that I call Vieira Park is not whether this seventeenth-century prophecy is, as Lourenço maintains, "symbolically coherent" (21), much less whether it is desirable, useful, or just, especially when such considerations would invariably be subject to our own contemporary perspectives. Instead, I prefer to focus on how these claims of being able to predict the future, both systematically and infallibly, are indicative of a much more fundamental human impulse: the attempt to will a particular chosen future narrative into being by way of the recurrent rhetorical instrument of prophecy. As the contemporary Dutch-Indonesian social theorist Jan Nederveen Pieterse concludes in his discussion of transnational imaginaries from the early modern period to the present day: "Prophetic and utopian visions of human integration and unity have often been wide in spirit but not specific in the forms this might take. When they have been specific, they have often turned oppressive . . . failed blueprints of social engineering litter the record of history. The point is not to be anti-utopian but to be loosely utopian, not to give up on emancipatory human integration as a myth of Sisyphus, but to take the forms it takes sufficiently lightly" (38).

Are we perhaps not already part of this elusive "history of the future" by simply affirming our irrefutable presence, in all of its plurality, in the here and now? In much the same way, that baseball diamond and grove of trees on an island off the coast of southeastern Massachusetts becomes something different, a deterritorialized and translated "common place" that marks not only the continuation of migrant and other cultural presences in this most obscured of lusophone Atlantic archipelagoes, but also a connecting point to a much more extensive transnational narrative.

The green baseball diamond at its center is made not only of soil, bases, and mowed grass but is presumably also the site of a game, or, as some say, the *most American of games*. But where is this game really taking place? Yes, at times it is here at V(i)eira Park, but it is also being played continually across a vast network of other fields spread out over endless expanses of ocean and airspace, each part of a transcontinental ritual of athletic activity, spectatorship, and play-by-play commentary.

By now it should be clear that this space called V(i)eira Park—and the ever-expanding "game" associated with it—were not invoked just to serve the "national pastime" but as the means of simultaneously recontextualizing the memories and renegotiating the loyalties that connect an entire series of cultural identities. Likewise, when we view the field from the edge of this space, we can see that even when we are on what appear to be the sidelines, or even in the trees beyond the outfield, we are invariably at the center of something.

So by reconsidering the semantic density of this and other marginal fields, it may yet become possible to create an opening in the present order of signification and perhaps even make room for other interpretations: not to impose any one of them as the definitive turn toward yet another inevitably totalizing system, but as parts of an incomplete project that not only allows for but actually encourages multiple levels of linguistic and cultural differentiation. Don't worry: if the earth were actually to open up in V(i)eira Park, it would hardly be considered "the end of the world"; it is, after all, just one tiny point on the map, a virtual nowhere on a larger grid of transoceanic contacts. The opening I refer to here is not necessarily apocalyptic, but it could nonetheless affect the ways in which the ends of our divergent futures might be interpreted. For some, it might call attention to those often suppressed yet still enduring narratives of those emigrants who chose to opt out of the serial projects of Portuguese empire, even if many of them were only to be reassimilated into later and even more ambitious projects of global expansion and hegemony; for others, it might serve as a continuing reminder of the destabilizing potential of this and other flows of transnational migration, a challenge to institutional moves to delegitimize any and all forms of migrant mobility and culture. Of course, there will always be those for whom it simply "is," or is what it appears to be at first glance: an out-of-the-way and common place, marked by an obscure sign that few will ever bother to read.

Even so, there will still be those who choose to read this (post-)bilingual sign aloud, and it is in this way that V(i)eira Park may come to signal an opening in present conceptions of time and space, an actual semantic hole in the fabric of globalizing processes, an "outside" in the innermost recesses of what is presumed to be the "inside," a place deserted and, at the same time, full of localized and semantic complexity. This resistant and plural space called V(i)eira Park is both here and there, everywhere and nowhere, and like the rapidly unfolding future narratives that envelop it, it does not exist if not in that incipient and alternating state of erasure and revelation. It might even qualify as the kind of "non-place of Empire" that Michael Hardt and Antonio Negri attempt to map out by way of another set of question marks: "Where is the standpoint from which critique can be possible and effective? In this passage from modernity to postmodernity, is there still a place from which we can launch our critique and construct an alternative? Or, if we are consigned to the non-place of Empire, can we construct a powerful non-place and realize it concretely?" (Hardt and Negri 2000, 208). It is thus in the spirit of this sort of transformational project of critique, one that emerges from the very place that seems culturally subsumed and theoretically deactivated, that I wish to depart from the prophecies, letters, and other writings of António Vieira and move toward the sort of critically active "non-place" that Hardt, Negri, and others actually create and inhabit.

This is necessary for me, especially from where I stand at the moment, not only in a corner of V(i)eira Park but also in a corner of a present-day world ruled by an even more complex and potentially dangerous set of social, political, and economic forces. It might be necessary to examine the possibility of this and other "histories of the future," to attempt a more contemporary rearticulation of the terms of scholarly prognosis (especially those formulated under the rubric of "futurity"), present-day critiques of historiography, complete with its "numbered empires," and other more recent geopolitical projects of exploration, globalization, empire, and hegemony. Central to this discussion is yet another question: how might Vieira's future, when read more as a recurrent rhetorical strategy than an actually realized prediction, find a relevant place in discussions of diasporic cultures on the "far side" of the lusophone Atlantic and beyond, cultures no less preoccupied with their own transoceanic and future "places in the world"?

In the present discussion of futurity, there are notable examples of scholars and academics who, like Vieira, attempt to reframe ongoing historical processes in such a way as to privilege established institutional narratives under the rubric of globalization. In these more recent versions of futures foretold, some may still recognize the same kind of conclusions that can be drawn from a reading of Vieira: above all, the notion that the only forms of acceptable difference from, and resistance to, established Western cultural norms are those that have been effectively neutralized, assimilated, subjugated, or even eliminated by those norms. By referencing this kind of scholarship, which aims to validate and maintain discursive hierarchies with regard to national identity and security (and their attendant institutional structures of domination and control), I hope to make clear that the point of this investigation is not merely to reiterate, catalogue, and thereby legitimize the established structural and epistemological paradigms in which such theories of futurity have all too often been complicit, but actually to attempt to reorganize them by offering both my own and at least a few other points of resistance.

Many of the points of resistance already in place today involve theoretical explorations and concrete political movements linked to the development of alternative forms of globalization. Many of these theories and movements might be identified by way of emergent sites, most notably the World Social Forum, an event that brings together not only well-known intellectuals but also representatives of social groupings often underrepresented in or excluded from the main streams of global communication and power. As these voices are heard, recognized, translated, and disseminated, we may move toward what the Portuguese social theorist Boaventura de Sousa Santos has in mind when he and other global scholars and activists elaborate upon the slogan that emerged from Porto Alegre and that projects itself as part of a wide range of potential futures: "um outro mundo é possível." Sousa and his interlocutors accomplish this not only by stating but also by demonstrating through a broad-based compilation of indigenous and non-Western subaltern voices that indeed "another knowledge is possible" (Santos 2002; Polet et al. 2004; Santos 2007).

There is and no doubt will continue to be disagreement as to the specific terms in which critiques of present-day globalizing hegemonic structures are understood and articulated. The current lack of consensus on the subjects of globalization and empire might actually be necessary to counter ongoing attempts such as that of Vieira to impose a single, totalizing narrative on the diversity of human thought and experience; even so, no vision—not even a partially displaced, multiple, or hybrid vision—of a past, present, and future world can ever be said to represent the sum total of our potential existence. We are all, at least in part, a result of the diverse set of narratives that we inherit, whether by way of those linguistic terms that still intervene in the definition of our ethnic and cultural identities, the national ideologies rooted in hometown patriotisms and localized cultural practices, or the necessary questions shaped by subsequent reconfigurations of belief and understanding, combined with our own developing capacities for critical agency. If it turns out in the end that we are indeed a continually developing amalgam of what we experience over the course of our lives and what we imagine ourselves to be, then this multiple set of futures is already at work in the here and now.

A baseball diamond on an island off the coast of Massachusetts can thus also become a kind of *brasão*, or topographical emblem, much like all the others that mark the Portuguese-American cultural presence in these "outermost Azores," as well as a monument to a far more extensive cultural narrative reaching back over hundreds of years, one part of a much larger "playing field" made not only of soil and mowed grass but also of vast expanses of ocean, cultural cross-references, and the most intimate and fragile memories of ethnicity that continually renew and complicate our sense of identity. And if the message that comes out of this brief rewalking of the bases is that any one of us can in fact still invent, expand upon, and disseminate a measure of our own semantic complexity, then perhaps even further-reaching interventions in future time and space are not just possible but already inseparable from the terms and territories of our lived experience.

NOTES

1. All translations are my own unless otherwise noted.

2. To Vaz's recourse to the invisible imagery of airwaves I cannot help but juxtapose my own introduction to the Portuguese language through the radio and television broadcasts that I grew up with. One of my earliest memories of Portuguese being spoken is associated not with any particular person but rather with being in my living room alone, watching on television locally produced Portuguese-language programs broadcast to my island from WTEV in New Bedford, programs with names like *The Portuguese Around Us* and *Passport to Portugal*. Often, the program was not about Portugal proper but about points in its rapidly disappearing overseas empire. I recall one program on Macau, for

example, and how transfixed I was by the images of this tiny, faraway territory where the Portuguese flag waved exactly as it did at the Portuguese-American Club down the street from my house, as well as on any number of Portuguese-American homes in my neighborhood alongside the U.S. Stars and Stripes. As I grew older and actually began to learn the Portuguese language, these television programs were replaced by radio broadcasts of news and music on the New Bedford station WJFD-FM. While actual Portuguese speakers would eventually arrive on my island in the 1990s in the form of a sizable Brazilian immigrant community, my first experiences of Portuguese on this cold and tiny island in the North Atlantic were much like those I imagined taking place in Portugal's faraway Asian colonial outpost: I was perhaps one of the loneliest and most isolated of all Lusophones.

3. "Allora si ricordò della rubrica 'Ricorrenze' e si mise a scrivere. 'Tre anni or sono scompariva il grande poeta Fernando Pessoa. Era di cultura inglese, ma aveva deciso di scrivere in portoghese perché sosteneva che la sua patria era la lingua portoghese. Ci ha lasciato bellissime poesie disperse su riviste e un poemetto, *Messaggio*, che è la storia del Portogallo visto da un grande artista che amava la sua patria.' Rilesse quello che aveva scritto e lo trovò ributtante, sostiene Pereira. Allora gettò il foglio nel cestino e scrisse: 'Fernando Pessoa ci ha lasciato da tre anni. Pochi si sono accorti di lui, quasi nessuno. Ha vissuto in Portogallo come uno straniero, forse perché era straniero dappertutto. Viveva solo, in modeste pensioni o camere d'affitto. Lo ricordano gli amici, i sodali, coloro che amano la poesia.'"

4. A *pelourinho* is a stone column in the public square marked with the emblems of the Portuguese state, to which criminals were once tied and publicly punished. Yes, a pillory of sorts, to use a Yankee term, and yet today it serves primarily as an emblem of Portuguese culture, no longer a place of public humiliation but one where the global reach of the Portuguese cultural presence (if not always Portuguese rule) is both remembered and celebrated (cf. *Dicionário Aurélio*). An *azulejo* is a tile, yet not the red *tijolo* used for roofing but that of the decorative variety used for murals, often identified by the predominance of two colors: blue and white. The *porto* is the port or harbor; for me, those of Oak Bluffs or Vineyard Haven, to others, perhaps those of Lisbon, New Bedford, or Oporto. A *galo* is a rooster, whether the typical emblem from Barcelos or the more common Red variety from Little Compton, Rhode Island, both equally symbolic and part of everyday life. Juxtaposing these two words, *porto-galo*, we hear the name Portugal, though not one bound by history or etymology but another, more poetic and historically "ex-centric" Portugal. And yes, *pão* means bread, but as George Steiner points out in his seminal book on translation *After Babel* (1975), bread is not exactly what we imagine when we hear the French word *pain* or the German word *Brot*; all are culturally distinct and thus unequivalent to one another by nature. I wonder what Steiner would have thought of the Portuguese *folar de Pascoa* baked on my island at Easter, in the shape of a fish with a dyed hard-boiled egg

baked into the center for an eye. During the 1970s, my mother, Dorothy Larkosh Roberts, would prepare these loaves in the special education class she taught with her assistant, an Azorean-American woman by the name of Helen de Bettencourt, and they would give them out as gifts to those in the community who had supported them over the course of the year. One year, one school principal's wife from another island town, a recent arrival from off-island and thus unfamiliar with the tradition, had imagined upon receiving her loaf that my mother's pupils had simply forgotten to crack the egg into the dough before they kneaded and baked it! Regardless of her own ethnic origin, my mother participated in and passed on a number of Portuguese-American folkways and traditions, especially in the festivals to which she first brought my brother and me, and in the food that she in turn prepared and shared with others in her community. So regardless of the diverse criteria by which one could evaluate the pertinence of this and other short anecdotes from everyday life within academic-literary discourse, it serves to make all the more clear just how many different meanings and culturally distinct histories a simple word like "bread" can hold.

WORKS CITED

Botelho, Afonso. *Da saudade ao saudosismo*. Amadora: Bertrand Editora, Biblioteca Breve, 1990.

Bronner, Stephen Eric, ed. *Planetary Politics: Human Rights, Terror, and Global Society*. Oxford: Rowman and Littlefield, 2005.

Camões, Luiz Vaz de. *Os lusíadas*. With an introduction by Silvério Augusto Benedito and Notaspor António Leitão. Lisbon: Biblioteca Ulisseia de Autores Portugueses, 1988.

Cortesão, Jaime. *Os descobrimentos pré-colombinos dos portugueses*. Lisbon: Portugália Editora, 1966.

da Silva, Manuel Luciano. *Os pioneiros portugueses e a pedra de Dighton*. Porto: Brasília Editora, 1974.

Espanca, Florbela. *Poesia completa*. Amadora: Bertrand Editora, 1994.

Fein, Ian. "Rural, Urban Values Collide in Rooster Tale." *Martha's Vineyard Gazette*, 2 February 2007, 1.

Fisher, William F., and Thomas Ponniah, eds. *Another World Is Possible: Popular Alternatives to Globalization at the World Social Forum*. With a foreword by Michael Hardt and Antonio Negri. London: Zed Books, 2003.

Gaspar, Frank X. *A Field Guide to the Heavens*. Madison: Wisconsin UP, 2002.

———. *Leaving Pico*. Hanover, N.H.: UP of New England, 1999.

———. *Night of a Thousand Blossoms*. Farmington, Maine: Alice James Books, 2004.

Hardt, Michael, and Antonio Negri. *Empire*. Cambridge, Mass.: Harvard UP, 2000.

Hopper, Paul. *Understanding Cultural Globalization*. Cambridge: Polity Press, 2007.

Lopes, Teresa Rita, and Maria Fernanda de Abreu, eds. *Fernando Pessoa: Hóspede e peregrino*. 2nd ed. Catálogo da exposição evocativa de Fernando Pessoa. Lisbon: Divisão de Actividades Criativas e de Montagens do Ministério da Cultura e Coordenação Científica de Portugal, 1985.

Lourenço, Eduardo. *O labirinto da saudade*. Lisbon: Dom Quixote, 1978.

———. "Portugal and Its Destiny." Trans. Kenneth Krabbenhoft. In *Chaos and Splendor and Other Essays*, ed. Carlos Veloso, 109–71. Dartmouth, Mass.: Center for Portuguese Studies and Culture, University of Massachusetts–Dartmouth, 2002.

Martinho, Fernando J. B. *Pessoa e a moderna poesia portuguesa (do "Orpheu" a 1960)*. Amadora: Bertrand Editora, Biblioteca Breve, 1983.

Pessoa, Fernando. *Mensagem*. Lisbon: Edicões Ática, 1952.

———. *Ode marítima: Poema de Álvaro de Campos*. Lisbon: Imprensa Nacional–Casa de Moeda (Parque Expo 98), 1996.

Pieterse, Jan Nederveen. *Globalization and Culture*. Oxford: Rowman and Littlefield, 2004.

Polet, François, and CETRI, eds. *Globalizing Resistance: The State of Struggle*. London: Pluto Press, 2004.

Santos, Boaventura de Sousa, ed. *Another Knowledge Is Possible: Beyond Northern Epistemologies*. London: Verso, 2007.

———. *Globalização e ciências sociais*. São Paulo: Cortez, 2002.

———. "The World Social Forum: Towards a Counter-Hegemonic Globalization." In Polet and CETRI, *Globalizing Resistance*, London: Pluto Press, 2004.

Saramago, José. *O ano da morte de Ricardo Reis*. Lisbon: Editorial Caminho, 1984.

Silva, Reinaldo. "The Ethnic Garden in Portuguese-American Writing." *Journal of American Culture* 28.2 (2005): 191–200.

Steiner, George. *After Babel*. New York: Oxford University Press, 1992.

Tabucchi, Antonio. *Requiem: Uma alucinação*. Lisbon: Quetzal Editores, 1991.

———. *Sostiene Pereira*. Milan: Feltrinelli, 1994.

Vaz, Katherine. "My Hunt for King Sebastião." In Vaz, *Fado and Other Stories*, 16–41. Pittsburgh: Pittsburgh UP, 1997.

———. *Saudade*. New York: St. Martin's Press, 1994.

Vieira, António. *Esperanças de Portugal, quinto império do mundo*. Vol. 6 of *De Obrasescolhidas*. Lisbon: Livraria Sá de Costa, 1952.

———. *História do futuro*. With an introduction and notes by Maria Leonor Carvalhão Buescu. Lisbon: Casa de Moeda, Imprensa Nacional, 1982.

CHRISTOPHER LARKOSH teaches Portuguese language and lusophone cultures at the University of Massachusetts Dartmouth. His main areas of scholarly interest include lusophone and comparative literatures and cultures, translation studies, gender and sexuality, and studies of multilingualism, ethnicity, and diaspora. He is the editor of the volume *Re-Engendering Translation: Transcultural Practice, Gender/Sexuality, and the Politics of Alterity* (St. Jerome, 2011), as well as articles on a wide range of topics not only within, but also beyond the official limits of the lusophone world: from Quebec and Argentina on the one hand to Central Europe, Turkey, and South and East Asia on the other. He is currently co-editing another volume on German-Brazilian interculturalities, and working on a single-author monograph on cultural relations between the lusophone world and Asia. He may be reached at clarkosh@umassd.edu.

LUÍS MADUREIRA

For my sister Bela, in loving memory

Lusofonia
From Infancy to Necrology, or The Peregrinations of a Floating Signifier

ABSTRACT: Between 1926 and 1933, the Portuguese regime enacted legislation defining Africans as a separate element of the colonial population, as "natives" or *indígenas*. Those who learned to speak Portuguese, took commercial or industrial jobs, and conducted themselves as Portuguese citizens were labeled *assimilados*. The colonial administration stringently applied the conditions for assimilation. However, the logic of assimilation demanded the wholesale rejection of indigenous religions and cultural practices. This article analyzes the contradictions in this situation.

KEYWORDS: assimilation, colonial administration, Mozambique.

> L'institutionalisation de la CPLP [Comunidade dos Países de Língua Portuguesa] s'est faite dans la douleur . . . césarienne.
> —Francisco Santana Ferra

> Subtil mas constantemente, sente-se perpassar na atmosfera política nacional um sopro gélido, muito necrofílico, que à força de exaltar o passado, compromete o presente, e ainda mais o futuro.
> —Alfredo Margarido

It took me nearly half a lifetime to get back home. Unlike Odysseus, however, I returned not to violently reclaim a legacy of patriarchal rule but, in a half-intuited way, to relinquish any lingering notion of rightful appurtenance to my estranged and largely imagined homeland. In a sense, I came home in order to leave it. Or at least that is the story I now like to tell myself. I was born in Nampula, Mozambique, in the year when the hackneyed winds of change were sweeping across the African continent. I left colonial Lourenço Marques (present-day

Maputo) for Boston, Massachusetts, by way of Lisbon in early 1975, twelve days before my fifteenth birthday and about three months before Mozambique achieved its independence. Unbeknownst to me at the time, thirty-five years would pass, almost to the day, before I was to fly back to Maputo on a Fulbright grant. Driven no doubt by a vocational proclivity to look for "deep meanings" even in the most anodyne practices of everyday life, when I was kindly invited to contribute to a special issue on Lusofonia, the putatively Odyssean cast of my deferred homecoming appeared to me as exemplary of the construct that Eduardo Lourenço has famously designated as a "lusophone mythology" (2001, 176). For, what ultimately defines Lusofonia—according to its critics, at any rate—is a return as well.

Michel Cahen, for example, calls it a nostalgic (*saudosista*) discourse, still haunted by mythic caravels (*caravéliste*) and harking back to Lusotropicalist theories positing the Portuguese colonizing enterprise as exceptional, predisposed to miscegenation and the formation of affective ties among the peoples it allegedly brought together (quoted in Ferra 2006, 161). This assessment is echoed by Manuel Villaverde-Cabral, who considers it a dream shared in common by Portugal's elites, a democratized version of a hoary yet resilient Lusotropicalism (ibid., 162). By the same token, Francisco Santana Ferra regards a certain dominant strain of Lusofonia as "the last avatar of the Portuguese 'dream' of an empire and greatness that have disappeared forever" (163),[1] while Maria Manuel Baptista deems it a sort of return of the colonial repressed (2006, 102). Alfredo Margarido, on the other hand, in a renowned rebuke of the concept, which Onésimo Almeida describes as "a forceful and bitter tirade" (2005, 3–4), identifies Lusofonia's underlying purpose as "to recuperate at least a fraction of the former Portuguese hegemony so as to maintain colonial domination, albeit having renounced the vehemence or the violence of any colonial discourse" (2000, 76).[2] Whatever links the truncated and roughly parabolic trajectory of my own return journey may have with this complex symbolic structure are likely incidental rather than metonymic (let alone metaphoric), but I should like to sustain my opening conceit for a while longer (under erasure, as it were) as an expedient means of broaching the brief and rather personal analysis of Lusofonia that follows.

As far-ranging as my travels may seem at first blush, they never strayed far beyond the confines of the symbolic space that Fernando Alves Cristóvão, one of Lusofonia's more prolific proponents, terms the first of "three concentric circles" encompassing the values of a common language. Mozambique is of course one of the eight nation-states whose official language is Portuguese, and the particular corner of New England where I ended up (around twenty miles outside of New Bedford, Massachusetts) constitutes one of those regions that belong to non-lusophone nations and cultures but share a language and history with "lusophone reality," which Cristóvão likewise locates within Lusofonia's first concentric circle.[3] I should concede at the outset that my initial encounter with Maputo was marked by estrangement rather than identification, by difference rather than identity.

I recall walking the shabby, dilapidated streets that were once the epitome of colonial chic ("the mortal remains of colonial Lourenço Marques," as a Portuguese expatriate would later describe them) in the first days following my arrival. I recall trying to gather up the scattered shards of what I could remember of my former life in Lourenço Marques and arrange them in a seamless sequential narrative. I remember trying hard to will this jumble of memories to line up obligingly in chronological order against the uncanny and yet familiar world that now unfolded before my eyes. I remember trying to coax a smile of recognition from the face of the decidedly foreign homeland that the tourist brochures proclaimed *O País dos Sorrisos*. And I recall trying in vain. At the same time, however, there was some portion of that reality that I insisted on claiming as my own. The roots of the man I have become lay somewhere under that red dust—or so I stubbornly wished to believe—and those roots could not but remain visible beneath the deceptively alien surface of things. Yet this sense of identification was probably little more than a soothing fiction. Indeed, it was during the years I spent away from my homeland that I commenced inchoately to measure the immense cultural distance separating the former colonizer from the colonized in Mozambique. Only after I left the colony did I begin to glimpse what Eduardo Lourenço calls the Other's "unimaginable" modes of living, perceiving, and feeling that the Portuguese colonizer had for centuries refused or neglected to recognize (2001, 190).

As Alfredo Margarido asserts, it was always the colonizing nation that bestowed historical meaning upon the colonized. The latter became, as a result, mere footnotes in a multisecular epic of expansion and conquest (2000, 52). The colonized signified only insofar as they ratified the conqueror's will to conquer. As Frantz Fanon memorably puts it, "the colonizer makes history; his life is an epic, an Odyssey. He is the absolute beginning" (2004, 51). This epos, to paraphrase Margarido, cannot heal the colonial wound or mask the harrowing stench of death (2000, 54). It is graven in blood (52) upon native bodies rendered inert and "almost inorganic" by this very violent inscription (Fanon 2004, 51). It is pertinent to question, therefore, whether my alleged identification with an "imaginary" that, although expressed in a common language, derives from a radically different culture (Lourenço 2001, 188, 192), was a product of my colonial upbringing or of a cultural and historical knowledge that I acquired only after my departure.

My insistence on tracing a line of continuity between the colony I left and the nation I returned to may well have been cut from the same cloth as the exclusively Portuguese myth of Lusofonia that "imagines" the "community" of Portuguese-speaking countries (CPLP) as "an ideal totality compatible with the cultural differences that characterize each one of its members" (Lourenço 2001, 179). In this context, the question Mozambican scholar Lourenço Rosário raises about Lusofonia becomes critical: "African countries, including those whose official language is Portuguese, being in general colonial in origin, but exhibiting a bipolar socio-cultural reality by virtue of their ethno-linguistic adversity, how legitimately will we be able to designate them as lusophone?" (2007).[4] To put it in alternate but perhaps equally compelling terms, the key question concerning Lusofonia is whether it can, as Eduardo Lourenço solemnly proposes, ever emerge as the world of the Other, of a subject who shares "our" language but not "our" cultural memory, who has become Other precisely by refusing, transforming, or resignifying the cultural legacy with which the Portuguese language has been historically linked (2001, 189).

The historical memory in question here pertains to the violent imposition of the Portuguese language during the colonial period. Language, as Margarido remarks, functioned as an agent of domination during the empire (2000, 66) and, despite evident differences, it maintains a dominant role in the era of Lusofonia as well. As even a cursory glance at the pronouncements by high Portuguese officials will attest, the promotion of the Portuguese language on the international scene is invariably upheld as one of the principal tasks of Lusofonia. At the same time, the scholarly production of its academic proponents, habitually suffused with reverential citations of the obligatory line by the Pessoan heteronym Bernardo Soares ("A minha pátria é a língua portuguesa"), often advances the correlate claim that Portuguese serves as a coalescing cultural factor across a plural, heterogeneous lusophone space (Cristóvão 1995, 99).

Russell Hamilton argues cogently that the history of the Portuguese language in Africa has been ambivalent. Its violent inception notwithstanding, Portuguese played a significant role in the liberation movements, not only in mobilizing and politicizing, and indeed building a "national culture" across ethnolinguistic lines, but as the idiom of "cultural revindication, primarily in the form of literary expression," during both the protracted anticolonial struggle and the postindependence period (1991, 325). As Hamilton appositely observes, for Amílcar Cabral, for instance, the only thing Africans should thank the Portuguese for is having bequeathed them their language (325), which the nationalist leader famously considered not just the incontestable language of written communication but the single means of improving the Guinean people's well-being as well as securing scientific progress. Unlike Hamilton, though, I would hesitate to relegate Lusofonia to "a moot point" because at present "most lusophone African writers and intellectuals" have shifted beyond a resigned accommodation to their dependence on the language of Camões and come fully to accept "the place of the former colonial language in their own political sovereignty and cultural autonomy" (334).

The imperial specter that continues to haunt Lusofonia cannot simply be laid to rest because lusophone writers have, to borrow Mia Couto's well-known rejoinder to Pessoa, ingeniously claimed *their own* Portuguese language as their homeland: "Minha pátria é a minha língua portuguesa . . . a *minha* língua portuguesa que estou inventando para mim" (2009, 195, 196). As Couto himself is quick to add, Portuguese is merely one of Mozambique's multiple languages (one of its many "nations," as he writes), which a scant 3 percent of the population speak as their mother tongue. It is of course this tiny minority, composed of urban blacks, mulattoes, Indians, and whites, who wield political and cultural power. Perhaps, to cite Couto again, Portuguese was adopted "not as a legacy but as the most valuable war trophy" (191). Perhaps, as Cabral insisted and as Mozambique's liberation movement (Frelimo) decided at its inception, adopting the colonizer's language was the inescapable condition of possibility for the emergence of a single nation out of an unwieldy ethnic plurality and linguistic heterogeneity. Yet it remains an open question whether this colonial genealogy can be stricken with the wave of the pen.

Wole Soyinka has memorably impugned the nation-state in Africa as "an artificial creation . . . which did not take into consideration either the wishes or the will or the interests of the people who were enclosed and lumped together within [its] boundary" (1993, 33). The question, then, pertains not only to the selection of a national language but to the nation's form itself, which is neither natural nor inevitable but always provisional, contingent, and performative. Along with Partha Chatterjee, we should thus inquire into the ways in which the "regulative logic" of the postcolonial nation derives from colonial structures, into the modes in which emergent national discourses reproduce an order of knowledge "whose representational structure corresponds to the very structure of power nationalist thought seeks to repudiate" (1993a, 38). Couto is keenly aware of the irony that the Mozambican government has done more to foster the growth of the Portuguese language than five hundred years of Portuguese colonialism (2009, 192–93). In the same vein, Lourenço writes that "even in their imperial hour, the Portuguese were far too weak to 'impose' their language" (2001, 123), while Margarido mordantly adduces that the Portuguese themselves never considered "the Portuguese language a suitable, or even indispensable means of ensuring colonial operations" (2000, 64). As Couto recalls, Portugal's colonial enterprise in Africa was geared in part toward the formation of a social stratum (the *assimilados*) that would be able to run the "colonial state machinery" and reproduce colonial institutions (2009, 187, 188).

In effect, between 1926 and 1933, the Portuguese regime enacted legislation defining Africans as a separate element of the colonial population, as "natives" or *indígenas*. Those who learned to speak Portuguese, took commercial or industrial jobs, and conducted themselves as Portuguese citizens were labeled *assimilados*. The colonial administration stringently applied the conditions for assimilation. According to a 1950 official census, for instance, *assimilados* represented less than 0.01 percent of the total population in the colonies. Male *indígenas* were required to carry identification cards and pay a head tax. If unable to raise the tax money, they were compelled to work for the colonial government for up to six months out of each year without wages. This compulsory labor system remained in force until 1962. Although the 1951 constitutional amendments officially abolished the distinction between *indígenas* and *assimilados*, reclassifying Angola, Mozambique, and Guinea as provinces with the same status as those in metropolitan Portugal, and attributing Portuguese citizenship to all their inhabitants regardless of status, most of its degrading and discriminatory aspects remained firmly in place until independence.

Couto reminds us that the logic of assimilation demands the wholesale rejection of indigenous religions and cultural practices (2009, 187–88). It establishes concomitantly that the process of assimilation remains perforce deficient, asymptotic. The citizenship assimilation ascribes is, therefore, "second rate" as well (188). In his overview of the paltry efforts of the Portuguese colonial regime to disseminate the Portuguese language, Margarido posits, as one of the main reasons for this failure, the racist conviction that Africans are incapable of grasping the phonetic and syntactical subtleties of the Portuguese language, a conviction that, he notes, metropolitan literary production has historically reflected (2000, 60). Thus, for example (and to limit ourselves to theater), until the waning years of Portugal's colonial rule, the roles of black characters in Portuguese plays are, with few exceptions, generally restricted to "naïve and devoted servants" who express themselves in some variety of a largely invented "Guinea Portuguese" or *pretoguês*, harking back at least to Gil Vicente's early sixteenth-century farces (Cruz 2006, 41). To cite Margarido again, in the course of the expansion, the Portuguese continually "discovered" peoples who had already forged coherent and lasting social structures, peoples whom they invariably proceeded to transform, upon discovery, into "more or less infantile objects of human history" (2000, 54).[5] As the politicocultural by-product of this perdurable colonial domination, Lusofonia inescapably arises out of an enforced linguistic and cultural silence, an infantilization, as it were. For a colonized subject to adopt the Portuguese language in these circumstances, then, is ineluctably to consign her native language to infancy (in its original, etymological sense: an early developmental stage characterized by the inability to speak). *Infancy* represents, in this specific historical sense, Lusofonia's condition of possibility.

If, as Couto intimates, the "colonial order" persists in the national phase (2009, 188), then it behooves us to ask whether the promotion of Portuguese in the name of national unity plays a fundamental role in perpetuating the hierarchical social structure that has been in place since independence, whether in the end the postindependence adoption of Portuguese as a national language discloses, in the last instance, a continuity between colony and nation. Couto mentions that it is Mozambique's urban, Portuguese-speaking minority that comprises "lusophone Mozambique" (187). It is the privileged, lettered few who wield the power to make decisions and issue official proclamations about Lusofonia. "The other Mozambicans of the other Mozambican nations run the risk of remaining outside, removed from decision-making processes, excluded from modernity" (187).[6] But it is not merely from debates about Lusofonia that those who belong to Mozambique's "other nations" risk being excluded. The central issue underlying this sociolinguistic divide concerns the relationship that the centralized state, subscribing to authoritarian modernization, establishes not just with local or "national" languages but with local forms of community and authority (both prior to and after Frelimo's official abandonment of Marxism-Leninism).

Ironically for a movement whose success stemmed to a large degree from its ability to mobilize large segments of the rural population, the first generation of Mozambican nationalist leaders proved themselves astonishingly incapable of imagining the nation without expunging "the concrete historical heterogeneity of the social groups which they wished to unite and integrate under the sign of a single national identity" (Geffray 1991, 15). Geffray and other historians of Mozambique have maintained that one of the major causes of the postindependence civil war was the exacerbation of the urban-rural divide by the administrative enforcement of development. In this way, and despite their radically different aims, the nature of power exerted by Mozambique's independent nation-state (during the revolutionary and neoliberal democratic periods alike) resembles that of the former metropolis. As Mahmood Mamdani asserts in reference to "radical African states," the conviction that social revolution can be imposed from above builds on the legacy of colonial power (1996, 135). Hence, by abrogating local forms of authority and instituting Portuguese as the national language, by effectively refusing to "recognize within its jurisdiction any form of community except the single, determinate, demographically enumerable form of the nation" (Chatterjee 1993b, 238), the Mozambican state revealed itself as one of "the true inheritors of the colonial tradition of rule by decree and rule by proclamation, of subordinating the rule of law to administrative justice so as to transform society from above" (Mamdani 1996, 135). In the years since Mozambique's aggressive and often brutal insertion into the neoliberal global exchange circuit, this reproduction of the structural logic of colonial power becomes even more striking.

Despite the lofty rhetoric issuing from the presidential office about the "battle against poverty," both poverty and social inequality have been steadily rising in Mozambique for the past seven years, at least. Thirty-seven years after the country gained its independence, and notwithstanding the record economic growth it has been posting since the end of the civil war in 1993, the overriding majority of Mozambicans continue to be excluded from the benefits and privileges of Mozambique's dominant social order. I glimpsed the signs of this social divide on the night I arrived in Maputo, as I drowsily watched an amalgam of tumbledown shanties unfurling like some peri-urban equivalent of Hegel's bad infinity from behind the window of the late-model, air-conditioned U.S. Embassy van that drove me from the airport. I was to become better acquainted with the meanders of those suburban precincts in the course of my research in 2010. Yet they remained, not just for me but probably for most of those who dwell in the urban zone of economic privilege, citizenship, and sociability, largely a foreign country. As Mozambican sociologist Carlos Serra asks in a recent interview: "What do we know of our compatriots' lives in the suburbs? What do we know of their dreams, their sorrows, their ambitions? We talk about them and make projects that involve them without ever contacting or listening to them" (Ricardo 2011).

In a study of social vulnerability, Serra argues that the inhabitants of what Mia Couto calls "the other nations of Mozambique" constitute a hybrid "counter-society" that produces new rules, new values, new identities, and new forms of social representation. While those who live in the urban centers enjoy full citizenship rights, the rural populations and shantytown dwellers engage in a grueling and unremitting struggle for daily survival, forever poised "on a knife's edge," immured in a kind of "infra-citizenship" (Serra 2003, 19). Ironically, not only has a kind of avatar of the rapacious "comprador bourgeoisie," against whose emergence early nationalist leaders solemnly pledged to struggle, returned in full force, but so has a particularly overreaching form of financial "neocolonialism."

As Mozambican economist Carlos Castel-Branco points out, dependence on foreign aid and investment represents a "fundamental characteristic" of Mozambique's economy at the turn of the millennium (2010, 64). In 2007, for instance, 22 percent of the country's gross national product stemmed directly from development aid, a figure that is five times greater than the average for sub-Saharan nation-states, making Mozambique the eleventh-most foreign-aid-dependent country in the world (69). As it happens, foreign "donors wield immense and detailed power, and are at the very heart of decision-making and policy formulation, from the conception of issues and options through to writing the final policy. There is a real sovereignty question here: 'to what extent should non-Mozambicans be playing such a central role?'" (Hanlon and Smart 2008, 131). Concomitantly, as Castel-Branco emphasizes, Mozambique's emerging capitalist class uses its control over natural resources (obtained via its stranglehold on the state apparatus) to facilitate the largely unregulated penetration of foreign capital and thereby ensure its own unrestrained "primitive accumulation" (77–78). Most of the country's professed "liberators," who also happen to make up "lusophone Mozambique," according to Couto, have, in sum, aggressively embraced neoliberalism, while the majority of their fellow citizens can hardly eke out a living.

It may be elucidatory, at this point, to pose once again Lourenço Rosário's question regarding the *legitimacy* of the epithet "lusophone" to classify former colonized countries in which this level of extreme inequality and ethnolinguistic heterogeneity prevails. In the light of such strikingly inequitable socioeconomic relations, produced and sustained, to a substantial degree, by an enduring legacy of colonial power, the question of Lusofonia's legitimacy assumes a more definitive scope. According to Eduardo Lourenço (as we saw), if Lusofonia is to retain any meaning and efficacy in a postcolonial epoch, it must be enunciated by the Other; it must unequivocally unmoor itself from its colonial provenance and forsake once and for all its imperial home: "The lusophone imaginary has definitely become one of *plurality* and *difference*, and it is from this actuality that it suits, or behooves us to discover the community and brotherhood inherent in a fragmented cultural space whose Utopian unity, in the sense of something shared in common, can only exist through the increasingly deeper and more serious study . . . of that plurality and that difference" (2001, 112).[7]

It is difficult not to concur readily and wholeheartedly with this "pious wish" (*voto piedoso*), as Lourenço himself queryingly designates it. At the same time, I cannot but wonder if the path leading to a rigorous and profound inquiry into the plurality and difference that now arguably define the "Utopian unity" posited by "lusophone mythology" can, in the end, bring us back to Lusofonia. Does the "dialogue and exchange" between the Portuguese language and the other languages and cultures of Portuguese-speaking nations and regions (the reciprocal cultural and linguistic transaction that allegedly defines Lusofonia's "second concentric circle," according to Cristóvão) ever occur in the indicative mode, or is it always inevitably expressed in the imperative?

Is there space within Lusofonia for the Other who cannot "speak Portuguese like us" (Lourenço 2001, 189), or for the plural "nations" that must be either silenced or expunged so that "the single, determinate, demographically enumerable form of the nation" (Chatterjee 1993b, 238) may arise? Is there room within the "lusophone imaginary" for a protean community in which interethnic distinctions as well as those between the rural and urban spheres will "be more fluid than rigid, more an outcome of social processes than a state-enforced artifact" (Mamdani 1996, 301), for a Mozambique where indigenous or "national" languages will play as key a role as Portuguese in the nation's political life, where literacy in Portuguese will finally cease to be one of the unwritten and yet fundamental requirements for inclusion in civil society and political decision making? Whether or not it is enunciated by the Other "who speaks Portuguese like us but does not share our cultural memory" (Lourenço 2001, 189), can Lusofonia ever become anything other than a dream shared in common by elites not just within Portugal (as Villaverde Cabral asserts) but within the sovereign nation-states that now occupy the lingeringly affective territory of its lost empire?

Given its close affinity with an economic and political order that seeks precisely to erase cultural and linguistic heterogeneity in the name of national unity, an order that deliberately relegates the majority of the population to unrelenting indigence and the outer rim of citizenship and civility, it remains an open question whether Lusofonia can ever be fully commensurate with the plurality and difference that Lourenço "piously" invokes. As a full-fledged account of the political and sociocultural complexity and contradictoriness of "lusophone" African nations, Lusofonia seems destined to fall irremediably short.[8] To borrow Soyinka's definition of the nation-state in Africa, Lusofonia, too, is apparently "an artificial creation . . . which did not take into consideration either the wishes or the will or the interests of the people who were enclosed and lumped together within [its] boundary" (1993, 33). It seems at best a polysemic term that its proponents tend to fill with whatever content they most ardently desire (Ferra 2006, 151), a contemporary "*rose-colored map* where all . . . empires can be inscribed . . . glowing like a flame in the atrium of our [Portuguese] soul" (Lourenço 2001, 177). At worst it resembles "a myth and a mystique" (Margarido 2000, 15), comparable in scope and content to the derisory wish-fantasy of Lusotropicalism or the discredited fable of Portugal's imperial exceptionalism.

I began this brief meditation with a personal anecdote. I should like to close with another autobiographical vignette, upon which I shall also seek to impose, by "vocational proclivity" (so to speak), a tropological reading. The episode I now turn to took place in late April 2011, during my second return to Maputo. I had been invited to participate in the Maputo Book Fair and, as always, had unrealistically taken along work with me: a preface I was asked to write (and that would never be published) for the Portuguese translation of *Da Gama, Cary*

Grant, and the Elections of 1934, a coming-of-age novel by Portuguese-American writer Charles Reis Felix. As George Monteiro indicates in the book's English edition, Felix's novel belongs to the same genre as Hemingway's Nick Adams stories or Sherwood Anderson's stories about George Willard in *Winesburg, Ohio* (Felix 2005, x). The interwoven but self-sustained episodes that compose the novel re-create the variegated experiences of an immigrant community living in a small corner of the city of Gaw, the fictional equivalent of New Bedford (decidedly the most "Portuguese" of North American cities) during the Depression years. *Da Gama* is thus a novel of initiation, in the course of which Seraphin, the young and naif ("angelical"?) protagonist gradually forsakes his illusions about the minuscule, self-contained universe he inhabits. In this way, each of the title's nominal syntagmas ([Vasco] da Gama, Cary Grant, the elections) relates to a distinct phase in Seraphin's ambiguous learning process; or rather, each one of these illusions will have irremediably crumpled by the end of the novel. The world the novel portrays, although arguably lusophone, could not contrast more sharply with the tropical setting of my colonial upbringing, or indeed 1930s Portugal, which Salazar had only recently minted as *estadonovista*.

I read the last pages of the novel on the terrace of a cultural center in the Maputo borough of Alto Maé, about a block away from the modest, third-floor flat where I grew up. When I looked up, I saw the corner where I used to play cowboys and Indians with shotguns fashioned from wooden slats ripped out of beer crates, and the broken sidewalk where I learned to ride my bicycle. As I tried to reconstruct the sense of despondent estrangement I experienced when I first saw New Bedford, another, classic bildungsroman came to mind: Flaubert's *Sentimental Education*, in particular the well-known first epilogue, in which the protagonist Frédéric Moreau encounters, several years after their initial meeting, the woman he had desperately loved as a young man. And it occurred to me that the street scene unfolding chaotically below me, compared to my childhood memory of it, was like the frail and aged body we meet by chance decades later compared to the object of our overpowering adolescent desire. Nevertheless, if there was one figure that linked 1930s New Bedford to *estadonovista* Portugal and colonial Lourenço Marques, it was that of Vasco da Gama—also, in large measure, a mythic or imagined entity—whose inaugural landfall in Mozambique happened only a few hundred miles up the coast, according to Álvaro Velho's *Roteiro*.

Before I turn to this slightly odd emergence of a hero of the Portuguese expansion in Depression-era New England, I should like to reproduce, as a matter for reflection, Lourenço Rosário's closing question regarding Lusofonia: "why have Mozambique and India not commemorated along with Portugal [the voyage of] Vasco da Gama, symbol par excellence of the Portuguese saga . . . of Maritime Expansion?" (2007).[9] In Felix's novel, the celebrated navigator's presence relates to Seraphin's painful and gradual comprehension of the irrevocably subaltern status of the inhabitants of the tiny ethnic enclave of Heap Square. During the eponymous (mayoral) elections of 1934, the contestants line up in strict accordance with their ethnic affiliation, and it is in the thunderous stump speech that the Luso-American candidate, Secundo B. Alves, delivers to an obscure audience of credulous Portuguese immigrants that the intrepid sea captain makes his inaugural appearance:

> I see a ship plowing bravely through the unknown sea, a sea full of peril and danger. And in the dark of night comes a violent storm. . . . The ship groans in the ferocity of the storm's attack. And on the storm-drenched deck I see Da Gama at the helm. His grasp is firm. And when so many on the voyage have lost hope, I hear his calm voice—"Do not despair, my countrymen. I shall take you to a safe harbor."
>
> The spirit of Da Gama lives in each of you, my dear friends. He sailed off into the unknown. So did you. He sailed through storms. So did you. He was a man of great courage. So are you. . . . To your sons, tell them—"Never forget! You are Portuguese! Be proud of it!" (102–3)

The image is of course well known: Portugal as harbinger of new worlds, as Atlantic exception. Yet even the demagogic Alves appears tacitly to concede that the exceptionalism he invokes here is destined to be consigned to oblivion, to the irrevocable anonymity of a pebble cast into the ocean. As Alves himself will demonstrate, when he replicates the very same speech in support of the French-American candidate, who now replaces Vasco da Gama at the helm of the storm-tossed ship, the exceptionalism he calls upon is ultimately exchangeable, artificial, and polysemic, second-rate, in sum, as his first name (Secundo) and middle initial (B) perhaps suggest. This may well be Seraphin's most painful discovery and, in my estimation, it is a revelation worth underscoring. Like the figure of Vasco da Gama in Felix's novel, Lusofonia, too, has become a sort of floating signifier whose elusive referent is consistently displaced, always deferred, reappearing endlessly in the guise of a nostalgia for the lost empire. If, as in a Lacanian structure of desire, the place of the empire (desire) always remains unchanged, then Lusofonia operates alternately as one in a chain of signifiers (Lusotropicalism, exceptionalism, etc.) that always remit us to the same meaning: the void that was once the empire. I believe the time may be ripe for us to begin understanding it as an illusion of home that we must learn to forsake once and for all.

NOTES

The epigraph from Francisco Santana Ferra may be translated as, "The institutionalization of the CPLP was done in . . . Caesarean pain"; the epigraph from Alfredo Margarido as, "Subtly but constantly, one feels a chilly and very necrophilic wind that, by dint of glorifying the past, compromises the present, and the future even more."

Unless otherwise indicated, all translations are my own.

1. "Le dernier avatar du 'rêve' portugais d'un empire et d'une grandeur à jamais disparus."

2. "Recuperar pelo menos uma fracção da antiga hegemonia portuguesa, de maneira a manter o domínio colonial, embora tendo renunciado à veemência ou à violência de qualquer discurso colonial."

3. As Cristóvão defines it, Lusofonia functions on three interrelated levels (or in terms of "three concentric circles"). The "first circle," or more restricted definition, refers to the eight nation-states, including Portugal, Brazil, and the so-called CPLP (Comunidade de Países de Língua Portuguesa), in which Portuguese is the official language. It also encompasses the other nations or regions within other countries and cultures "with whom [Portugal] shares its Language and History," as well as territories where Portuguese-based Creole languages have been or are currently spoken. The second level or circle comprises the other languages and cultures of Portuguese-speaking nations and regions that "remain in contact through a common language, which, through dialogue and exchange, promotes and enriches each one of these languages and cultures." To the third and broadest level belong institutions and individuals who are not from Portuguese-speaking countries or regions but "maintain a learned and friendly dialogue based on affinity ties and various other interests with the common [Portuguese] language and the cultures of the eight Portuguese-speaking countries and regions" (Cristóvão et al. 2005, 654–55).

4. "Sendo os países africanos, na sua generalidade, incluindo os de língua oficial portuguesa, de origem colonial, mas com uma realidade sócio-cultural bipolar, pela natureza da adversidade etno-linguística, com que legitimidade os poderemos designar de lusófonos?"

5. "Coisas mais ou menos infantis da história humana."

6. "Os outros moçambicanos das outras nações moçambicanas correm o risco de ficar de fora, afastados dos processos de decisão, excluídos da modernidade."

7. "O imaginário lusófono tornou-se, definitivamente, o da *pluralidade* e da *diferença* e é através desta evidência que nos cabe, ou nos cumpre, descobrir a comunidade e a confraternidade inerentes a um espaço cultural fragmentado, cuja unidade utópica, no sentido de partilha em comum, só pode existir pelo conhecimento cada vez mais sério e profundo, assumido como tal, dessa pluralidade e dessa diferença."

8. In a recent interview, Mia Couto argues that "even though Mozambique is a lusophone country, it must construct its own Lusofonia, even if it bears another name" (mesmo que Moçambique seja um país lusófono, tem que construer a sua própria lusofonia; Lopes 2012, 26). The question I am asking is essentially whether this Lusofonia bearing another name remains Lusofonia.

9. "Por que razão Moçambique e Índia não festejaram com Portugal Vasco da Gama, símbolo maior da saga portuguesa no que toca à epopéia da Expansão Marítima?"

WORKS CITED

Almeida, Onésimo T. "Lusofonia: Some Thoughts on Language." Institute of European Studies, University of California at Berkeley, 21 May 2005. http://escholarship.org/uc/item/6sp4b6j6.

Baptista, Maria Manuel. "A Lusofonia não é um jardim ou da necessidade de perder 'o medo às realidades e aos mosquitos.'" *Ellipsis* 4 (2006): 99–129.

Cabral, Amílcar. *Return to the Source: Selected Speeches of Amílcar Cabral*. Ed. Africa Information Service. New York: Monthly Review Press, 1973.

Castel-Branco, Carlos Nuno. "Economia extractiva e desafios da industrialização em Moçambique." In *Economia extractiva e desafios da industrialização em Moçambique*, ed. Luís de Brito, Carlos Nuno Castel-Branco, Sérgio Chichava, e António Francisco, 19–109. Maputo: Instituto de Estudos Sociais e Económicos, 2010.

Chatterjee, Partha. *Nationalist Thought and the Colonial World: A Derivative Discourse*. Minneapolis: University of Minnesota Press, 1993a.

———. *The Nation and Its Fragments: Colonial and Postcolonial Histories*. Princeton: Princeton UP, 1993b.

Couto, Mia. *E se Obama africano e outras interinvenções*. Lisboa: Caminho, 2009.

Cristóvão, Fernando Alves. "Fernando Pessoa e a Lusofonia a Haver." *Letras* 85 (January–July 1995): 85–101.

Cristóvão, Fernando, Maria Adelina Amorim, Maria Lúcia Garcia Marques, e Susana Brites Moita., eds. *Dicionário temático da lusofonia*. Lisboa: Texto Editores, 2005.

Cruz, Duarte Ivo. "O Teatro em português: Da expansão às independências." *Camões: Revista de Letras e Culturas Lusófonas* 19 (December 2006): 14–61.

Fanon, Frantz. *The Wretched of the Earth*. Trans. Richard Philcox. Foreword by Homi K. Bhabha. New York: Grove Press, 2004.

Felix, Charles Reis. *Da Gama, Cary Grant, and the Elections of 1934*. Dartmouth, Mass.: Center for Portuguese Studies and Culture, 2005.

Ferra, Francisco Santana. "Entre héritage impériale et diversité culturelle: La lusophonie, une réalité à multiples facettes." *Cahiers de l'Institut Linguistique de Louvain* 32.1–4 (2006): 149–79.

Geffray, Christian. *A Causa das Armas: Antropologia da guerra contemporânea em Moçambique*. Trans. Adelaide Odete Ferreira. Porto: Afrontamento, 1991.

Hamilton, Russell. "Literature in Africa: Lusofonia, Africa, and Matters of Language and Letters." *Callaloo* 14.2 (1991): 324–35.

Hanlon, Joseph, and Teresa Smart. *Do Bicycles Equal Development in Mozambique?* Woodbridge, UK: James Currey, 2008.

Lopes, Humberto. "Mia Couto: 'Moçambique tem que construir a sua própria lusofonia.'" *Tempo Livre* (June 2012): 24–28.

Lourenço, Eduardo. *A Nau de Ícaro e Imagem e miragem da lusofonia*. Lisbon: Companhia das Letras, 2001.

Mamdani, Mahmood. *Citizens and Subjects*. Princeton: Princeton UP, 1996.

Margarido, Alfredo. *A Lusofonia e os Lusófonos: Novos Mitos Portugueses*. Lisboa: Edições Universitárias Lusófonas, 2000.

Ricardo, Celso. "Manifestações para além do custo do pão." *O País*, 9 July 2011.

Rosário, Lourenço. "Lusofonia: Cultura ou Ideologia?" *Notícias*, 6 June 2007.

Serra, Carlos. *Em cima duma lâmina: Um estudo sobre a precariedade social em três cidades de Moçambique*. Maputo: Imprensa Universitária, UEM, 2003.

Soyinka, Wole. "The Shape of Things to Come." *Index on Censorship* 22 (1993): 32–33.

LUÍS MADUREIRA is an associate professor in the Department of Spanish and Portuguese at the University of Wisconsin–Madison. His major areas of specialization include Luso-Brazilian colonial and postcolonial studies, as well as modernism and modernity in Latin America, Africa, and the Caribbean. He is author of *Imaginary Geographies in Portuguese and Lusophone-African Literature: Narratives of Discovery and Empire* (2007) and *Cannibal Modernities* (2005). Dr. Madureira has published several articles on topics ranging from Luso-Brazilian literature and cinema to early modern travel narratives and postcolonial theory. His current research focuses on Mozambican theatre and the politics of time in contemporary lusophone fiction. He may be reached at lmadureira@wisc.edu.

MICHELLY CARVALHO AND ROSA CABECINHAS

The Orthographic (Dis)Agreement and the Portuguese Identity Threat

ABSTRACT: This article analyzes the Portuguese people's opinion of the orthographic agreement recently implemented among the members of the Community of Portuguese-Speaking Countries. This agreement aims to make Portuguese orthography uniform. A survey was conducted about this issue in Portugal. Our hypothesis was that the Portuguese people would reject this agreement because it would be seen as an identity threat, a kind of submission by the former colonizer (Portugal) to the former colony (Brazil). As expected, the level of rejection of the agreement was very high. In this essay, the discourse of the rejection of the agreement and the kinds of motives invoked by Portuguese respondents are discussed, integrating the contributions of social representations theory.

KEYWORDS: orthographic agreement, identity threat, social representations.

Introduction

This article analyzes Portuguese opinion on the orthographic agreement recently implemented among the members of the Community of Portuguese-Speaking Countries (Comunidade dos Países de Língua Portuguesa, or CPLP).[1] The CPLP, established in 1996, is a highly heterogeneous and dispersed geolinguistic community of eight "lusophone" countries: Angola, Brazil, Cape Verde, East Timor, Guinea-Bissau, Mozambique, Portugal, and São Tomé and Príncipe.

According to Luís António Santos (2003), this community institutionally formalized a postimperial relationship between Portugal and its former colonies. One of the difficulties Portugal faced in establishing this community was the need to avoid the charge that the CPLP was designed to support a "neocolonialist" agenda. According to its constitutive declaration, the CPLP aims to "promote and expand the Portuguese language" and to preserve "a historical link and a shared patrimony resulting from centuries of common experiences" (17 July 1996, http://www.cplp.org). The establishment of an orthographic agreement among the Portuguese-speaking countries was one of the CPLP's major goals. Several early attempts failed, but recently, after years of tense negotiations among its members, especially between Brazil and Portugal, the agreement was formalized. The agreement entered into force in January 2009 in Brazil and in May 2009 in Portugal. However, the period of transition has been longer in Portugal, and the deadline for implementing the orthographic agreement there is 2015, whereas in Brazil the deadline falls in 2012.

This agreement aims to make Portuguese orthography uniform by reducing substantially the discrepancy between the Brazilian and the Portuguese versions of the language. However, these changes are not symmetrical, since the orthographic agreement implies more changes in Portuguese spelling than in Brazilian. Taking into account the importance of this agreement and the anticipated resistance to it by Portuguese people, we conducted a survey in Portugal in October 2009, in order to analyze the factors that might contribute to this resistance.

In light of previous studies of Portuguese identity, our hypothesis was that Portuguese university students would reject this agreement, viewing it as an identity threat, that is, as entailing a kind of submission by the former colonizer to a former colony (some people labeled it the "Brazilian Agreement").

In this essay we analyze the discourse of nonacceptance of the agreement and the reasons participants gave for their positions. We then discuss the results in the context of other studies of lusophone issues, integrating the contributions of social identity theory (Tajfel 1982) and social representations theory (Moscovici 1988).

The Orthographic Agreement

The orthographic agreement is a treaty that unifies the writing systems of the Portuguese-speaking countries. The attempt at unification is not new, having been tried since 1924 (Fiorin 2008). In 1945 unification became law in Portugal but was not approved by the Brazilian National Congress. According to Fiorin, Brazil rejected unification because, after Brazilian independence from Portugal, Brazil's leaders believed that independence had to be not only political but also cultural. For this reason, Fiorin observes, "Brazil has never recognized the linguistic authority of Portugal."

In 1971 in Brazil and 1973 in Portugal, legislation was enacted that reduced orthographic differences between the two countries. Even with these efforts, disparities continued to exist between the two orthographic systems. Thus in

1975 another attempt at unification was made, but it too failed because of political differences. A decade later, in a 1986 meeting in Rio de Janeiro attended by representatives from Portugal, Brazil, and five African countries, a new agreement was reached, but it was subsequently rejected owing to controversy and opposition, mainly in Portugal (*Diário da República* 193 [1991]: 4382). According to the *Diário da República*, one of the biggest obstacles to all of the agreements attempted between 1945 and 1986 was their effort to impose absolute, 100 percent unification.

In Fiorin's view, the orthographic differences between Brazilian Portuguese and Portugal's version of the language are minimal, which is why texts in either spelling are easily understood by Portuguese speakers. But the orthographic diversity affects the international dissemination and use of Portuguese. For example, official documents from organizations that adopt Portuguese as their official language need to be written in two versions, because the variations are considered unacceptable. The writer Geoffrey de Oliveira Neto, president of the Committee on Portuguese Language of the Ministry of Education during the government of Lula da Silva (see Leoni 2008), points out that this problem does not exist in the cases of British and American English or Spanish and Argentinian Spanish.

In 1990 another attempt was made to reach an agreement to reduce the inconsistencies between the different spellings of the Portuguese language. According to Fiorin (2008), this agreement was to take effect on 1 January 1994, after its ratification by the eight countries of the CPLP. Once again, however, ratification was not forthcoming. Ten years later, in 2004, yet another attempt was made; this agreement was designed to take effect when ratified by at least three of the eight Portuguese-speaking countries.

Although Cape Verde, São Tomé and Príncipe, Brazil, and Portugal ratified this latest orthographic agreement in 2008, it was not implemented at the same time in all four countries. In Brazil and Portugal, for example, the agreement took effect in 2009.

Imperial Nostalgia

To understand Portuguese public opinion on this issue, one must take into account the role that colonial empire has played in the development of Portuguese identity. The Portuguese empire was the last European empire to fall, a process competed only in 1975, in an era usually considered postcolonial. Brazil was the first colony to declare independence, in 1822 (it was recognized by Portugal in 1825). The African colonies achieved independence only after the Carnation Revolution (25 April 1974), which ended the longest dictatorship in Western Europe and triggered the process of decolonization. Despite the huge socioeconomic and cultural changes that have taken place in Portugal since the decolonization process, and the country's entrance into the European Union (1986), some observers maintain that the experience of empire has left a lasting impression on many people's minds (Cabecinhas and Feijó, 2010).

In fact, in Portugal today, lusophone rhetoric frequently assumes the form of "imperial nostalgia" (Martins 2006, 80), giving rise to conflicts and misunderstandings, both in international affairs and in interpersonal relations. Despite the lusophone rhetoric, people from the former Portuguese colonies still suffer discrimination, and old racial stereotypes and paternalistic prejudices (even if more subtle than in the past) persist (e.g., Cabecinhas and Feijó 2010; Vala, Lopes, and Lima, 2008).

The poem *Os Lusíadas*, an icon of Portuguese literature that tells through an idealized narrative the story of Portugal from its early days until the period of Camões, plays an important role in Portuguese education. According to its author, it became a symbol of Portuguese identity, especially in difficult moments of the country's history. During the Spanish occupation, or dual monarchy, it was read aloud regularly at moments of crisis, as when Portugal was under hostile siege, and gave the Portuguese the moral strength to resist their enemies (Rebelo 2003, 116). More recently, during Salazar's dictatorship, it was used as colonialist propaganda. Even today the poem is held up as representative of Portuguese identity.

According to Reiter (2005, 89), "the legacy of colonialism still strongly informs the ways in which Portugal defines national belonging." Reiter argues that Portugal's position as a "nation in between" (81), occupying an ambivalent position in the international hierarchy, has created a double tension: "On the one hand, national pride, damaged by potentially humiliating comparisons with richer and more powerful European nations, demanded the evocation of Portugal's 'glorious past.' But distance from aspects of that past was also required. . . . The result was a kind of Portuguese neurosis over its colonial past" (87).

Baptista adds, "From a national perspective, it seems that the time for a serious, dispassionate, thorough and systematic look in the direction of our colonial past has not been reached yet. We are currently in a moment that, psychoanalytically and symbolically, might be called 'repression and denial'" (2006, 25). According to Baptista, looking at the past requires a certain detachment that Portuguese society has not yet mastered. The very recentness of decolonization has discouraged the kind of searching self-analysis that the Portuguese need. Much distance remains to be traveled before a productive political, economic, cultural, and historical relationship with the lusophone countries can be achieved.

Several empirical studies conducted in the past decade point to the importance the Portuguese attribute to their "glorious past"—the "golden age" associated with the voyages of discovery (e.g., Cabecinhas, Lima, and Chaves 2006; Vala and Saint-Maurice 2004). Cabecinhas et al. (2006) conducted research on the historical perceptions of young Brazilians and Portuguese in which participants in both countries were asked to identify the events and personalities they saw as most important in world history and in the national histories of the respective countries.

The Portuguese participants considered the Portuguese discoveries the fourth-most important event in world history, and chose many Portuguese statesmen and navigators as among the world's most outstanding personalities. Moreover, more than two-thirds of the participants saw the Portuguese discoveries as having a major positive impact for all humanity, and associated them with such positive emotions as pride, admiration, and happiness. These results suggest the hegemonic social representation (Moscovici 1988) of the Portuguese discoveries as the "golden age" of the nation. Brazilian participants, by contrast, expressed mixed feelings about the Portuguese "discovery" of Brazil.

These findings are consistent with those of other studies, conducted in both Brazil and Portugal, of representations of the "discovery of Brazil" on the occasion of the quincentennial commemoration (e.g., Möller, Sá, and Bezerra 2004; Sá, Oliveira, and Prado 2004; Vala and Saint-Maurice 2004). According to Möller, Sá, and Bezerra (2004), Brazilians recognized some merit in the colonization but identified more negative aspects of the Portuguese occupation. Brazilians' feelings about the colonization were more varied than those of the Portuguese.

According to Wertsch, "collective remembering typically provides an essential basis for the creation and maintenance of groups" (2002, 67). Collective memory provides a "usable past" that can serve present-day purposes, namely, fostering collective identity claims. Wertsch argues that collective remembering has three important dimensions. First, it is an active process: "rather than being a thing, or possession, remembering is best understood as a form of action. Specifically, it is a form of mediated action, meaning that it is fundamentally distributed between active agents, on the one hand, and the cultural tools—especially narrative texts—that they employ, on the other." Second, it is essentially mediated by textual resources: "Instead of being neutral, or asocial, the textual resources employed in collective remembering bring with them a social position and perspective" (172). Third, collective remembering is dynamic, even if it often makes claims of stability and constancy.

Similarly, Cunha argues that images of the past generally legitimate the present-day social order. But such images can also serve to refute that order; thus social memory can be understood "as a field of battle, for social control and the exercise of power, the ability to define what is memorable and what to be forgotten" (2003, 86).

There is constant interplay between social identity and social representations of history. As Liu and Hilton point out, history "defines a trajectory which helps construct the essence of a group's identity, how it relates to other groups, and ascertains what its options are for facing present challenges" (2005, 537).

Portugal is one of the poorest countries in the Eurozone today, while Brazil is an increasingly important player in the global economy. Brazil's rise relative to Portugal's economic weakness represents a perceived threat to Portuguese identity, which has exacerbated the difficulty of reaching agreement on the orthographic issue as an attempt to preserve the cultural heritage of the Portuguese language.

Methodology

We designed a survey composed of both narrow and open-ended questions, allowing Portuguese respondents to express, explain, and support their opinions. We used the criteria of place of birth; citizenship and previous migration experiences; socioeconomic and cultural background; contact with Brazilian immigrants; feelings toward and stereotypes of Brazilian immigrants; opinions about cultural diversity, and so on. On the issue of the orthographic agreement, we posed a specific, narrowly defined question: "Do you agree with the orthographic agreement among the Portuguese-speaking countries?" Participants were to check "yes" or "no" and then justify their answers.

The sampling was nonprobabilistic, so the results should not be extrapolated to the entire Portuguese population. We were interested in the opinions of university students in particular, since they could be expected to constitute a more informed group than the general population. The survey was administered to a sample of 198 undergraduate students at the University of Minho, 95 females and 103 males, between the ages of eighteen and twenty-five. The survey was conducted in university classrooms and participation was voluntary.

We subjected the data to a thematic analysis, a methodological approach that consists in looking at the main themes presented in the data set. According to Braun and Clarke, thematic analysis is "a method for identifying, analysing and reporting patterns (themes) within data. It minimally organizes and describes your data set in (rich) detail" (2006, 79). The thematic analysis is a suitable methodological approach for exploratory studies like the one reported here because of its flexibility, in terms of both the variety of data sets to which it can be applied and its compatibility with different research paradigms for the in-depth analysis of one or more of the themes that emerge as structuring a particular data set.

Fereday and Muir-Cochrane (2006) corroborate the soundness of this approach and cite Daly, Kellehear, and Gliksman (1997, 82) to make the point that "thematic analysis is a search for themes that emerge as being important to the description of the phenomenon."

Findings

This essay is concerned only with the results of the question "Do you agree with the orthographic agreement among the Portuguese-speaking countries?" In our sample of 198 respondents, 140 (70.7 percent) opposed the agreement. When asked to explain their position, the respondents offered three basic arguments. Most linked their rejection of the agreement to the need to protect Portuguese cultural identity and preserve the cultural heritage of Portugal's leading role during the period of empire. Typical responses included the following:

> I believe the agreement will facilitate the homogenization of Portuguese orthography among the countries that have Portuguese as their official language, but its implementation means the loss of the cultural/traditional roots of our country, we are losing our identity. (23-year-old male)

> Because somehow we are destroying more and more the essence of our language. (18-year-old female)

> Destruction of cultural heritage of our specific language/culture. This agreement is due more to economic than social reasons, is unacceptable. The other Portuguese-speaking countries contributed to the degradation of the language and now the country's native language is going to adopt this degradation! Is unacceptable! (21-year-old male)

> I am firmly against globalization, I consider this agreement as a loss of identity by those who signed it. (17-year-old female)

> I think we should try to maintain our cultural identity, even considering that the language is not something static. The various Portuguese-speaking countries should maintain their differences. (18-year-old female)

> I feel that we may lose our identity, I think our "Portuguese" is the correct one, and is vital to learn how to communicate correctly. (27-year-old male)

These participants saw the orthographic agreement as undermining the historical hegemony and sovereignty of the Portuguese people, who still glorify the age of discovery. They viewed the agreement as menacing the perceived high status of Portugal in relation to its former colonies. Everything that might compromise this perceived high status was to be avoided, especially in view of the fact that the former colony of Brazil was gaining international economic influence relative to Portugal (Pires 2000, 8). In this respect, the majority of the participants refused to acknowledge any influence on the part of Brazilian Portuguese, which they saw as a threat to the more authentic and more sophisticated original Portuguese language. They claimed that the Portuguese of Portugal was the "correct" version of the language, evoking the importance of Portugal's historical importance, which, they felt, should be respected.

Participants also reacted negatively to the leading role played by Brazil in the negotiations on the agreement, and felt that Portugal should play a more decisive role.

> I think we should teach the proper Portuguese to the Brazilians instead of changing our language, because what is better for one will be worse for the other, the rules should not be changed to the advantage of some majorities. (20-year-old male)

The Brazilians do not know how to write or conjugate verbs. The language is "Portuguese" and not "Brazilian." The agreement is disadvantageous, because the Portuguese language is very rich and very historic. (20-year-old male)

I do not agree with the orthographic agreement among the Portuguese-speaking countries because, I think, we were the colonizers and we should not submit our mother tongue to some details created by the colonized peoples. (18-year-old female)

The agreement undoes former spelling rules of our language and makes the European Portuguese a copy of the Portuguese of Brazil. (17-year-old male)

Especially for Portugal, since this is the old country, the orthographic agreement came disproportionately, since it implies a new approach to learn the language. (18-year-old female)

We are proud of our language because it is complex and refined, it will lose its value with these adaptations. (18-year-old female)

Because if the language is originally from Portugal, the Portuguese-speaking countries should write Portuguese as we do, never the originating country of the language writing as they do. (24-year-old male)

With the agreement, many words would be more like the Brazilian Portuguese than the Portuguese of Portugal. (28-year-old female)

It might even be good for all Portuguese-speaking countries to have the same spelling, but doesn't make any sense that Portugal, from which the Portuguese language comes, changes the original spelling. Countries that deviate should adapt. (20-year-old male)

These answers not only show how the historical argument predominated among the Portuguese students but also reflect a strong resistance to change. As several authors have stressed, change is not always easy, and people generally are afraid of the new. McLuhan (2003), for example, says that when technology changes, humankind changes. People are often unwilling to change, and in some cases the resistance to change will override curiosity. However, our respondents did not express their resistance to change as an individual preference but attempted to justify it with dispassionate arguments, citing, for example, the difficulties that this change would cause in pedagogical terms:

> For people of my generation such an agreement would be absurd now because we will need to learn everything again, we are used to writing and reading in a certain way. There are things more important to be solved in our country. (21-year-old female)
>
> ---
>
> Because I do not see any advantage in unifying the records of Portuguese-speaking countries. I also disagree since it will make it difficult for children to learn new rules. (18-year-old male)
>
> ---
>
> I do not agree because we have learned a particular form of grammar so far, and suddenly, this change happens. (18-year-old male)
>
> ---
>
> Because if these spelling differences exist I don't see any reason to change it. This is a characteristic of each country, and for whoever learned it in this way it is difficult to change from one moment to another. (19-year-old female)

These excerpts also reflect a lack of information about the potential benefits of the orthographic agreement. Many of these responses focus on a feared loss of identity and the complete displacement of the Portuguese of Portugal by Brazilian Portuguese. In fact, the orthographic agreement involves spelling changes only in some words and not the language as a whole. Under the agreement, some spelling variations will continue to exist.

Concluding Remarks

In this paper we analyzed the results of a survey about Portuguese students' opinions on the orthographic agreement recently approved among the Portuguese-speaking countries. The vast majority of the participants in this research declared their opposition to the orthographic agreement on the grounds that, in their view, the language originated in Portugal and not in other countries. For this reason they considered it "unacceptable" that Portugal would have to adapt to the "perverted" spelling rules of Brazilian Portuguese.

Portuguese students saw the agreement as a threat to Portuguese identity, as a kind of submission by the former colonizer to a former colony, a former colony that they perceived as leading the outcome of the agreement. They argued that Portugal should not submit to the agreement because it benefits the Brazilian version of Portuguese, which they saw as a simplified and distorted version of the "authentic" Portuguese language.

Research carried out on the Web sites of two Portuguese newspapers (*Expresso* and *Jornal de Notícias*) produced different results. According to Carvalho (2011) those who took part in the newspaper surveys supported the orthographic agreement. This outcome may be explained by the extensive reporting of the issue in both newspapers. According to Carvalho, the newspapers reflected the ideas of the elite more than of the general public, taking into account the dominance of institutionalized voices in both newspapers.

None of the student respondents in our survey mentioned the importance of the Portuguese language worldwide, which, according to the latest edition of *Ethnologue: Languages of the World* (Lewis 2009) is the seventh-most spoken language on the globe, although it has yet to be formally adopted by international bodies. According to experts, the biggest problem until now has been the inconsistency between the Portuguese language of Brazil and that of Portugal. Standardizing the language, they argue, will increase the influence of Portuguese internationally. None of our respondents referred to the "real reason" for the agreement which, according to its proponents, is to reinforce the importance of the Portuguese language worldwide.

Another factor to be considered in the discourse of rejection is the lack of information concerning the degree of change expected to result from the orthographic agreement. Our respondents believed that adjusting to the new written language would constitute a hardship for students who have already learned the language in a certain way. They claimed that the agreement would change the language as a whole, although this is not in fact the case, since, as noted above, the number of changes is limited.

In summary, our findings are consistent with results obtained in previous studies conducted among the Portuguese population in documenting the persistence of "imperial nostalgia" among Portuguese participants, who referred repeatedly to Portugal's historical role in colonization in support of their conviction that Portugal should have played a leading role in the negotiations on the orthographic agreement. Moscovici (1961, 26), in his theory of social representations, mentions that the social process generally occurs as a dynamic of familiarization in which objects and people are understood and distinguished on the basis of previous models or perceptions. What we observe in the Portuguese imagination about the orthographic agreement is thus a reflection of the cognitive and social processes resulting from the privileged position of the country in the past, which serves as a paradigm for understanding positions taken in the present. Demystifying the agreement, especially among young people, is thus a challenging but necessary task. Changing these social representations can have a positive impact not only on the issue of the orthographic agreement but also in international relations with countries of the CPLP, as well as in daily interpersonal relations.

NOTE

1. This article was developed under the scope of the project "Identity Narratives and Social Memory: the (Re)making of Lusophony in Intercultural Contexts," funded by the Fundação para a Ciência e a Tecnologia (PTDC/CCI-COM/105100/2008). All translations are our own unless otherwise noted.

WORKS CITED

Alexandre, V. "O império e a ideia de raça (séculos XIX e XX)." In *Novos racismos: Perspectivas comparativas*, ed. J. Vala, 133–44. Lisbon: Celta Editora, 1999.

Baptista, M. "A Lusofonia não é um jardim ou da necessidade de 'perder o medo às realidades e aos mosquistos.'" In *Comunicação e Lusofonia: Para uma abordagem crítica da cultura e dos media*, ed. M. Martins, H. Sousa and R. Cabecinhas, 23–44. Porto: Campo das Letras, 2006.

Braun, V., and V. Clarke. "Using Thematic Analysis in Psychology." *Qualitative Research in Psychology* 3 (2006): 77–101.

Cabecinhas, R., and J. Feijó. "Collective Memories of Portuguese Colonial Action in Africa: Representations of the Colonial Past Among Mozambicans and Portuguese Youths." *International Journal of Conflict and Violence* 4.1 (2010): 28–44.

Cabecinhas, R., M. Lima, and A. Chaves. "Identidades nacionais e memória social: hegemonia e polémica nas representações da história." In *Identidades Nacionais em Debate*, ed. J. Miranda and M. I. João, 67–92. Oeiras: Celta, 2006.

Carvalho, M. "Análise da cobertura jornalística do novo Acordo Ortográfico da Língua Portuguesa na Web em Portugal." Congress Minutes of SOPCOM, 2011. http://sopcom2011.up.pt/.

Cunha, L. *Entre espaço e representação: Comunidade e memória social*. PhD diss., University of Minho, Braga, 2003.

Daly, J., Kellehear, A. & Gliksman, M. *The Public Health Researcher: A Methodological Approach*. Melbourne, Australia: Oxford UP, 1997.

Fereday, J., and E. Muir-Cochrane. "Demonstrating Rigor Using Thematic Analysis: A Hybrid Approach of Inductive and Deductive Coding and Theme Development." *International Journal of Qualitative Methods* 5 (2006): 80–92.

Fiorin, J. L. *E agora, Portugal?* 2008. http://www.marcosbagno.com.br/conteudo/arquivos/for_fiorin.htm.

Leoni, F. "Acordo ortográfico: Os prós e os contras de uma unificação." 2008. http://opiniaoenoticia.com.br/opiniao/tendencias-debates/acordo-ortografico-os-pros-e-os-contras-de-uma-unificacao/.

Lewis, M. P., ed. *Ethnologue: Languages of the World*. 16th ed. Dallas: SIL International, 2009.

Liu, J. H., and D. Hilton. "How the Past Weighs on the Present: Towards a Social Psychology of Histories." *British Journal of Social Psychology* 44 (2005): 537–56.

Lourenço, E. *Nós e a Europa ou as duas razões*. Lisbon: Imprensa Nacional Casa da Moeda, 1990.

Martins, M. "A lusofonia como promessa e o seu equívoco lusocêntrico." In *Comunicação e Lusofonia: Para uma abordagem crítica da cultura e dos media*, ed. M. Martins, H. Sousa, and R. Cabecinhas, 79–87. Porto: Campo das Letras, 2006.

McLuhan, M. *Understanding Me: Lectures and Interviews*. Ed. David Staines and Stephanie McLuhan. Cambridge, Mass.: MIT Press, 2003.

Möller, R. C., C. P. Sá, and F. C. C. Bezerra. "Representações sociais vivas do descobrimento do Brasil: a memória social atualizada de brasileiros e portugueses." *Psicologia* 17.2 (2004): 405–17.

Moscovici, S. "Notes Towards a Description of Social Representations." *European Journal of Social Psychology* 18 (1988): 211–50.

Moscovici, S. *La Psychanalyse, son image et son public*. Paris: PUF, 1961/1976.

Pires, N. "O contributo dos descobrimentos na ampliação vocabular." 2000. http://ruc.udc.es/dspace/bitstream/2183/2589/1/RGF-3-6-def.pdf.

Rebelo, L. "O mito do lusíada: uma tentativa de superação." In *Fantasmas e fantasias imperiais no imaginário português contemporâneo*, ed. M. Ribeiro and A. Ferreira, 115–26. Porto: Campo das Letras, 2003.

Reiter, B. "Portugal: National Pride and Imperial Neurosis." *Race and Class* 47 (2005): 79–91.

Sá, C. P., D. O. Oliveira, and L. A. Prado. "As memórias colectivas do descobrimento do Brasil: imagem comum e juízos diferenciados nas populações brasileira." *Psicologia* 17.2 (2004): 275–91.

Santos, L. A. "Portugal and the CPLP: Heightened Expectations, Unfounded

Disillusions." In *The Last Empire: Thirty Years of Portuguese Decolonization*, ed. S. Lloyd-Jones and A. Costa Pinto, 67–81. Bristol, UK: Intellect, 2003.

Tajfel, H., ed. *Social Identity and Intergroup Relations*. Cambridge: Cambridge UP, 1982.

Vala, J., D. Lopes, and M. Lima. "Black Immigrants in Portugal: Luso-Tropicalism and Prejudice." *Journal of Social Issues* 64 (2008): 287–302.

Vala, J., and A. Saint-Maurice. "Representações sociais sobre o descobrimento do Brasil: os actores e a colonização." *Psicologia* 17.2 (2004): 385–404.

Wertsch, J. V. *Voices of Collective Remembering*. New York: Cambridge University Press, 2002.

MICHELLY CARVALHO has a degree in communication sciences and a master's in information and journalism from the University of Minho. Currently she is developing a PhD in communication sciences in the area of sociology of communication, "The Orthographic Agreement and the Meaning of Lusofonia: Comparative Analysis," at the University of Minho. She has a scholarship from the Foundation for Science and Technology (FCT) and is a researcher at the Communication and Society Research Center (CECS). She may be reached at michellyscarvalho@gmail.com.

ROSA CABECINHAS has a PhD in communication sciences (the social psychology of communication) and is associate professor at the Social Sciences Institute of the University of Minho. Currently she is director of the Communication Sciences Department at the same university. She is the principal investigator of *Identity Narratives and Social Memory: The (Re)making of Lusophony in Intercultural Contexts*, financed by the Fundação para a Ciência e a Tecnologia (PTDC/CCI-COM/105100/2008). She may be reached at cabecinhas@ics.uminho.pt.

VINCENT BARLETTA

Lusofonia and Eternal Empire
Notes from the Sixteenth Century

ABSTRACT: Framed as love and commonality, as a shared patrimony, as the eternal spirit of empire, or as a "sad and ridiculous" attempt to exert influence long after the fact, the workings of Lusofonia may or may not have evolved over the past five centuries. What seems clear, however, is that the Portuguese language has been understood since at least the sixteenth century as not only the "companion" or tool of Portugal's empire, but rather as its most enduring and ontologically *real* aspect.

KEYWORDS: Lusofonia and empire, neo-colonialism, Renaissance, grammar.

"Today," Eduardo Lourenço has observed, "Lusofonia is our Pink Map, where all those empires can be inscribed, invisible and even ridiculous to anyone who looks in from the outside, but shining for us like a flame in the atrium of our soul" (1999, 177).[1] In this brief but densely poetic statement, Lourenço describes the existence of something akin to a metaphysics of empire within postimperial Portugal (the inhabitants of this Portugal being the "us," one assumes, to whom Lourenço refers) that has somehow unmoored itself from the contingencies and embarrassments of history and found its ground instead within the seemingly limitless and explicitly prophetic promise of language. As Lourenço frames it, what has emerged since the collapse of the empire, and even seen itself formalized through the CPLP, is a more or less quixotic (and thus hardly innocent) belief in the promise of a global set of speech communities somehow joined, rather than divided, by a common language.

Looking in from the outside, the new map of empire that Lourenço describes—sketched out within and between the bodies and tongues of the formerly colonized—is anything but ridiculous or invisible; rather, there is something ominously Borgesian to this vision, as though all the caravels, *padrões*, churches, and trading forts of Portuguese empire had merely been transferred by cartographers (all with unimpeachable liberal credentials) to an image the exact size of the former empire and corresponding "point for point with it" (Borges 1974,

847). Miguel Tamen, speaking more recently on the questionable politics that underlies the latest round of orthographic accords and the broader issue of Lusofonia, has expressed this situation perhaps most succinctly: "In Portugal, the idea of *lusofonia* corresponds historically to a kind of liberal colonialism, the idea that with the disappearance of the Portuguese Empire, it might be possible to maintain its spiritual substitute" (Pereira 2012, par. 4).

Lourenço and Tamen are right to call attention to the inherently neocolonialist ideologies that support contemporary notions of Lusofonia from the Portuguese perspective; however, one wonders if these notions have really emerged over the past forty years as a "spiritual substitute" for Portugal's lost global empire or if they were not understood from the very beginning to be the essence of the empire, that part of it that would endure, perhaps eternally, long after the rest had crumbled. My point here is not that Portugal's overseas empire was in some objective sense *not real* (and certainly it was real for those who found themselves on the business end of its lances and grenades); rather, I am arguing that the earliest formal theorizations of Portugal's language and empire, articulated by sixteenth-century humanists, reveal something akin to a belief in the ontological priority of the Portuguese language and its metaphysical possibilities even over the physical realities of empire. To give Borges another turn, so to speak, we might say that in sixteenth-century Portugal there existed a tendency to invert the conventional relation between "world" and "map" in such a way that the former became, in fundamental ways, the infelicitous simulacrum of the latter.

In this essay I examine the ways in which Portuguese humanists Fernão de Oliveira (1507?–1581?) and João de Barros (1496–1570) framed the question of language, empire, and immortality. Of particular concern is the special importance that these writers gave to the Portuguese language and the broader question of Lusofonia within their theories of empire. Focusing on selected passages from the grammars of Portuguese that Oliveira and Barros published within four years of each other (1536 and 1540, respectively), as well as the broader account of language and the divine found in Barros's first volume of the *Décadas da Ásia* (1552), I argue that Lusofonia has served, from its earliest origins in the Renaissance, not as the "spiritual substitute" for empire so much as its metaphysical ground.

Oliveira's Army

Oliveira's *Grammatica da lingoagem portuguesa*, published in 1536, is the earliest known Portuguese grammar and, like other vernacular grammars produced in the Iberian Peninsula during the period, it is also a self-consciously political project. Oliveira was born in Aveiro in 1507, and his active (if somewhat unfortunate) life placed him in close contact with the workings of empire and language. Entering the Dominican Order in 1520, he became a student of André de Resende while residing in the Dominican convent in Évora. In 1532 he left the Dominicans and moved to Castile, entering the lay clergy. He returned to Lisbon four years later, finding work as a private tutor for the children of figures such as João de Barros and Fernão de Almada. In the same year, he published his Portuguese grammar, which is dedicated to Almada.

After a few years of (mostly undercover) service to João III, Oliveira found work in 1545 as a pilot in the French navy and was soon afterward taken prisoner by the English. While imprisoned in England, Oliveira developed an affinity for ideas circulating around the court of Henry VIII. Upon his return to Portugal in 1547, he was imprisoned by the Inquisition. Oliveira was set free in 1551; in the following year, he participated in a naval expedition in North Africa. His bad luck holding, Oliveira found himself once again taken prisoner. He managed to return to Lisbon the next year, and in 1554 João III appointed him typographic editor at the University of Coimbra, where he also taught courses in rhetoric. In 1555 the Inquisition once again saw fit to imprison him; the events of his life become difficult to determine after this point. He seems to have once again obtained his freedom in 1557, and is thought to have died in 1581.

Apart from his Portuguese grammar, Oliveira also composed a series of works dealing with navigation and naval warfare. Among these are his *Livro da fábrica das naus* (Book of Shipbuilding; ca. 1580); *Arte da guerra do mar* (The Art of Naval Warfare; Coimbra, 1555); and the *Ars nautica* (Art of Sailing; ca. 1570). Near the end of his life, he also composed a history of Portugal that is extant in manuscript form.

Focusing on Oliveira's 1536 grammar, we see that he goes to great lengths to mix in a good deal of myth and political theory with his marginally systematic account of Portuguese phonology and morphology. In so doing, Oliveira persistently situates the Portuguese language, and the broader notion of Lusofonia, within a notion of empire that actively seeks a decisive break with Rome and Greece. He writes, for example, at the beginning of the book's fourth chapter:

> The liberal arts extend the glory of the land in which they flourish. It is because of [the liberal arts] that Greece and Rome still survive; because when they ruled the world they ordered all of their subject peoples to learn [Greek

> and Latin]; and in these languages they wrote many good teachings, and they wrote in them not only what they thought but they also translated into them all the good things that they read in other languages. In this way, they have compelled us even now to work to learn their language and forget our own. Let us not do this; rather, let us focus on ourselves now that it is our time to be masters, because it is better that we teach Africa than allow ourselves to be taught by Rome, even if the latter still had all of its prestige and merit. And let us not doubt the worth of our own language, as people make language and not the other way around. (7)[2]

Particularly striking is Oliveira's statement that as imperial "masters" in Africa (certainly an exaggeration in 1536), it is incumbent upon the Portuguese to shake off the continued cultural dominion of Rome. Unlike Antonio de Nebrija, who in 1492 had argued in his *Gramática de la lengua castellana* that one of the singular benefits of standardizing the Castilian language was that this would facilitate the study of Latin (Barros would argue something quite similar), Oliveira argues rather forcefully that the Portuguese should leave aside Latin, the continued study of which constitutes for him a form of continued, albeit "soft," Roman imperial rule.

A corollary of Oliveira's stance with respect to Rome and the Latin language is his truly striking argument that the Portuguese language can itself operate as a form of lasting, even eternal dominion in Africa and beyond. In this, Oliveira effectively goes beyond Nebrija's famous axiom, according to which language serves as the "companion of empire." For while Nebrija argues that language follows empire in all the stages of its formation, development, and decay, Oliveira instead places language—and particularly the Portuguese language—on a very different ontological footing from the physical empire on the ground. In essence, what emerges from Oliveira's argument at the start of the fourth chapter of his Portuguese grammar is a call not for a broader lusophone empire in Africa (with the latter understood to be a concrete geographical space) so much as an *empire of Lusofonia* within a metonymic Africa: "It is better that we teach Africa than allow ourselves to be taught by Rome." This, to be clear, is a vision of empire in Africa that sees Portugal operating and existing first and foremost not *through* but rather *as* the use of Portuguese. As Oliveira has it, the continued use of Latin and Greek—which is not wholly voluntary but rather operates within a strict economy of symbolic power and prestige—signifies the continued dominion of the Roman and Greek empires long after their fall. The argument that underlies Oliveira's grammar is that, by the sixteenth century, it is Portugal's turn to establish a realm of shared linguistic practice—a "regime of language" (Kroskrity 2000) that might endure, as in Greece and Rome, long after the physical empire has ceased to exist.

Within Oliveira's grammar, the notion of a Portuguese regime of language is less suggestive of the institution of a common, standardized language within a group of territories under the control of a single supreme authority than of the idea that language itself can be the form or enduring *spirit* of that earthly authority. In other words, as the soul outlives the body, so will the Portuguese language outlive the other, more material elements of Portuguese rule. How does such a regime establish itself and operate? Oliveira provides a glimpse of his own answer to this question near the end of the fifth chapter of his grammar:

> And let us focus our efforts on our language and people so that the memory of these efforts will be more enduring [*ficará com maior eternidade*]. And let us not work in a foreign language, but rather let us perfect our own with sound doctrines that we might teach to many other peoples; and in this way we will always be praised and loved, because similarity engenders love and all the more so with languages. For we see that in Africa, Guinea, Brazil, and India, those who are born among us but do not speak Portuguese do not love us owing to the difference in language, but those who grow up speaking Portuguese love us well and refer to the Portuguese as "their own" because they speak as we do. (10)[3]

Oliveira's explicit invocation of the eternal is significant, in that he consciously works to project a kind of afterlife for the actions of his contemporaries as well as for the Portuguese empire itself. He also speaks of how, through the dissemination of their language, the Portuguese will "always be praised and loved" by other peoples. The use of the term "always" is significant here, in that Oliveira is referring as much to actions and attitudes in a distant future as he is to habitual actions in the present or proximal future. Put another way, "always" (*sempre*) here can simultaneously suggest that the Portuguese will be both *consistently* praised and loved and *forever* praised and loved. In fact, given that this statement comes directly after another one that underscores the links that Oliveira wishes to forge between linguistic expression and eternity (*ficará com maior eternidade*), the issue of the distant future—potentially an endless one—seems to be paramount.

What of the question of praise and love? Oliveira argues that by teaching sound doctrines to other peoples *in Portuguese* (one infers here that Africans, Brazilians, and Asians are implied, before Oliveira removes any doubt in the following sentence, mentioning them by name), these "other peoples" will always praise and love the Portuguese. What underlies this potentially endless process of praise and love, and even serves as its cause, is nothing other than the common use of Portuguese: "those who grow up speaking Portuguese love us well and refer to the Portuguese as 'their own' because they speak as we do." This is Lusofonia writ large and linked explicitly to imperial dominion, and it is noteworthy that Oliveira frames it not in terms of military conquest and forced submission but rather as a seduction—as a Lusotropical love affair induced through early socialization into (and through) a common language.

Another significant aspect of Oliveira's theorization of (Portuguese) language and empire is the question of human agency and action. When he calls on his readers to focus their scholarly efforts (*trabalho*) on the Portuguese language and people, for example, what is the notion of agency that underlies such effort? Turning once again to the very end of the grammar's fourth chapter, we see that Oliveira argues forcefully that the Portuguese should not doubt the worth of their language, because "people make language and not the other way around." What follows from this reasoning are two related ideas: the first holds that the Portuguese are not limited by their language any more than the Greeks or Romans were; and the second (a consequence of the first) maintains that Portuguese is in no way inherently inferior to Greek or Latin, in large part because the Portuguese are in no way inferior to the Greeks and Romans. Through the Portuguese language, Oliveira is once again arguing, the Portuguese may have a share of the enduring dominion—framed explicitly as the love and praise of the African Other—then still enjoyed by the Romans through Latin.

What is perhaps most interesting about Oliveira's statement at the end of the fourth chapter of his grammar regarding human agency and language (which found common expression in sixteenth-century Portuguese chronicles and other texts of empire) is that he uses it as a kind of launching pad to move immediately into the realm of myth. In this case, the legend that he cites situates the origins of human speech itself in the Iberian Peninsula:

> If you wish to hear legends, I'll tell you how the people of the earth first learned to speak: Vitruvius says, in the second book of his *On Architecture*, that

people used to come together at a certain fire that, owing to strong winds, had ignited in the woods; conversing there with one another, people learned to form words and speak. Vitruvius does not tell us where this fire was, but Diodorus Siculus tells us in the sixth book of his *Library of History* that it was in the Pyrenees, which extend between France and Iberia." (7)[4]

The second book of Vitruvius's *On Architecture* does in fact include an account of a storm that ignites a certain forest, and Vitruvius goes on to tell how people gathered there and eventually learned to form words and communicate. Oliveira is also correct in stating that Vitruvius gives no hint regarding the location of this forest. One searches in vain, however, within the sixth book (or any book for that matter) of Diodorus Siculus's *Library of History* to find a passage that links this fire, and the formation of human speech, to the Pyrenees. All that one finds in Diodorus, in fact, is the following brief passage in book five, chapter 35, of the *Library of History*, in which he discusses the richness of Iberian silver mines: "And since they contain many thick and deep forests, in ancient times, we are told, certain herdsmen left a fire and the whole area of the mountains was entirely consumed; and due to this fire, since it raged continuously day after day, the surface of the earth was also burned and the mountains, because of what had taken place, were called the Pyrenees." There is a false etymology at work in this passage, according to which the Greek word for "fire" (*pyr*), rather than the Celtic word for "mountain" (*byrin*), is the source for the mountain range's name, and Oliveira leaps on Diodorus's creative misreading to situate the origins of human speech and verbal interaction within the Iberian Peninsula (Smith 1857, 687). In this way we come back to Oliveira's concern with the "ancient and noble" (7) status of the languages of the Iberian Peninsula and the possibility of their primacy over Greek and Latin.

Beyond the more politicocultural concerns that run through Oliveira's grammar, this text also reveals a pronounced concern on Oliveira's part with questions of eternity and divine knowledge that seem to transcend the merely political. In this matter, too, Oliveira argues that the Portuguese language plays a central role, and in his approach we find, once again, a recognizable debt to at least the prologue of Nebrija's Castilian grammar. The common idea, for example, that linguistic standardization and the liberal arts (Nebrija's *artes de la paz*) can in some manner preserve the memory of a nation's achievements is a conceit that runs through both texts. As Nebrija puts it in the prologue to his *Gramática*:

> I have decided before all else to systematize [*reduzir en artificio*] our Castilian language, so that from now on all that is written in it may follow the same standard and so extend itself for all time to come, as has been the case with Greek and Latin. . . . Because if we do not standardize our language as was done for those languages, in vain will our chroniclers and historians write and entrust to immortality the memory of your praiseworthy deeds, and [likewise in vain] do we try to translate into Castilian foreign and strange things. Such a project can only be short-lived. In fact, one of two things will necessarily occur: either the memory of your deeds will perish along with the language or it will travel along through foreign nations, as it will not have its own home in which to reside. (15–16)[5]

While the specific link between linguistic standardization and the eternal is much more implicit in the body of Oliveira's grammar than in Nebrija's prologue, it nonetheless remains the case, at a very basic level, that both authors consider their respective grammars to be tools for systematizing their national languages, and believe that the success of this process, as with Greek and Latin, will confer a share of immortality, insofar as the accomplishments and learning of Castile and Portugal will live on in their languages even after these kingdoms' respective *imperia* have fallen into decay.

As I have suggested, however, there are also definite limits to any comparison between Oliveira and Nebrija. Some of these limits, as in the case of their treatment of Greek and Latin, are ideological, but there are also deeper philosophical differences between the two humanists' treatment of their respective national vernaculars. For example, while Nebrija justifies his grammar as an instrument for better executing Castilian laws in conquered lands and exhorts Queen Isabel I to help the liberal arts flourish in the wake of her kingdom's military conquest of Granada (the study of Greek and Latin presumably taking center stage in this program), Oliveira is much more focused on the deeper meaning of Portugal's role as both Africa's teacher and the object of its undying love. Put another way, if Nebrija is more or less narrowly concerned with linguistic standardization as a way to forestall political decline and oblivion within the culturally and politically diverse Castilian Crown (for Nebrija as for other fifteenth-century Castilian humanists, the term *imperio* still most commonly signified "dominion" or "rule" in a general sense, and not necessarily the more restricted modern concept of "empire"), Oliveira has his sights set on the development of something much more deeply metaphysical, ambitious, and fraught.

From a philosophical standpoint, Oliveira's approach to the Portuguese empire and the Portuguese language emerges from his broader understanding of language itself. At the beginning of the first chapter of his grammar, Oliveira speaks of language in terms of Thomist notions of cognition and understanding embedded (albeit superficially) within an Augustinian framework of understanding, memory, and will. Seeking to define language, he argues, "Language is a figure of understanding [*entendimento*], and it is true that the mouth says what the heart commands it to say and nothing else; and nature creates no more deformed monster than those who say something other than what is in their will, because words are the proof of the man. As the greatest Truth, our Lord Jesus Christ says: 'Words are the image of works'" (4).[6] Here Oliveira speaks explicitly of understanding, memory (with the heart as its recognized seat), and will; but what exactly does he mean to say by juxtaposing the axiomatic statement that language is a "figure" of understanding with an account of human praxis encoded within a paraphrase of Jesus's claim that "each tree is recognized by its own fruit" (Luke 6:44)? What of his monster of dissimulation? Where does he situate understanding (and action), and what do his ideas on this issue mean for his arguments regarding the Portuguese language, the Portuguese empire, and the eternal? One way to answer these questions is to approach them as aspects of the broader philosophical project that informs Oliveira's grammar, namely, to link particulars to universals and thus the temporal to the eternal.

In the first place, we might say that for Oliveira language exists as the shape or form of our understanding (*entendimento*)—that which brings the workings of the passive intellect (Lat. *intellectus possibilis*; Gr. *nous pathetikos*; Ar. *al-ʿaql al-hayūlānī*) and active intellect (Lat. *intellectus agens*; Gr. *nous poetikos*; Ar. *al-ʿaql al-faʿāl*) into view and presents them as objects for analysis and judgment. The compound structure of understanding and its link to universal reason find perhaps their clearest and most influential exposition (especially in the immediate context of the Council of Trent) in the philosophy of Thomas Aquinas, who had argued that the active intellect serves as the cognitive power, linked to the eternal *logos*, by which we form general concepts (in language and even language itself) from sense experience: "[The active intellect] confers generality upon the thoughts (*species expressa*) of the passive mind. Without the work of the former no concepts would be available; and without these cognition could not take place, for the sensuous presentation of the environment could not be ordered. The active intellect is thus not something separate and external to the subject—neither a common storehouse of ideas nor a metaphysical 'starting-handle' pushing forms into the mind or jerking it into action. Rather it is a power of deriving intelligible forms from experience" (Haldane 1992, 205). In other words, for Aquinas, in our sense experience particulars (presented before the imagination or *passive intellect* as phantasms) become general concepts through the power of the active intellect, which is linked to the mind of God through the principle of universal reason. Our *understanding* is thus a composite of the images that our passive mind derives from sense experience and the generation of general concepts linked to the universal and eternal through the work of the active intellect.

As the figure of our understanding, language is thus itself a generalized concept linked to divine knowledge; however, it is also instantiated through words (*palavras*) that we experience as images (*phantasms*, as Aquinas puts it) linked to our actions, through both intentionality and use. Put another way, if Jesus's parable of the tree and its fruit is largely concerned with intentionality and ethics, Oliveira seems more concerned with deriving abstract principles from concrete forms and instances of language use and praxis. It is through these abstract principles, embodied in language as a system of signification linked both to universal reason and to particulars experienced through sight and sound, that Oliveira seeks to join the Portuguese language to the imperial project and so imbue the latter with something akin to an immortal soul.

Barros and the Eternal Spirit of Empire

João de Barros was both a towering figure in Portuguese humanism and Oliveira's contemporary (Oliveira even served for a time as the tutor of Barros's children), and his theories of language, empire, and the eternal intersect with those expressed in the 1536 *Grammar* in many respects. Educated in the royal court in Lisbon, Barros led an active life in the service of three successive Portuguese kings: Manuel I, Joaõ III, and Sebastião I. In 1532 he was put in charge of the Casa da Índia in Lisbon, the administrative center of Portugal's Asian empire, a post he held until 1568, two years before his death. Barros was also an active writer over the course of his life, composing chivalric, philosophical, and didactic works.

Barros's early chivalric work is *Chrónica do Emperador Clarimundo, donde os reys de Portugal descendem, tirada da linguagem ungara em a nossa portugueza* (Chronicle of the Emperor Clarimundo, from Whom Are Descended the Kings of Portugal, Translated from Hungarian into Portuguese; 1520). His best-known philosophical and didactic works include *Rhopicapnefma, ou mercadoria espiritual* (Rhopicapnefma, or Spiritual Merchandise; 1532), *Cartinha para aprender a ler* (Epistle for Learning to Read; 1539), *Gramática da língua portuguesa* (Grammar of the Portuguese Language; 1540), *Diálogo em louvor da nossa linguagem* (Dialogue in Praise of Our Language; 1540), *Diálogo da viciosa vergonha* (Dialogue of Corrupted Shame; 1540), and *Diálogo de preceitos moraes com prática delles em modo de jogo* (Dialogue of Moral Precepts with Their Practice in the Form of a Game; 1540). Barros also composed four volumes of his vast history of the Portuguese empire in Asia (the last of them published posthumously) before Diogo do Couto picked up the project and produced nine more volumes (not all of which have survived). While Barros's *Décadas da Ásia* was overshadowed in terms of popularity by Fernão Lopes de Castanheda's much less detailed (and less accurate) *História do descubrimento e conquesta da Índia pelos portugueses* (History of the Discovery and Conquest of India by the Portuguese), it has remained a central source for piecing together the history of early modern India and east Asia even to the present day.

In the introduction to the first volume of his *Décadas da Ásia*, Barros speaks directly to the Portuguese king João III, offering the ailing monarch a dense and complex theorization of empire, human works, language, and immortality. At the start of the text, Barros gives his king a brief lesson on the principle of reproduction as a means of achieving a form of immortality through the body and within nature:

> All things, very powerful king and our lord, are so committed to the preservation of their being that they work as much as possible, and however they can, to give themselves perpetual life. Natural beings, upon which humans have no influence, have in each of them a generative capacity; and when they are divinely disposed, although they are menaced by their own corruption, Nature itself renews them in the form of a new being, through which they remain alive and preserved in their own species. (xiv–xv)[7]

Barros here begins with a philosophical commonplace about the desire for immortality before moving into a discussion of the question of generation and corruption.[8]

For Barros (as for Aristotle), human actions are denied even the distributive immortality achieved through reproduction. As Barros puts it (borrowing in part from a historiographical conceit that dates back to Herodotus), because human actions (*feitos*) lack any sort of regenerative power, and die with the individuals who perform them, it has been necessary for humans to develop some sort of instrument by which their actions might approach at the very least the sort of mediated immortality achieved by natural beings through reproduction. Barros speaks of this instrument as a "divine artifice":

> And other things, which are not the work of Nature, but rather human achievements and actions, these die with their author due to both their lack of any animate ability to generate something like themselves and the brevity of human life. These same humans, in order to conserve their name and memory, sought out some divine artifice that might represent in the future that which they did in the present. This artifice, although its development has been attributed to various authors, seems more likely to have been inspired by God than invented by some human intellect. (1, xiv)[9]

According to Barros, the means—that is, the artifice or system—by which humans might collaboratively resolve this seemingly intractable conflict with human mortality, action, and the process of forgetting that accompanies individual death is language. As Barros presents it, language, framed explicitly as verbal practice, is a system with roots not in human industry but in divine intellect. Perhaps more radically, Barros goes on to suggest, following the thirteenth-century Mallorcan polymath Ramon Llull, that the human capacity for verbal practice is itself a sense, like hearing, sight, touch, taste, and smell, but superior to all of these.

Barros seems to accept Llull's account of the embodied physicality of speech, but he also takes this idea in a new direction. In essence, Barros seeks a kind of compromise between the dictates of universalist reason and morality and the wholly contingent features of verbal interaction and human being-in-the-world. Barros's notion of language as both "divine" and an "artifice" (or "system") designed to mitigate the undesired effects (in this world and the next) of human mortality essentially allows him to walk a thin line between the idea, on the one hand, of verbal discourse as an intra- and intersubjective tool and the Llullian concept, on the other, of its status as an innate human sense linked in some direct way to the divine and the moral finality of our existence.

Having presented language as an inherently pragmatic and embodied system of signification linked to the divine order (a "divine artifice"), Barros quickly points out the limitations of verbal communication for any attempt to overcome the durational and ontological challenges that language in general is called on to resolve. Having thus established both the promise and the limitations of verbal language, Barros moves on to the powers of written language. As Barros puts it, written letters, because they are not animate, do not suffer the sort of corruption that affects natural beings and phenomena such as verbal language use. As inanimate, artificial things, letters endure and, in addition, do not cause the corruption of the elements from which they are composed. What complements this freedom from corruption and imbues written language with force and meaning, however, is the "living spirit" (*espírito de vida*) that nonetheless resides within writing:

> And written letters, being inanimate characters, yet contain within them the spirit of life, given that they speak to us of all things. They are elements that provide assistance to nature and make things last into the future, with the multiplication of the years, in the most excellent way that Nature can achieve; for we see that Nature, in order to generate something, corrupts and alters the elements from which it is composed; and written letters, being the elements from which the form and meaning of things are composed, corrupt neither these things nor human understanding. (I, xv–xvi)[10]

Here Barros extends the Llullian theory of *affatus* in important ways. Most significantly, he argues that written language serves as a mediating means or instrument by which speech, an embodied faculty or sense linked to the *logos* of creation and salvation, does not die with the body or degenerate over time but endures in uncorrupted form. Barros goes on to argue that "the fruit of human actions is very different from our natural fruits, which are made from semen through the innate mortality found within all humans (for whose use all things were created). The fruit of human actions is eternal, given that it proceeds from the understanding and the will, where all actions are produced and received and, given that the understanding and the will are components of the soul, they make these actions eternal" (xvi–xvii).[11] Like Oliveira before him, Barros moves into Augustinian territory here (speaking of will, understanding, and memory—and all linked to the individual soul), though he also retains a strong link to Llull, Aquinas, and Aristotle (by way of, most probably, some version of Avicenna's metaphysics). For Barros, written language offers to human beings an approximation to divinity, expressed both as a form of immortality/permanence and as a means of moral perfection within the social sphere of action and interaction (with origins in the soul). This idea departs in marked ways from Marsilio Ficino's more ambivalent treatment of writing, elaborated in his commentary on Plato's *Phaedrus* (as well as Jacques Derrida's much later, deconstructionist reading of the dialogue). Glossing Socrates' story of the Theban king Thamus's rejection of writing on the grounds that it would make people forgetful and convert them into sophists who "seemed" to have wisdom but did not, Ficino says that "writing would make them negligent in their learning [*ad inventionem*], given that they would rely on the talent [*ingenium*] of their superiors and not on their own" (Allen 1981, 211). In this and other passages, it becomes clear that for Ficino (and Neoplatonists working in both Italy and Portugal), writing is decidedly lacking in the *espírito da vida* with which Barros seeks to imbue it.

In Barros's hands, however, written language (and especially historical writing) emerges as a hybrid inanimate/animate construct that offers the possibility, through the use of cultural tools, of an unending and progressively perfect life. But where does Barros's syncretic theorization of language, written history, immortality, and progress take us as we work to understand the ideologies that informed both the development of the Portuguese empire in Asia and the evolution of Iberian humanism during the sixteenth century? One crucial place to begin, as was the case with Oliveira, is with the implicit theories of the Portuguese language that underlie Barros's broader theorization of language and immortality. It is, after all, in Portuguese that Barros writes his *Décadas da Ásia*, and it is in that language that the histories of Portuguese achievements that he describes will also presumably be written. How do Barros's ideas on language and immortality intersect with his understanding of the Portuguese language, its link to empire, and the broader concept of Lusofonia?

Four years after the publication of Oliveira's Portuguese grammar, Barros published his own *Gramática da língua portuguesa*, which was bound together with his *Diálogo em louvor da nossa linguagem*, a conversation between a father and son on the virtues of the Portuguese language in relation to other European languages. Barros begins his Portuguese grammar, which is shaped in significant ways by the grammars of Priscian and Nebrija, with a brief definition of grammar itself. It is a short passage, but it presents many of the elements that he would include in his 1552 introduction to the *Décadas da Ásia*:

> Grammar is a Greek term that means the science of letters. According to the definition that the grammarians have given it, it provides a certain and just

> mode of speaking and writing, collected from the usage and authority of wise men. We can call it a system of words put in their natural places in such a way that, in speech and writing, we might come to know the intentions of others. Because written letters enter through our sight just as spoken words enter through our ears—the instrument with which our understanding receives the majority of things. (293)[12]

This paragraph, at its most basic level, is an application of Thomist notions of the active and passive intellect. As Barros sets things up, our understanding (*intendimento*) receives utterances as sense impressions (whether through our ears or, in the case of written texts, through our eyes), and grammar serves as a systematization or "art" of utterances (quite literally framed as "acts of speech") that allows us to determine meaning—in essence, to extract general concepts from particular impressions left upon our imagination. Insofar as it is seen to be the fruit of the *active intellect*, grammar is thus linked to the universal and the divine.

Building upon an understanding of language and grammar rooted in philosophical conceptions of knowledge and the eternal, Barros moves into more openly political and ideological territory in his *Diálogo em louvor da nossa linguagem*. Mirroring and even expanding Oliveira's arguments regarding the role of Portuguese in the workings of the empire, the father in the dialogue makes the following claim:

> With respect to material things, we say that which endures possesses greater excellence, just as in matters of honor we consider things retained in the memory to have greater glory. We find examples in all kingdoms, and while [the Romans] inevitably saw political decline owing to the variability of time and fortune, they left the Latin language as a sign of their empire, which will endure forever. The arms and *padrões* of the Portuguese, established in Africa, Asia, and in more than a thousand islands beyond the three known parts of the earth, are material things, and with the passing of time they might deteriorate, but what will not deteriorate are the teachings, customs, and language that the Portuguese left in these lands. (404–5)[13]

What emerges from this statement is that the Portuguese language, like Latin before it (as well as many other imperial languages), can serve as that part of the Portuguese empire that will never decline or end. Barros frames it, in a very explicit sense, as the eternal soul of empire, embedded forever within the bodies and minds of the colonized and their descendants. In his response to the father, the son presents this idea as axiomatic: "It is certain that a good custom and word can outlast a *padrão*" (é çerto que mais pode durar um bom costume e vocábulo que um padram; 405).

Barros's framing of language and Lusofonia as the eternal spirit of empire becomes even more apparent in the father's next statement regarding Portugal's language socialization and evangelical efforts within its colonies. In a statement that adds the full weight of Portugal's perceived missionary responsibility in Africa, Asia, and Brazil to Oliveira's account of Portugal's regime of language in those regions, the father in Barros's dialogue argues that "there is certainly no glory that compares to the fact that, through our grammar [*a nossa arte*], Ethiopian, Persian, and Indian children—living on this and the far side of the Ganges and within the jurisdiction of their temples and pagodas, where the word 'Roman' had never been heard—have learned Portuguese and may thus become instructed in the precepts of our faith, which are written in that language" (405).[14]

Here the achievements of the grammarian outstrip those of the explorer and conqueror, and Barros opens up yet another path by which the concept of Lusofonia—here linked not just to philosophical accounts of universal reason and knowledge but directly to processes of Christian conversion—serves the empire even centuries after the decay of *padrões*, outposts, forts, and other such monuments of worldly dominion.

Conclusions

In the linguistic work of Oliveira and Barros, the notion of Lusofonia—articulated in its infancy as the spread of Portuguese throughout Portugal's colonized territories—emerges as something akin to the eternal spirit of empire. This occurs on many levels. First, on what one might term the historico-imperial level, both Oliveira and Barros discuss the spread of Portuguese as a means of following and even exceeding the example of the Greeks and especially the Romans, who had achieved through their languages a form of lasting power and even immortality. On a second, more deliberately philosophical level, we see the elaboration of theories regarding the Portuguese language, and language in general, in terms of a somewhat sophisticated discussion of theories of cognition and immortality current in the Iberian Peninsula at the start of the sixteenth century. On a third, more ideological level, the Portuguese language emerges as an instrument of language socialization by which the Portuguese might carry out Christian conversion and initiate a kind of perversely reciprocal love affair with their colonized subjects—an emotional bond with all the characteristics of a transhistorical form of Stockholm syndrome.

Framed as love and commonality, as a shared patrimony, as the eternal spirit of empire, or as a "sad and ridiculous" attempt to exert influence long after the fact, the workings of Lusofonia may or may not have evolved over the past five centuries. What seems clear, however, is that the Portuguese language has been understood since at least the sixteenth century as not only the "companion" or tool of Portugal's empire, but rather as its most enduring and ontologically *real* aspect.

NOTES

1. The "Pink Map" (*mapa cor-de-rosa*) was a nineteenth-century document that represented Portugal's claim to sovereignty over Angola, Mozambique, and the wide strip of land between the two (modern-day Malawi, Zambia, and Zimbabwe). The Portuguese government discarded the Pink Map in 1890, in the wake of a British ultimatum that laid claim to the territory between Angola and Mozambique. All translations are my own unless otherwise noted.

2. "Esses estudos fazem mais durar a glória da terra em que florecem. Porque Gréçia e Roma só por isto ainda vivem: porque quando senhoreavão o mundo mandarão a todas as gentes a elles sogeytas aprender suas línguas: e em ellas escrevião muytas bõas doutrinas e não somente o que entendião escrevião nellas: mas também trasladavam parellas todo o bo que lião em outras. E desta feyção nos obrigarão a que ainda agora trabalhemos em aprender e apurar o seu, esqueçendo-nos do nosso: não façamos assy mas tornemos sobre nos agora que he tempo e somos senhores porque milhor he que ensinemos a Guine ca que sejamos ensinados de Roma: ainda que ella agora tevera toda sua valia e preço. E não desconfiemos da nossa lingua porque os homens fazem a língua, e não a lingoa os homens."

3. "E com tudo apliquemos nosso trabalho à nossa língua e gente; e ficará com maior eternidade a memória delle. E nam trabalhemos em língua estrangeira, mas apuremos tanto a nossa com boas doutrinas que a possamos ensinar a muytas outras gentes e sempre seremos dellas louvados e amados porque a semelhança he causa do amor e mays em as línguas. E ao contrayro vemos em África, Guiné, Brasil e Índia não amarem muytos os Portugueses que antrelles naçem so polla diferença da língua: e os dela nacidos querem bem aos seus portugueses e chamanlhes seus porque falão assi como elles."

4. Vitruvius's text, found in the first chapter of the second book of his *On Architecture*, reads as follows: "Mankind originally brought forth like the beasts of the field, in woods,

dens, and groves, passed their lives in a savage manner, eating the simple food which nature afforded. A tempest, on a certain occasion, having exceedingly agitated the trees in a particular spot, the friction between some of the branches caused them to take fire; this so alarmed those in the neighborhood of the accident, that they betook themselves to flight. Returning to the spot after the tempest had subsided, and finding the warmth which had thus been created extremely comfortable, they added fuel to the fire excited, in order to preserve the heat, and then went forth to invite others, by signs and gestures, to come and witness the discovery. In the concourse that thus took place, they testified their different opinions and expressions by different inflexions of the voice. From daily association words succeeded to these indefinite modes of speech; and these becoming by degrees the signs of certain objects, they began to join them together, and conversation became general."

5. "Acordé ante todas las otras cosas reduzir en artificio este nuestro lenguaje castellano: para que lo que agora y de aquí adelante en él se escriviere pueda quedar en un tenor: y estenderse en toda la duración de los tiempos que están por venir. Como vemos que se a hecho en la lengua griega y latina. . . . Porque si otro tanto en nuestra lengua no se haze como en aquellas: en vano vuestros cronistas y estoriadores escriven y encomiendan a inmortalidad la memoria de vuestros loables hechos: y nos otros tentamos de passar en castellano las cosas peregrinas y estrañas: pues que aqueste no puede ser sino negocio de pocos años. I será necessaria una de dos cosas: o que la memoria de vuestras hazañas perezca con la lengua: o que ande peregrinando por las naciones estranjeras: pues que no tiene propria casa en que pueda morar."

6. "A lingoagem é figura do entendimento e assi é verdade que a boca diz quanto lhe manda o coração e não outra cousa; antes não devia a natureza criar outro mais difforme monstro do que são aquelles que falão o que não tem na vontade, porque se as obras são prova do home. Como diz a suma verdade Jesu Christo nosso Deus: e as palavras são ymagem das obras." The source for this idea is Luke 6:43–45: "No good tree bears bad fruit, nor does a bad tree bear good fruit. Each tree is recognized by its own fruit. People do not pick figs from thorn bushes, or grapes from briers. A good man brings good things out of the good stored up in his heart, and an evil man brings evil things out of the evil stored up in his heart. For the mouth speaks what the heart is full of."

7. "Todalas cousas, muito poderoso rey, e senhor nosso, tem tanto amor á conservação de seu proprio ser, que quanto lhe he possivel trabalham em seu modo por se fazerem perpétuas. As naturaes, em que sómente obra a Natureza, e não a industria humana, cada huma dellas em si mesma tem huma virtude generativa, que quando Divinamente são dispostas, ainda que periguem em sua corrupção, essa mesma Natureza as torna renovar em novo ser, com que ficam vivas, e conservadas em sua propria especie."

8. See, for example, Aristotle's *De anima* (2.4): "The acts in which [the nutritive soul] manifests itself are reproduction and the use of food—reproduction, I say, because for

any living thing that has reached its normal development and which is unmutilated, and whose mode of generation is not spontaneous, the most natural act is the production of another like itself, an animal producing an animal, a plant a plant, in order that, as far as its nature allows, it may partake in the eternal and divine."

9. "E as outras cousas, que não são obras da Natureza, mas feitos, e actos humanos, estas porque não tinham virtude animada de gerar outras semelhantes a si, e por a brevidade da vida do homem, acabavam com seu author: os mesmos homens por conservar seu nome em a memoria dellas, buscáram hum Divino artificio, que representasse em futuro o que elles obravam em presente. O qual artificio, pero que a invenção delle se dê a diversos Authores, mais parece per Deos inspirado, que inventado per algum humano entendimento."

10. "E as letras, sendo huns caracteres mortos, e não animados, contém em si espirito de vida, pois a dam ácerca de nós a todalas cousas. Cá ellas são huns elementos, que lhe dam assistencia, e as fazem passar em futuro com sua multiplicação de annos em annos per modo mais excellente do que faz a Natureza; pois vemos, que esta Natureza pera gerar alguma cousa, corrompe, e altera os elementos de que he composta; e as letras, sendo elementos de que se compõe, e fórma a significação das cousas, não corrompem as mesmas cousas, nem o entendimento."

11. "[O] fruto destes actos humanos he mui differente do fruto natural, que se produz da semente das cousas, por este natural fenecer no mesmo homem, pera cujo uso todas foram creadas; e o fruto das obras delles he eterno, pois procede do entendimento, e vontade, onde se fabricam, e aceptam todas, que, por serem partes espirituaes, as fazem eternas."

12. "Gramática é vocábulo grego; quér dizer çiência de lêteras. E, segundo a difinçám que lhe os gramáticos déram, é um módo çérto e justo de falar e escrever, colheito do uso e autoridade dos barões doutos. Nós podemos-lhe chamar artefíçio de palavras postas en seus naturáes lugares, pera que, mediante elas, assi na fála como na escritura, venhamos em conhiçimento das tenções alheas. Porque bem assi entram as lêteras pela vista como palávras pelos ouvidos—instrumento com que o nosso intendimento reçebe as mais das cousas."

13. "E quanto, antre as cousas materiais, é de maior excelênçia aquela que mais dura, tanto açerca das cousas da honra, sam de maior glória as que a memória mais retém. Exemplo temos em todalas monarquias, cá, se perderam com a variedade do tempo e fortuna das coisas humanas, pero leixou a língua latina este sinal de seu império, que durará eternalmente. As armas e padrões portugueses, postos em África e em Ásia, e em tantas mil ilhas fora da repartiçam das três partes da terra, materiaes sam, e pode-as o tempo gastar, pero não gastará doutrina, costumes, linguagem, que os portugueses nestas terras leixarem."

14. "Çerto é que nam há glória que se possa comparar a quando os mininos etíopas,

persianos, indos, d'aquém e d'além do Gange, em suas próprias terras, na força de seus templos e pagodes, onde nunca se ouviu o nome romano, per esta nossa arte aprenderam a nossa linguagem, com que possam ser doutrinados em os preçeitos da nossa fe, que nela vam escritos." For more on the use of Portuguese missionary grammars in Africa, Asia, and Brazil, see Zwartjes 2011.

WORKS CITED

Allen, J. B. *Marsilio Ficino and the Phaedran Charioteer: Introduction, Texts, Translations.* Berkeley and Los Angeles: University of California Press, 1981.

Aristotle. "On the Soul." In *The Basic Works of Aristotle*, ed. Richard McKeon, 535–606. New York: Random House, 1941.

Barros, João de. *Da Ásia de João de Barros.* 24 vols. Lisboa: Sam Carlos, 1973.

———. *Gramática da língua portuguesa.* Ed. Maria Leonor Carvalhão Buescu. Lisbon: Facudade de Letras/University of Lisbon, 1971.

Borges, Jorge Luis. *Obras completas.* Buenos Aires: Emecé, 1974.

Haldane, John. "Aquinas and the Active Intellect." *Philosophy* 67.260 (1992): 199–210.

Kroskrity, Paul V. "Regimenting Languages: Language Ideological Perspectives." In *Regimes of Language: Ideologies, Polities, and Identities*, ed. Paul V. Kroskrity, 1–34. Santa Fe: School of American Research Press, 2000.

Lourenço, Eduardo. *A nau de Ícaro seguido de Imagem e miragem da Lusofonia.* Lisbon: Gradiva, 1999.

Nebrija, Antonio. *Gramática de la lengua castellana.* Barcelona: Lingkua, 2009.

Ochs, Elinor, and Bambi B. Schieffelin. "Language Acquisition and Socialization: Three Developmental Stories and Their Implications." In *Linguistic Anthropology: A Reader*, 2nd ed., ed. Alessandro Duranti, 296–328. Malden, Mass.: Wiley-Blackwell, 2008.

Oliveira, Fernão de. *Grammatica da lingoagem portuguesa.* Lisbon: Galhardo, 1536.

Pereira, Nelson. "Miguel Tamen: 'A lusofonia é uma espécie de colonialismo de esquerda.'" *iOnline*, 24 April 2012.

Siculus, Diodorus. *Library of History.* Ed. Bill Thayer. *Lacus Curtius.*

Smith, William. *Dictionary of Greek and Roman Geography.* 2 vols. Boston: Little, Brown, 1857.

Vitruvius. *On Architecture.* Ed. Bill Thayer. *Lacus Curtius.*

Zwartjes, Otto. *Portuguese Missionary Grammars in Asia, Africa, and Brazil, 1550–1800.* Amsterdam: John Benjamins, 2011.

VINCENT BARLETTA is an associate professor of Iberian and Latin American cultures at Stanford University. His research tends to focus, within a comparative framework, on the literature of Iberian empire in Africa and Asia. Dr. Barletta is also concerned with broader anthropological and philosophical questions that arise out of readings of this literature. His current book project focuses on these philosophical issues, examining theories of rhythm as ethics from fifth-century-BCE Greece through to the end of the (Iberian) sixteenth century. His most recent book is *Death in Babylon: Alexander the Great and Iberian Empire in the Muslim Orient*. He is also the author of *Covert Gestures: Crypto-Islamic Literature as Cultural Practice in Early Modern Spain*, and editor/translator of Granadan Morisco Francisco Núñez Muley's *A Memorandum for the President of the Royal Audiencia and Chancery Court of the City and Kingdom of Granada*. He may be reached at vbarletta@stanford.edu.

JOANA PASSOS, SANDRA ATAÍDE LOBO,
CONSTANTINO XAVIER, AND DUARTE DRUMOND BRAGA

Inside/Outside Lusofonia
The Case of Goa

ABSTRACT: In answer to the call for papers on "Lusofonia and Its Futures," a group of researchers from the academic community focusing on Goa decided to reflect collectively on this topic. The individual statements compiled below represent the productive dissonance in this community, where everyone contributes and listens. They address the concept of Lusofonia in the context of issues of identity, self-definition, academic visibility, cultural memory, and global networks.

KEYWORDS: global mappings, Lusosphere, genealogies, invisible Lusofonia.

Alternative Global Mappings

JOANA PASSOS

The term Lusofonia has been used as a descriptive concept to define the borders of a particular academic field whose object of study coincides with the use of the Portuguese language across a variety of geographical locations, expressing their respective cultures. Such a transversal definition of the term seems neutral enough, and promotes the idea that a network of affinities and spontaneous empathy might connect different peoples, favoring a productive global network. I have nothing against this celebratory view of Lusofonia, nor do I reject its positive potential to structure solid networks of cultural (and economic) exchange, relying on Portuguese as a convenient working language. However, after Foucault, Derrida, and Gramsci, we know that there is no such thing as an innocent use of language and that subtle hegemonic agendas have often relied on discourse, dominant ideologies, and cultural production as effective means of social and political control. Its positive potential notwithstanding, what are the perverse meanings inherent in the notion of Lusofonia? My tentative answer considers two elements of the concept: the visibility of the Portuguese language and the geographies the word invokes.

If the principle defining the limits of the lusophone universe is the dominant status of the Portuguese language in a given society (regardless of token references to minority languages and cultures), then Lusofonia refers to a set of Portuguese-speaking national units. As such, the geography of the use of the Portuguese language (and of English, French, and Spanish) in fact emulates old colonial mappings of the world, hidden under postindependence uses and appropriations of the language. I believe that the historical heritage underlying these linguistic maps is not neutral, and that collective amnesia is neither cathartic nor wise when it comes to working toward positive outcomes in international relations. Lusofonia, Francofonia, and World English are collective concepts that inscribe an agenda and point to one horizon of preferential relations instead of others. In addition, these concepts undermine the concepts of diversity and difference in their assertion of a collective project. And what are the centers of decision in this collective project? Did the new orthographic agreement on the writing of the Portuguese language include references to standard Portuguese in several African countries? And do graduation courses in English studies devote the same number of hours to English, American, and Nigerian literature? Languages, in other words, have their hegemonic centers and peripheries in spite of being shared. Consequently, if the Portuguese language unites us in our diversity, I would prefer actual references to the language itself, instead of an umbrella term like Lusofonia.

Another point worth making in discussing the negative reverberations associated with the lusophone world is the invisibility of communities that lack the status of nations. If Lusofonia refers to countries where Portuguese is the dominant language, then communities of Portuguese-speaking emigrants are not properly acknowledged by the term. Consider the residual scholarly work on the cultural activity produced within these emigrant communities, and you will understand the dimensions of their marginalization. Working with a notion of Portuguese-speaking communities might give such communities the visibility and acknowledgment they deserve.

While writing a postcolonial history of Goan literature in Portuguese, I became even more aware of the limits one adjusts to when going along with the established debate.[1] If Portuguese is becoming a language of the past in Goa, why does the invisibility of Goa in the core debates around Lusofonia change into visibility when accompanied by Timor and Macau? The answer must be that within this set Goa gains new symbolic meaning. These are colonial geographies of cultural encounters being translated into contemporary epistemologies.

In Europe, within the frame of postcolonial theory, there is growing awareness of the necessity to think about alternative networks and working platforms that do not necessarily reproduce colonial logic. Otherwise, the West remains perpetually the center and the norm in shaping global relations. However, if you replace certain types of hierarchical world order for multicentered networks, the balance of knowledge or power distribution shifts in a democratic direction.

Goa seems a good place to start thinking along these alternative lines. Its written culture, ancient and multiple, evolved as a hybrid that accommodated tension, fragmentation, and forms of synthesis. As Goa related to different sources of influence in an active way, studying Goa offers knowledge on a great variety of issues. Not only did it produce forms of resistance and subversion against colonialism and Western influence, but it also assimilated romantic aesthetics, modernism, and neorealism, integrating them in an Eastern cultural location. Moreover, its ex-centric situation in relation to Portuguese late colonialism, to British India, and to Indian core cultures creates a unique vantage point that illuminates other realities. Consequently, it is productive to think about concepts such as Lusofonia (and its respective theoretical mappings) from the perspective of Goa, suggesting that alternative, ex-centric mappings of cultural heritages in Portuguese may prove productive vantage points from which to question established epistemologies, or at least to confront their hidden agendas and ambiguities.'

These Languages That Separate Us

SANDRA ATAÍDE LOBO

If we accept as a given among the different ideas supported by the concept of Lusofonia that it implies the existence of Portuguese-speaking communities, then in the case of Goa this community is not only insignificant but also confined to an older generation. Consequently, it seems probable that it will vanish with its last members. It is true that the search for a basic knowledge of Portuguese has increased in the territory, but this seems connected more to migratory fluxes than to a new appropriation of Portuguese. On the other hand, there are a number of scholars interested in studying Portuguese: those who take degrees in Portuguese language and literature at the University of Goa, and those whose research interests "force" them to learn at least written Portuguese. I do not know whether somewhere, somehow, these scholars coincide or work on common projects, but these academic interests do not necessarily mean that these scholars use the language in colloquial or even academic communication. In view of this panorama of divergent interests, it seems reasonable to assume that Goa would generally be forgotten or marginalized to a subaltern space in the debate around Lusofonia.

However, considering a relevant part of contemporary Goan intellectual tradition, between 1921 and 1961 or even later, it seems rather unfair, and thus unacceptable, to relegate Goa to this subaltern status, for there has been a huge amount of Goan scholarship in the Portuguese language, in such diverse fields as literary criticism, historiography, medicine, law, economy, politics, ethnography, colonial debates, cultural and political identity—the list goes on and on. Furthermore, the invisibility of Goa in lusophone debates is equally unjustified because of the intervention of a significant group of Goan intellectuals in Portuguese public debates, which has contributed to the development of different trends in contemporary Portuguese thought. Goan scholars have also played an active role in promoting Portuguese language and culture abroad. Note that I am not referring exclusively to the role they have played in Africa, an issue that is only now beginning to garner the attention it merits. There are other dimensions to this stream of Goan activity: Plácido and Vicente de Bragança Cunha, brothers of T. B. Cunha, were responsible for the first lectures on Portuguese language and literature at the universities of Calcutta and Bombay, respectively. When Vicente de Bragança Cunha was in England, he played the same role at the University of London. Other examples could be mentioned, including scholarly contributions in the United States. All of these Goan scholars are important to the adequate construction of a collective memory concerning Portuguese language and cultures and their international context, as well as to the memory of Goan culture itself.

Returning to the subject of Goan contemporary reality, I would submit that both local intellectual activity and the construction of collective memory have much to gain from a wide and extensive dialogue with their own diverse scholarly heritage, but this dialogue depends in part on access to texts that were produced in the past, in Portuguese. Thus the role that the Portuguese language played in Goa until 1961 in the medium of print reveals how serious and disruptive the cultural consequences of obliterating this Portuguese heritage would be. When I try to explain the object of my studies, I'm often met with ironic questions like "Where are there intellectuals in Goa?" Goan acquaintances, most of them well educated, have made such comments, reflecting the local perception of Goa as a subaltern realm in terms of intellectual life and scholarly production. In my view, this question goes beyond the problematic concept of Lusofonia and the debates surrounding it, for the focus of study needs to be shifted from the preservation of Portuguese memory in Goa to the importance of Goan memory in Portuguese expression. Contrary to the common belief that the Portuguese language in Goa would be exclusively related to the Catholic community (where it was undeniably dominant), this heritage also concerns the Hindu community, for relevant Hindu intellectuals sometimes had their works published in Portuguese. This problem has begun to be tackled by a group of Goan intellectuals, several of them less than fluent in Portuguese. They are doing what they can to address this difficulty, promoting the local appropriation of Portuguese and investing (within financial constraints) in translations of local Portuguese texts into English. There is also an increasing trend to publish studies of Goa's diverse intellectual traditions. The limited institutional impact of these efforts becomes clear on a visit to the Goan university website. The recommended reading in the social sciences and humanities is in English, in contrast to the multilingual character of Goa's past and present. In the case of Konkani and Marathi literature, local tradition at least receives the attention of the respective departments. But one cannot find a definition of Goan Portuguese literature on the webpage of the Portuguese department.

I would like to examine a final aspect of the issue by looking at the academic situation in Portugal. Most history syllabuses in Portuguese schools and universities fail to grant Portugal's former colonies any historical autonomy; they are always viewed through the lens of Portuguese colonialism. Nor does the study of these ex-colonies take into account their reciprocal influence on Portuguese politics and culture. Only now are some Portuguese scholars beginning to take a broader approach to the study of the former colonies, one that appreciates their diversity, autonomy, and historical importance in their own right, and not merely in their relation to Portugal, but this trend has yet to make a significant impact on mainstream curricula. Finally, in the area of Oriental studies in Portugal, it is very strange that one can take classes in Sanskrit, Hindi, Arab, Japanese, Chinese, and Persian, but there is not a single course in Konkani or Marathi. This makes it difficult for Portuguese historians of Goa to gain access to fundamental sources. Moreover, most Portuguese scholars do not consider the absence of courses in these languages a problem, which in itself suggests the extent of the invisibility of these cultures in most Portuguese eyes.

Goa as India's Hub to the Lusosphere

CONSTANTINO XAVIER

India today is affected by a "lusophone paradox" that sees many of its efforts to internationalize its economy lost in translation. While its economic engagement with the eight Portuguese-speaking countries (CPLP) and Macau is booming (now at US$15.3 billion, up by 400 percent since 2005), diplomatic and cultural engagement lags far behind. For example, India makes many scholarships and educational programs available to students and officials from the CPLP countries, but they are administered in English. And only a handful of Indian diplomats are fluent in Portuguese, and they are often posted in non-CPLP capitals.

But New Delhi's perception is changing fast, and Goa's historical and cultural specificity is now not only officially acknowledged but even seen as an asset in India's new focus on revitalizing relations with nations in the Southern Hemisphere. Indian prime minister Manmohan Singh emphasized this new focus on the occasion of the Portuguese prime minister's visit to New Delhi in 2007, when he noted that "the richness of Portuguese culture in Goa, Daman and Diu is well known to every Indian, and we celebrate this legacy."[2]

Whether strictly lusophone or not, as an Indian state that was intimately linked to other Portuguese-speaking regions of the world for several centuries, Goa plays a fundamental role in India's reengagement with this larger Lusosphere. If Punjab is used as a hub for Indian confidence-building measures toward Pakistan, Tamil Nadu as a bridge to Sri Lanka, and the seven northeastern states as a "Look East" platform, why not transform Goa into India's hub for the Portuguese-speaking countries?

China, which assumed formal sovereignty over the former Portuguese colony of Macau in 1999, is already using the region (where Portuguese is an official language) as a hub for its lusophone diplomacy, most notably through the Macau Forum, set up in 2003, which serves as a biannual ministerial meeting between Beijing and all eight Portuguese-speaking states. There is no reason why Goa should not also host such an official (or, initially, an informal Track II) dialogue. This idea is supported by many decision makers in Brazil and Africa, including former Mozambican minister Oscar Monteiro, who recently called for Goa to play a "driving role" in India's reengagement with his country.[3] In India itself, former union minister for external affairs Eduardo Faleiro called in 2009 for a "biannual structured dialogue" between India and the CPLP countries.

Most important, India must in the meantime secure its status as an associate observer of the CPLP. Equatorial Guinea, Mauritius, and Senegal have all succeeded in acquiring such a status, and even China and Indonesia have expressed their interest. As an associate observer, the Indian government would have privileged access to the formal settings in which its Brazilian, Portuguese, Angolan, Mozambican, and other Portuguese-speaking counterparts regularly discuss crucial economic and political issues, including technical cooperation, exchange programs, and peacekeeping missions.

Beyond the political and economic arenas, other avenues of potential cooperation should be explored, including sports. For example, the Indian Olympic Association agreed in 2006 to become a member of the Association of Portuguese-Speaking Olympic Associations. Since then, New Delhi has agreed to send an Indian delegation to the first two editions of the Jogos da Lusofonia (Lusophone Games, held in Macau and Lisbon), and has also backed Goa's successful bid to host the third edition in 2013 (defeating Brazil's competing bid). Similar possibilities should be explored in the realms of science and technology (Goa hosts the Indian Institute of Oceanography), education (through Indian technical and other degrees possibly offered in Goa, in Portuguese, to CPLP officials), and other cultural exchanges (in 2008 the Brazilian government supported a successful Carnival parade in Goa).

I am not suggesting that India's reengagement with the Lusosphere should be *only* about Goa. But the region's immense potential should not continue to be ignored, either. As New Delhi looks for new opportunities to reactivate its "southern" and "non-anglophone" diplomatic ties, Goa has interesting opportunities to reinvigorate its historical identity as a hub linking not only East and West but also North and South.

Lost Dialogues, Uncertain Genealogies

DUARTE DRUMOND BRAGA

In a recent book by Miguel Real, *A vocação histórica de Portugal* (2012), we find a distressing prophecy of the birth of a new kind of Portuguese citizen within the next two or three centuries.[4] Ideally, Real believes, this citizen would be a *mestizo*, the result of impending political and social alliances among lusophone countries. The distressing element in such a prophecy is its ideological link to a Lusotropicalist heritage that a few Portuguese thinkers have reclaimed as the traditional means of promoting a certain idea of Lusofonia.

One must bear in mind that despite its ideological connotations, Lusofonia actually refers to the specific group of speakers that use the Portuguese language. However, the term carries ideological nuances, and it is imperative that we understand which discourses are molding the set of ideological implications related to this linguistic fact. It is important that we trace these implications and map their respective roots and influences. To that end, I would call attention to an article by Miguel Vale de Almeida, "An Earth-Colored Sea" (2000/2004), which introduces the question of Portuguese dialogues, adaptations, and projects converging upon Freyre's concept of Lusotropicalism. The key point to be made here is that beyond the colonial intelligentsia in the metropolis there were other scholars and thinkers, in the former Portuguese colonies, who directly or obliquely engaged in dialogue with Lusotropicalist tropes, creating new ramifications, forms, and meanings of this discourse, thus becoming complicit agents of Lusotropicalism. In order to get a full picture of the ideologies implicit in the Lusotropical version of Lusofonia, we must situate these thinkers in their specific contexts.

The abrupt ending of Portuguese colonialism in Goa in 1961—together with Goan marginality with respect to the Atlantic center of the lusophone map—makes Goa a revealing example of certain Portuguese discourses on Lusofonia. In terms of representation, Goa is usually placed in the lusophone symbolic map as a fragment or spillover inherited directly from the past. In the sixteenth and seventeenth centuries, Goa was part of the pragmatic construction of a social and economic empire, but its survival in or belonging to the postimperial Portuguese sphere is uncertain. In its current status as an inherited fragment, how have Goa and Portuguese India's ambiguous symbolic meanings been appropriated over time? One might argue that the flow of time, as a trope for Portuguese culture, has been stopped in India. From the late nineteenth century, in certain contemporary points of view, Portuguese culture has remained an uncorrupted symbol of empire itself. Consider, for example, the 1898 quadricentennial of Vasco da Gama's voyage and its ideological repercussions for the definition of the civic and literary agendas of Guerra Junqueiro, Teixeira de Pascoaes, and the young Fernando Pessoa, in which Portuguese India is often dissolved into the vague and mythical Indies (*as Índias*). One can trace the genealogy of this mythical heritage even to the recent quincentennial commemorations of the arrival of the Portuguese in India.

In contrast to the metropolitan appropriation of Lusotropicalism, local history and local scholars were rarely integrated into the ideological domain of Portugal. The myth of Goa and India as nineteenth- or twentieth-century symbols of colonial empire has overpowered any real acknowledgment of the independence and integrity of Goan writing and local authors. Yet one can find dialogues, forgotten sources, and neglected contributions among the Portuguese-language literature and scholarly writing produced in Goa, and in that way retrace the lost genealogy of a certain lusophone discourse. The focus of such an endeavor would be the Goan elite, brought up in the context of Portuguese culture and social references, which defined itself as part of the colonial empire, even as it criticized Portuguese colonialism. It would be a mistake, however, to generalize about the whole of Goan modern literary production written in Portuguese. I would argue, rather, that one must look for certain historical moments and texts that reveal Goa's dialogue with the "lusophone idea."

One example would be the poet and fiction writer Vimala Devi—part of that Goan elite—whose writing emerged during the transition between Goa's colonial and postcolonial history. Devi clearly uses the concept of Lusotropicalism to structure her literary history of Goan literature, *História da literatura indo-portuguesa* (1971), written in Portuguese in collaboration with her husband, Manuel de Seabra. On the one hand, this work views Goan literature as a literary system exogenous to Portuguese literature and does not refrain from criticizing aspects of Portuguese colonialism. On the other hand, it undeniably interprets Goan culture through a Lusotropicalist lens. Thus Devi engages in dialogue not only with Freyre but also with the dissemination and assimilation of his ideas during the final stage of the Portuguese colonial regime.

Consider the editorial affiliation of her research: the Junta de Investigações do Ultramar (Office for Research on the Overseas Provinces). I am not suggesting that Devi is a clear supporter of the Lusotropical project in its Portuguese late-imperial incarnation, but she does apply a Lusotropical perspective to Goan culture, mainly through her desire for Goa's postcolonial survival as a culturally miscegenational product, even if Portuguese influence is no longer a political reality. In this way Devi's book, as a written history and an epitaph for a certain cultural and literary tradition, embodies an important disruptive tension inherent in this tradition: it is not a part of lusophone literature, exhausted before 1975, and yet, from the limbo it inhabits, it relates to the ideological configurations at the root of the unfolding lusophone project. Goa would then be an important missing link in the discourse on Lusofonia, in dialogue with Gilberto Freyre and the appropriation of his theories by Portugal's late-imperial intellectuals.

NOTES

1. *Literatura goesa em língua portuguesa nos séculos XIX e XX: Perspectivas pós-coloniais e revisão crítica* (forthcoming, 2012).

2. "PM's Statement on India-Portugal Bilateral Summit," 1 December 2007, http://pib.nic.in/newsite/erelease.aspx?relid=33588.

3. "Call for Better Ties Between India, Mozambique," *Times of India*, 9 January 2010, http://timesofindia.indiatimes.com/articleshow/msid-5425432,prtpage-1.cms.

4. The ideas presented here are a work in progress for an article to be published in a critical anthology on Goan literature in Portuguese organized by Paul Melo e Castro of the University of Leeds.

WORKS CITED

Almeida, Miguel Vale de. *An Earth Colored Sea: "Race," Culture and the Politics of Identity in the Post-Colonial Portuguese Speaking World*. New York: Berghan Books, 2004.

———. *Um Mar da Cor da Terra. "Raça," Cultura e Política da Identidade*. Oeiras: Celta Editora, 2000.

Devi, Vimala, with Manuel de Seabra. *História da literatura indo-portuguesa*. Lisboa: Junta de Investigações do Ultramar, 1971.

———. *A Literatura Indo-Portuguesa 2. Antologia*. Lisboa: Junta de Investigações do Ultramar, 1971.

Real, Miguel. *A vocação histórica de Portugal*. Lisboa: Esfera do Caos, 2012.

JOANA PASSOS is an assistant researcher at the Universidade do Minho. She completed her PhD at the University of Utrecht (Netherlands), specializing in post-colonial and feminist studies. Her postdoctoral studies focused on the literary history of Goa, written in Portuguese. Dr. Passos is the co-editor of two anthologies of post-colonial theory, *Áfricas Contemporâneas* (2010), and *Itinerâncias Críticas* (2012). She has published articles in both English and Portuguese. She may be reached at jpassos@ilch.uminho.pt.

SANDRA ATAÍDE LOBO was born in Goa. She earned a Master's in the contemporary history of ideas, and since 2005 has been working on Goan intellectual history and the history of Goan intellectuals. In her PhD thesis, she approached Goan cultural and political history, particularly the period between 1890 and 1933, through the discourse of the Goan intellectual elite. She may be reached at andralobo@netcabo.pt.

CONSTANTINO XAVIER is a Fulbright scholar and PhD candidate at the School of Advanced International Studies, Johns Hopkins University, in Washington, D.C. His areas of research and publication include India's foreign-policy decision-making processes and institutions, South Asian security, and the political dimensions of migration and diasporas. He has an MA and MPhil in international politics from Jawaharlal Nehru University, with prior undergraduate studies in Lisbon and Paris. He may be reached at constantino.xavier@gmail.com.

DUARTE DRUMOND BRAGA is a researcher at the Universidade de Lisboa's Center for Comparative Studies (CEC). His PhD thesis (due 2014) discusses the issue of Orientalism in twentieth-century Portuguese poetry. He lectured in creative writing at the same university's undergraduate program in comparative arts and cultures, and is co-editor of the poetry anthology *Nau-Sombra: Os Orientes da Poesia Portuguesa do século XX* (forthcoming). He may be reached at duartedbraga@gmail.com.

Essays

WALNICE NOGUEIRA GALVÃO
Translated by Robert B. F. Stuart

Fernando Pessoa Crosses the Atlantic

ABSTRACT: The prehistory of Fernando Pessoa's reception in Brazil shows that Pessoa was warmly received. Three primary channels made this possible: literary magazines, writers on both sides of the Atlantic and, especially, the poetry troupe Os Jograis. Periodical writers were crucial to the reception of Pessoa's poetry, but Os Jograis did the most to popularize the work of the great Portuguese poet by presenting Pessoa's poems to a large audience through the immediacy of spoken words, without the mediation of writing. The dynamics of Pessoa's reception must be understood in the context of São Paulo, then in the process of becoming a major metropolis.

KEYWORDS: poetry, reception, literary magazines, Fernando Pessoa, Portuguese literature, *Crítica*.

A statement by Robert Bréchon, in the first great biography of Fernando Pessoa ever written by a foreigner (Bréchon 1996, 561), set me on the path that led to this article. Bréchon says that since the late 1950s there had been a pressing need for a systematic edition of Pessoa's poetry. Bréchon reached this conclusion after examining the several volumes of the Ática edition, with Almada Negreiros's Pegasus vignette on the cover, supervised by João Gaspar Simões and Luis de Montalvor, which came out between 1942 and 1946. Over the next thirty years other editions of Pessoa's poetry appeared, including the dramatic poems, the *quadras* (quatrains), the English poems, and many others—and that is just the poetry. Pessoa's prose and correspondence also began to be compiled and published in the second half of the twentieth century.

Bréchon finds it curious that the comprehensive edition of Pessoa's poetry so sorely needed, rather than being released in Portugal, came out in Brazil. Collected in a single volume by the publishing company Aguilar in 1960, it was prepared by Maria Aliete Galhoz, an expert on Pessoa, in an edition that was to become canonical. But only those who know nothing about the Pessoa fever that had spread across Brazil find it strange that the poet first became widely popular in the tropics rather than in Portugal.

While Pessoa's greatness as a poet had been appreciated in Brazil for some time, three main channels are responsible for the explosive growth of his popularity in the 1960s. The first channel, in an era before the hegemony of the visual media, consisted of journals and literary supplements in Brazil and overseas. Book production proceeded so slowly at the time that when Pessoa died in 1935, only *Message* had been published, and the edition of his complete works by Ática began only in 1942. The anthology *Fernando Pessoa—Poesia*, compiled by Adolfo Casais Monteiro, also appeared in 1942.

The second channel was the flow of writers, poets, and critics who saw the value of Pessoa's work and began to spread the word. A third channel, examined below, was a Rio de Janeiro theater company called Os Jograis (the Jesters), which helped build the foundations of modern theater in Brazil in the 1950s and '60s, and which based a large part of its early repertoire on Pessoa's poetry.

Journals in Brazil and Overseas

Among the most important Brazilian journals and literary supplements that took an interest in Pessoa's work was the *Boletim de Ariel*, the seventh issue of which (April 1938) included a study by Adolfo Casais Monteiro titled "O exemplo de Fernando Pessoa" that had first appeared in the newspaper *Diário de Lisboa*. The *Boletim de Ariel* also published several of Pessoa's poems in 1938, in its August and September issues (Saraiva 1986, 212). Another Brazilian journal, the *Revista do Brasil*, featured an article called "A apresentação de Fernando Pessoa," by João Gaspar Simões, in its November 1938 issue (Jackson 2011, 196). These were the first essays to appear on Pessoa by writers outside Portugal.

Other Brazilians also wrote about the poet in the early 1940s, among them Domingos Carvalho da Silva, with two articles in the newspaper *Correio Paulistano* (19 September 1943 and 6 February 1944) and a review of Casais Monteiro's anthology; Antonio Candido, who reviewed Ática's first volume of Pessoa's poetry, which contained the poetry of the *orthonym*, in the journal *Clima* (September 1944); and Murilo Mendes, who wrote about Pessoa in the Recife newspaper *Folha da Manhã* (10 December 1944). In addition, Geraldo Ferraz wrote an extensive feature for the newspaper *Diário de S. Paulo*'s literary and arts supplement titled "Quarta Seção" (1 December 1946), with a mini-anthology of the heteronyms and the *orthonym*. Lúcio Cardoso wrote two pieces, one in *Letras Brasileiras* (July 1946) and one in the Letras & Artes supplement of the newspaper *A Manhã* (December 1950). This supplement also published an article by J. S. Silva Dias (3 June 1948) and nine of Pessoa's poems (17 October 1948; Jackson 2011, 196–97). And the torrent only grew, its waters steadily increasing in volume throughout the 1940s.

Pagu

In the realm of journals, Patrícia Galvão, a modernist Pagu—Oswald de Andrade's partner in the journal *Revista de Antropofagia* and the newspaper *O homem do povo* (Galvão 2007, 56–58)—occupies a special place when it comes to promoting our poet, as she was an enthusiastic fan of Pessoa. Once she had left behind the modernist-activist phase, after many arrests and experiences in both proletarian and clandestine life, the Communist and feminist author of the novel *Parque industrial* severed her partisan ties and dedicated herself to professional journalism. Ever a libertarian spirit, however, she continued to wave the banner of modernism in her stories, always ready to fight a setback, whether aesthetic, political, or behavioral.

Galvão systematically defended the avant-garde and artistic experimentation, promoting Beckett, Nabokov's *Lolita*, Arrabal, Ionesco, Alfred Jarry's *Ubu Roi*, Brecht, André Breton, Saint-John Perse, Artaud, Stravinsky, and many others—but above all Fernando Pessoa, whom she championed indefatigably beginning with an article for the journal *Fanfulla* in 1950.

The recent revival of Galvão's journalistic work underscores the leading role she played in our poet's critical fate.[1] She penned news reports, chronicles, critiques, reviews, and articles on Pessoa, and even a review of the Fernando Pessoa recital by Os Jograis in 1955. She reviewed the *Estudos sobre Fernando Pessoa* by Casais Monteiro (1958), the Aguilar edition of *Obra poética*, and the anthology by João Gaspar Simões, published in Brazil in 1961. Closely attuned to the international art scene, she took note in 1960 of Pessoa's inclusion in the poetry series Poètes d'aujourd'hui by Seghers Editions, in a translation by Armand Guibert that included the *Ode marítima* (Jackson 2011, 194).

Galvão also founded the "Centro de Estudos Fernando Pessoa" in Santos, the city in which she lived for the rest of her life and where she was a leading cultural agitator. Her friendship with the great critic of Pessoa's work, Casais Monteiro, in his Brazilian phase (Monteiro wrote the preface to the second edition of *Doramundo*, a novel by Pagu in partnership with Geraldo Ferraz, in 1959 [Jackson 2011, 196]), ensured her communion in the worship of the poet.

The Mediators: Cecília Meireles

A precocious enthusiast of Pessoa's poetry, Cecília Meireles figures among those who first promoted it in Brazil, as well as in Portugal, so much so that Eduardo Lourenço stated that he first became acquainted with our poet by way of her anthology (Gouvêa 2001, 71). Meireles was the first Brazilian writer to recognize Pessoa's outstanding talent (Saraiva 1986, 213), and she gave him pride of place in the preface to her *Poetas novos de Portugal* (1944). As early as her 1929 thesis, *O espírito vitorioso*, Meireles transcribed excerpts of Pessoa's *Ode triunfal* (ibid., 67). She was one of the first to disseminate Pessoa's work in Brazil, and, after Casais Monteiro's *Fernando Pessoa—Poesia*, of 1942,[2] also one of the first to promote him in Portugal.

Cementing Meireles's prestige in Lusitanian lands, her book *Viagem*, published in Lisbon in 1938 by Ocidente, won first prize in a contest sponsored by the Portuguese Academy of Letters, much to the consternation of the native candidates and their patrons, prompting an argument in the newspapers. She also won a prize from the Brazilian Academy of Letters and, as this institution was still quite impervious to modernism, the accolade awarded to *Viagem* prompted protests there as well.

At that time Meireles was by far the most popular Brazilian poet in Portugal; indeed, she was more highly regarded there than in her motherland (Gouvêa 1986, 85). Married to a Portuguese painter and illustrator, Fernando Correia Dias, she had been visiting Portugal since 1934, and she often returned there, making friends with intellectuals and artists. Earlier, her husband and Pessoa had been contributors to the journal *Águia*. On one visit she had arranged to meet Pessoa, and waited several hours for him at A Brasileira do Chiado, where Pessoa was a regular, but the meeting did not take place, to her great frustration and disappointment. Pessoa left a copy of *Mensagem*, hot off the presses, at her hotel, inscribed: "To Cecília Meireles, high poet, and to Correia Dias, artist, old friend, and even accomplice (see *Águia* etc.), in invoking Apollo and Athena, / Fernando Pessoa / 10–XII–1934." This copy was one of the first that Pessoa gave, since the date is the same as that in the copies he gave to his girlfriend, Ofélia Queirós, and her nephew, his friend Carlos Queirós. Meireles replied with a thank-you card, signed jointly with her husband, now in the Fernando Pessoa Estate at the National Library in Lisbon (Saraiva 1986, 214). Later, her friendship with Os Jograis leader Ruy Affonso would influence the group's decision to base their debut repertoire on Pessoa's work.

In addition to Luis de Montalvor in 1913 and Correia Dias in 1914, the latter remaining in Brazil until his death, other Portuguese friends of Pessoa's who spent time in Brazil included Veiga Simões, Álvaro Pinto, Jaime Cortesão, Carlos Lobo de Oliveira, Antonio Ferro, and José Osório de Oliveira (Saraiva 1986, 211–12). They did less to promote Pessoa, however.

The Diplomats

Among Pessoa's fellow writers, Mário de Andrade did not give him much attention. Apart from the oft-cited "Uma suave rudeza" (1939), on Portuguese poetry, from *O empalhador de passarinho*, Andrade rarely mentions Pessoa. Nonetheless, he kept in his library (today at the Institute for Brazilian Studies at the University of São Paulo [IEB-USP]), the first issue of the journal *Contemporânea* (May 1922), in which Pessoa's "O banqueiro anarquista" was published. He also kept a copy of *Homenagem a Fernando Pessoa*, published by Carlos Queirós in 1936, one year after the poet's death (Saraiva 1986, 211–13).

It is also worth highlighting the mediating role played by Brazilian diplomats serving in Portugal in the 1930s and 1940s, as they were also writers, in general linked to modernism, among them Ronald de Carvalho, Ribeiro Couto, and the critic Álvaro Lins. Having gained prestige for his participation in the 1922 "Modern Art Week," de Carvalho was a career diplomat who failed to rise to the top of the hierarchy because of his untimely death. He met Pessoa in 1914, and they began a correspondence. He was the co-director, with Luis de Montalvor, of the important Portuguese modernist journal *Orpheu*, which Pessoa endeavored so strenuously to promote. Though an enthusiastic member of the *Orpheu* circle, de Carvalho was involved only in the first issue: his name did not appear in the second. In any case, he wrote nothing about Pessoa.

Another career diplomat, the modernist Ribeiro Couto, served as the chargé d'affaires in Lisbon from 1944 to 1946. Couto's friendship with Casais Monteiro was particularly influential, in that Couto introduced Casais to contemporary Brazilian literature. Casais became interested in his friend's work, publishing in 1935 a small book of poetry called *A poesia de Ribeiro Couto* (Perrone-Moisés 2002, 56–57). Their correspondence has recently been collected and edited.[3]

The critic Álvaro Lins, who, unlike his predecessors, was not a career diplomat but would hold high offices abroad, taught languages in Lisbon between 1952 and 1954, and went on to serve as ambassador to Portugal between 1956 and 1959. He co-wrote, with Aurélio Buarque de Holanda, the two volumes of the *Roteiro Literário do Brasil e de Portugal* (1956).

Adolfo Casais Monteiro

When Casais Monteiro's article on Pessoa was published in the *Boletim de Ariel* in April 1938, the Portuguese critic was setting out on the journey that would establish him as a great Pessoa scholar. Pessoa had addressed the famous handwritten letter of the heteronyms to him, a unique document in the genre. An influential critic, Casais Monteiro in 1931 became the director of the journal *Presença*, which closed down in 1940. His anthology *Fernando Pessoa—Poesia* of 1942, as noted above, was crucial to the study and growing reputation of our poet.

In 1954, after being arrested several times in Portugal and banned from teaching or publishing there, Casais Monteiro was left with no other alternative but to seek exile in Brazil. His immigration was carefully planned; in addition to the warm welcome and support he received from the Brazilians, his arrival coincided with the lavish celebration of São Paulo's quadricentennial. The events included the opening of Ibirapuera Park, with its gigantic Monumento às Bandeiras, modeled in stone by the country's greatest sculptor, the modernist Victor Brecheret. There were art exhibits, processions, parades, parties in the streets, a film festival attended by foreign celebrities and, last but not least, an international writers' congress featuring Nobel laureate William Faulkner and poet Robert Frost—a meeting that would prove of great importance for Casais Monteiro and for Fernando Pessoa's critical fortunes.

Ostensibly, Casais was traveling to Brazil only for the writers' congress, but plans had been made in secret for him to stay. To ensure that the plan would succeed and to discourage Salazar from intervening—with the disastrous consequences that might result—the spotlight was turned on Casais, granting him high visibility and the guarantee that he could remain in Brazil unscathed. It was he who made the speech opening the proceedings on the first day of the celebration. He was one of the party appointed by Congress to lay a bouquet of flowers on Mário de Andrade's tomb. He also joined the committee that wrote the Brazilian Declaration of Principles, a clear repudiation of dictatorship and a strong endorsement of freedom of expression. Formally appointed to act as a spokesperson for the foreigners who attended the quadricentennial, he spoke on their behalf at the opening ceremony.[4] In short, his presence was given the greatest possible attention so as to prevent obstacles to his being granted asylum in Brazil.

Casais was the only person at the writers' congress to be invited to contribute two articles (the other writers were asked to write only one) and both were published in the annals of the congress. He chose to write one of those articles on Pessoa: "Fernando Pessoa, o insincero verídico." *Alguns dos 35 sonetos de Fernando Pessoa* was published the same year in a bilingual edition, with translations by Casais and Jorge de Sena. This not only ensured Casais's visibility but also consolidated his status as a leading Pessoa critic, a status he would hold throughout his long and productive career in Brazil, where he worked as a university professor, newspaper critic, contributor to the famous literary supplement of *O Estado de S. Paulo*, and author of books on Pessoa. By then Casais had already secured two trump cards back in Portugal: the letter of the heteronyms and the organization of the first anthology of Pessoa's poetry.

Even so, when Agir Publishers decided in 1957 to publish the anthology *Nossos Clássicos* with the Portuguese Pessoa, Brazilian critics responded with nationalistic protest, a form of chauvinism that Casais Monteiro denounced (Perrone-Moisés 2002, 57). It was then that Casais began to address the convergences between the two Portuguese-speaking nations' cultural legacies, speaking and writing regularly on the subject with great vigor and analytical depth.

Casais's lifelong dedication to Pessoa culminated in the publication in Brazil of *Estudos sobre a poesia de Fernando Pessoa* (1958) and the anthology *A poesia de Presença* (1959). In addition to his published work, he lectured indefatigably at the universities where he taught, introducing Pessoa's work to countless students of language and literature. These students in turn broadcast Pessoa's importance in their secondary school classes. At the Department of Philosophy on Maria Antonia Street, whence most of them graduated, it became fashionable to carry under one's arm the Ática volumes, recognizable from the little winged horse on the cover, a sure sign that the bearer was one of the initiated.

Os Jograis: The Jesters

In the 1950s the city of São Paulo had an urban center where writers, performers, musicians, and other artists congregated and where "everything happened." Those years saw the rise of exciting initiatives like Vera Cruz and the TBC (Teatro Brasileiro de Comédia, or Brazilian Comedy Theater). Vera Cruz was a film company with Hollywoodian ambition that for some time produced films of the greatest relevance, jump-starting Brazilian cinema and lifting it out of amateurism and randomness. The TBC raised Brazil's theatrical art to a professional level and enlarged the local repertoire, thus laying the foundations of modern theater in Brazil.

The University of São Paulo's Faculties of Philosophy, Architecture, and Economics, and its School of Sociology and Politics, along with the Mackenzie secondary and university educational system and the high schools Rio Branco and Caetano de Campos, were all located downtown. Nearby were sophisticated bookstores like Pioneira, Duas Cidades, Jaraguá, Partenon, and Francesa. The design formed a metropolitan urban complex that had been in the making since the days of the foreign teaching body at the Faculty of Philosophy in 1934.[5]

The urban mesh of the city's center was made up of a great many rich and varied cultural offerings. There was the Municipal Theater, the Theater for Artistic Culture (Teatro de Cultura Artística), and the Mário de Andrade Municipal Library, open daily, especially for the "worshippers of the statue," who gathered at the foot of the statue of Minerva in the lobby. Concentrated in a dozen blocks one could find the Artists and Friends of Art Club (Clube dos Artistas e Amigos da Arte), affectionately dubbed the Little Club (Clubinho), the Children's Library, the Leopoldo Fróis Theater, and the Alliance Française school.

In addition to the Museum of Modern Art on 7 de Abril Street, with its bar, and a very active Filmoteca (as the future Cinematheque was called then), the city center offered a constellation of majestic movie theaters, all with at least a thousand seats, among them the Art Palácio, with more than three thousand seats, built by the illustrious architect Rino Lévi, and the Marabá, the Ipiranga, the Normandie, the República, and the Metro, among others (Simões 1999). The Marrocos hosted the international film festival at São Paulo's quadricentennial, which boasted not only a delegation of Hollywood stars to dazzle the crowds but also such monuments of the seventh art as Erich von Stroheim, Abel Gance, Henri Langlois, and André Bazin (*Festival Internacional de Cinema* 2004, 4–59). The film festival featured a retrospective of Stroheim's silent movies, as well as the great Gance's silent classic *Napoléon* (once the director's demands for several projectors had been met). Henri Langlois was the creator and, later, director of the Cinemathèque Française; his dismissal by the French government would trigger the protests of May 1968 in Paris. André Bazin is often considered the greatest critic cinema has ever had.

Including just a dozen blocks, this was the city's most effervescent perimeter. At its heart was the brand-new Arena Theater,[6] owned by José Renato, with the Redondo bar, always crowded, right next door. It was in this theater that

Os Jograis, at once a reflection and a disseminator of Pessoa's popularity, premiered the Fernando Pessoa Recital. It remained for a long season, becoming a must-see in São Paulo's entertainment world.

Os Jograis, a quartet of men who recited poetry dressed in tuxedos, debuted on 16 May 1955. Their leader, Ruy Affonso—whose friendship with Cecília Meireles (Affonso 2007, 299) would be decisive in the choice to launch the group with the Portuguese poet's work—was the only permanent member, while the others rotated, including over time Rubem de Falco, Felipe Wagner, Ítalo Rossi, Maurício Barroso, Carlos Vergueiro, Raul Cortez, Carlos Zara, and many others.[7] Pagu was one of the fans who would see the show and then write about it.

Os Jograis were an immediate and thunderous success, and when they went on tour to Rio de Janeiro the following year, the reputation earned in São Paulo preceding them, they performed on an extraordinarily prestigious stage, the auditorium of the Ministry of Education. Brazil's first modernist public building, designed by Lúcio Costa and Oscar Niemeyer, was celebrated by chroniclers and poets alike. To this building Vinicius de Moraes dedicated his poem "Azul e branco," the refrain of which honors the Portinari wall tiles as dubbed by Pedro Nava: "Concha e cavalo marinho." The building was the architectural incarnation of the new aesthetics at a time when Brasília, to be inaugurated in 1960, was barely a shimmering line on the horizon. Two thousand people squeezed into this eight-hundred-seat auditorium to see the group open their Rio de Janeiro season (Affonso 2007, 299).

Os Jograis soon recorded the album *Fernando Pessoa* (1957), which became so sought after that it required several releases. The group became a mandatory act in Brazil's national and cultural celebrations, including Rio de Janeiro's quadricentennial in 1965 and the fiftieth anniversary of Modern Art Week in 1972.

The success of Os Jograis, which has endured for more than half a century now, can be explained by its contribution to the Portuguese language, if not with a neologism then at least with a semantic shift. By using their labels as litotes, they sought in their humbleness to identify their performance with that of traveling artists like the minstrels and the troubadours. But as they began to be imitated in every school and parish party, "fazer um jogral" (to go jesting) became synonymous with any collective declamation. The new meaning did not make it into the Aurélio dictionary, but with the date of entrance into the Portuguese lexicon duly recorded, it did get listed in the Houaiss. The expression is still used today.

The name of the group prompted other uses. It christened the nightclub O Jogral, located in the Galeria Metrópole mall at the time, one of São Paulo's epicenters, a block behind the Mário de Andrade Municipal Library, the location also of the Paribar, the Barbazul, and the Arpège on São Luiz Avenue, among other pubs. A little farther along, the João Sebastião Bar, with its bossa nova shows, thrived for a while. Among the many nightclubs in the area, the Michel, the Baiúca, and the Oasis stood out for their ability to attract customers. O Jogral moved to Avanhandava Street, still downtown, in 1968, where it endured until 1971, when it closed its doors after the death of its owner, the composer Luiz Carlos Paraná, a partner of Adauto Santos, who used to play the guitar at the club. The bar was patronized by intellectuals and artists of all kinds, including Marcus Pereira and Paulo Vanzolini, who used to sing there for fun.

Back in 1948, Ruy Affonso had been one of the founders of the TBC, a theater initially intended for amateur troupe performances as part of the University Theater Group, led by Decio de Almeida Prado. As the offspring of the TBC, Os Jograis could not deny this connection, but even more important than mere affiliation, they represented TBC *diction*: typical São-Paulo-City-haute-bourgeoisie pronunciation, cleansed of any foreign traces (the Italian accent, mostly), as was common to São Paulo in general. The voice projection acquired in the laboratory of their masters gave them an air of family, with a slightly pompous delivery that can still be heard on their recordings.

Os Jograis dedicated their recitation shows to other poets as well. They performed twelve hundred recitals with thirty-five different programs in tours all over Brazil, Portugal, Angola, and Mexico. In Portugal, they performed at the D. Maria II Theater by invitation of the Portuguese government, and were so successful that they ended up touring the whole country in 1957, with forty shows, that contributed to popularizing Fernando Pessoa there. Celebrating a Portuguese Pessoa pundit, they did a show in Araraquara in late 1965 in homage to Jorge de Sena, who was moving to the United States.

After Ruy Affonso's death, Alex Ribeiro carried on the group's tradition. The Os Jograis archive is quite thorough in its documentation; the Web site contains photographs of every program, broken down into its tiniest details, plus historical background and comprehensive information on the recordings.

This brief account of Pessoa's critical reception in Brazil is dedicated to recapturing the first phases of its prehistory. Since that long-ago beginning, countless articles, courses, colloquia, and publications of all sorts on Pessoa have appeared, including the oft-cited 1960 Aguilar edition of *Obra poética*. Some of its volumes, focusing specifically on the work of Pessoa, have become highlights of Brazilian literary criticism.

NOTES

1. K. David Jackson is about to release a four-volume anthology of Galvão's work: vol. 1, *O jornalismo de Patrícia Galvão: A denunciada denuncia; Pagu e a política (1931–1954)*; vol. 2, *Da necessidade da literatura (de arte e literatura/lições de literatura)*; vol. 3, *Palcos e Atores: Teatro mundial contemporâneo*; vol. 4, *Antologia da literatura estrangeira: Os grandes autores mundiais*.

2. The anthology by Cecília Meireles (*Poetas novos de Portugal*, 1944) appeared two years after the publication of Adolfo Casais Monteiro's collection of Pessoa's poetry, in which Casais broke new ground in Pessoa scholarship, becoming one of the greatest authorities on Pessoa.

3. *Correspondência Casais Monteiro–Ribeiro Couto (1931–1962)*, ed. Rui Moreira Leite (São Paulo: Unesp Press, forthcoming).

4. For an account of these events, see Walnice Nogueira Galvão, "O Congresso Internacional de Escritores de 1954: A chegada de Adolfo Casais Monteiro," in *A missão portuguesa: Rotas entrecruzadas*, ed. F. Lemos and Rui Moreira Leite, São Paulo: Unesp/Unesc, 2002.

5. Only after 1968 would this harmonious complex be torn down, its debris scattered all over the city. Since then São Paulo has become polycentric—characterized by small centers distributed across the neighborhoods. As the downtown declined, the area's dwellers moved out and it became doomed to follow the fate of America's inner cities. After many years of abandonment, it still stubbornly resists efforts at revitalization.

6. Cláudia de Arruda Campos's book on the Arena Theater—*Zumbi, Tiradentes e outras histórias contadas pelo Teatro de Arena de São Paulo*—is fundamental for an analysis of the theater's origins, connections with the rest of the downtown area, and sociability.

7. On the creation of Os Jograis, see Ruy Affonso, "De como nasceram Os Jograis," *Teatro Brasileiro* 5 (23 March 1956).

WORKS CITED

Affonso, Ruy. "Cecília Meireles, amiga." In *Ensaios sobre Cecília Meireles*, ed. L. V. B. Gouvêa et al. São Paulo: Humanitas, 2007.

———. "De como nasceram Os Jograis." *Teatro Brasileiro* 5 (23 March 1956): 10–11.

Arruda Campos, C. de. *Zumbi, Tiradentes e outras histórias contadas pelo Teatro de Arena de São Paulo*. São Paulo: Perspectiva, 1988.

Articles by Adolfo Casais Monteiro published in Suplemento Literário de O Estado de S. Paulo. M. M. T. Gonçalves, Z. T. de Aquino e Z. M. Bellodi (eds.). Araraquara: Unesp, 1983.

Bréchon, R. *Etrange étranger*. Paris: Christian Bourgois, 1996.

Congresso Internacional de Escritores e Encontros Intelectuais—Realizados em São Paulo sob o Patrocínio da Unesco e da Comissão do IV Centenário da Cidade de São Paulo. São Paulo: Anhembi, 1957.

Festival Internacional de Cinema de 1954. São Paulo: Centro Cultural São Paulo, 2004.

Galvão, W. N. "O Congresso Internacional de Escritores de 1954: A chegada de Adolfo Casais Monteiro." In *A missão portuguesa: Rotas entrecruzadas*, ed. F. Lemos and Rui Moreira Leite, 23–26. São Paulo: Unesp/Unesc, 2002.

———. "Indômita Pagu." *Teoria e Debate* 23.87 (March/April 2007): 56–58.

Gama, L. H. *Nos bares da vida—Produção cultural e sociabilidade em São Paulo (1940–1950)*. São Paulo: Senac, 1998.

Gouvêa, L. V. B. *Cecília em Portugal*. São Paulo: Iluminuras, 2001.

———, ed. *Ensaios sobre Cecília Meireles*. São Paulo: Humanitas, 2007.

Jackson, K. D. "A denunciada denuncia [She who was denounced denounces]: Pagu and Politics, 1931–1954—An Introduction to the Journalism of Patricia Galvão." *Literature and Arts of the Americas* 39.73 (2006): 228–35.

———. "Uma evolução subterrânea: O jornalismo de Patrícia Galvão." *Revista IEB* 53 (March/September 2011): 31–52.

———. "Patrícia Galvão escreve sobre Pessoa no Brasil, 1955–1961." *Colóquio Letras* 176 (January 2011): 194–203.

Perrone-Moisés, L. "A crítica viva de Adolfo Casais Monteiro." In *A missão portuguesa: Rotas entrecruzadas*, ed. F. Lemos and Rui Moreira Leite, 53–60. São Paulo: Unesp/Unesc, 2002.

Ribeiro, A. www.futurart.com.br, www.futurart.com.br/ruy, www.jograisdesaopaulo.com.br, www.jograis.com.br. Accessed on May 1, 2011.

Saraiva, A. *O modernismo brasileiro e o modernismo português*. Porto: Gráfica Rocha, 1986.

Simões, I. *Salas de cinema em São Paulo*. São Paulo: Secretaria Municipal de Cultura/Secretaria Estadual de Cultura, 1999.

Vieira, N. H. *Brasil e Portugal—A imagem recíproca*. Lisboa: ICALP, 1991.

WALNICE NOGUEIRA GALVÃO is professor emerita of literary theory and comparative literature at FFLCH (Universidade de São Paulo). Dr. Nogueira Galvão is internationally acknowledged as one of the most important Brazilian scholars of the second half of the twentieth century. She has published thirty-six books on Guimarães Rosa, Euclides da Cunha, and literary and cultural criticism. Among her books are *Euclidiana*; *Mínima mímica*; and *O tapete afegão*. Her most recent book is *Sombras & Sons* (Lazúli: Companhia Editora Nacional, 2011). Her current research focuses on the relationship between literature and the arts. She may be reached at wngalvao@uol.com.br.

SANDRA GUARDINI TEIXEIRA VASCONCELOS

British Novels in Nineteenth-Century Brazil

ABSTRACT: From the most celebrated novelists to the most popular *feuilleton-romans*, French literature played an indisputable role in the making of Brazil's literary past. The aim of this essay is to argue that, though not fully acknowledged, British novels also were widely available in nineteenth-century Brazil, enabling the establishment of some links between their narrative paradigms and techniques and the making of the Brazilian novel, mainly with reference to common themes and conflicts. My hypothesis is that the presence of these novels in Brazil contributed to the formation and consolidation of the genre on Brazilian territory, resulting in the acclimatization of forms and procedures.

KEYWORDS: theory of the novel, circulation, acclimatization, comparative literature, book trade.

> In sum, foreign debt is as inevitable in Brazilian letters as it is in any other field, and is not simply an easily dispensable part of the work in which it appears, but a complex feature of it.
>
> —Roberto Schwarz

It has long been a commonplace among Brazilian literary historians and critics that French novels and novelists played a central role in the development and consolidation of the Brazilian novel during the nineteenth century. The received view has been that French novels were the predominant—almost exclusive—model available to Brazilian writers, and much of the evidence to date confirms the idea that these materials were pervasive in their influence. The pervasiveness of this French literature, and of French culture in general, stemmed not only from canonical works but also from popular fiction in French, as Antonio Candido makes clear in his *Formação da Literatura Brasileira*:

> Translated books belonged, in the main, to what one considers today third-rate literature; but they were frequently cherished novelties, just like the

> good works. Thus, side by side with George Sand, Merimée, Chateaubriand, Balzac, Goethe, Irving, Dumas, Vigny, lined up Paul de Kock, Eugène Sue, Scribe, Soulié, Berthet, Souvestre, Féval, besides others whose names do not mean anything today: Bard, Gonzalès, Rabou, Chevalier, David, etc. The vast majority of them were French, revealing in their titles the genre we call *feuilleton*. Who knows which and how many of these by-products influenced the making of our novel? Sometimes, they may have had more relevance than the important books on which we prefer to fix our attention.[1]

However, the question that Candido poses about the influence of less canonical literature and literature in French translation has not yet been explored fully. This essay takes up his challenge and argues that alternative sources of information—such as newspapers, catalogues, and literary periodicals—show that British novels also made a significant and hitherto unrecognized contribution to the formation of the Brazilian novel as a genre during this period.

These sources make it clear that although France always functioned as an intermediary in the literary marketplace, Britain brought to Brazil much more than a regular supply of merchandise and manufactured goods, like the chinaware, glass, pots and pans, cutlery, and tools found on the shelves of shops and warehouses in Rio de Janeiro in the nineteenth century. Not only were hardware and utensils from Britain available to the inhabitants of the still small and provincial Brazilian capital, but books and periodicals in general, and novels in particular, also found their way into the country, accompanying the introduction of new habits of consumption, new fashions, and a certain refinement of manners that even today is attributed to the British influence on everyday life in Rio de Janeiro after 1808.[2] The supply of British novels, sparse though it was at the beginning, intensified when bookshops and circulating libraries were opened some decades later. These novels often arrived in Rio's harbor via Lisbon, in Portuguese translation, or via Paris, translated into French, and circulated themes, narrative procedures, and techniques that had already become standard in European fiction.

In addition to reconstructing the history of the circulation of British novels in Brazil, this essay substantiates Roberto Schwarz's claim that "the novel had existed in Brazil before there were any Brazilian novelists" and explores the ways in which British narrative models were appropriated by the first Brazilian writers of prose fiction.[3] It does not, however, discuss the prominent role played by translation and by Portuguese and French translators in this process. Nor does it touch upon the issue of reading practices; although scholarship can establish which books were available on library shelves, it is nearly impossible to ascertain whether or how they were read.

Nonetheless, the history of the circulation of literary materials during this period, and of the appropriation of narrative techniques and processes drawn directly or indirectly from British literature, makes it clear that the unitary model of French influence is flawed and incomplete. From beneath the fragmentary references, misspellings, French titles, and anonymity—frequent in the advertisements and catalogues that publicized these works—a more variegated picture of the conditions governing the development of the genre in Brazil begins to emerge.[4] This picture encompasses a collection of eighteenth- and nineteenth-century novels, written by both famous and lesser-known novelists.[5] The Portuguese prince regent's decision to flee to Brazil during the Napoleonic invasion permanently altered life in Rio de Janeiro. Among other important changes, the country was suddenly and quickly integrated into the literary marketplace, thanks to the diligent and interested efforts of traders on both sides of the Atlantic. (Previously, censorship had been strict, and the Portuguese authorities had kept a close watch over the circulation of books.) Not only did the prince regent's act opening up Brazilian ports facilitate this integration, but it also came at a convenient time for European booksellers, who were eager to expand their sales and find new consumers for the books they printed and sold.

Despite Portuguese censorship and control prior to this period, recent research has shown that many books were available in colonial Brazil, and some novels could be found in private collections or for sale.[6] There is also evidence that books may have been smuggled into the country to circumvent official bans. Yet the policy of repressing the distribution of literature in Brazil differed markedly from patterns in Spanish America, where, as Irving Leonard notes, large shipments of Mateo Alemán's *Guzmán de Alfarache* (1599; second part 1604) to Mexico City in 1600 were soon followed by copies of Miguel de Cervantes's *Don Quixote*, which reached Peru in 1606, a year after its publication in Spain.[7]

The sheer diversity that characterizes Latin America makes it inadvisable to generalize about the nature of literary communities across the territory. As José Mindlin points out, "The history of the book and the press in Brazil is very different from that in Spanish America, for books in Spanish were already being published in the New World in the sixteenth century, while Brazil was to wait more than two centuries."[8] Nonetheless, it is important to situate Brazil in terms of the continent as a whole in order to elucidate the ways in which patterns of distribution and consumption were and were not similar across the linguistic and cultural divide. In fact, studies of the history of the book for Brazil do reveal some striking similarities with Spanish American countries, allowing us to draw some parallels and underscore some common features. For one thing, censorship on moral, political, and religious grounds seems to have exerted the same central role throughout the region, in what would be an often unsuccessful attempt to curb the free circulation of ideas and books. Moreover, Brazil was not alone in its position as the final destination for the books that French, British, and German booksellers had been printing in increasing numbers and at cheaper prices since the early nineteenth century. These sellers looked to the whole of Latin America as a potential marketplace.

While no full mapping has been made of which British novels circulated in which countries in the region, references to Oliver Goldsmith, Walter Scott, and Charles Dickens are endemic. These writers were figures in the "naturalization" of European novelistic conventions in Latin America, which, according to Antonio Benitez-Rojo, consisted of "the expropriation of a foreign discourse by subjects (writers) of a nation for the purpose of transforming it so that it may serve the nation."[9] At the same time, it appears that many translations of European texts into Spanish and Portuguese relied on identical sources, and that many of the novels circulating in Brazil also circulated in Hispanic America. For example, the French edition of Samuel Richardson's *Clarissa* (1747–49, 1785–86) was translated into Portuguese and found its way onto the shelves of an important circulating library in Rio de Janeiro.[10] This same edition was later translated into Spanish and published by Ackermann in Mexico.[11]

Certainly, the collection of British novels found in Brazil is highly representative of the history of the European edition and publishing market; the subscription and circulating libraries in Rio de Janeiro had on their shelves works of the most important publishers and booksellers in Europe, which was no doubt also true of the rest of Latin America. Of course, their presence in Rio is not surprising, since the most famous nineteenth-century publishers, such as Aillaud and Hachette in Paris, Routledge and Bentley in London, and Bernhard Tauchnitz in Leipzig, were businessmen who had a keen eye on the market and employed agents globally. Nor was this export trade insubstantial. The *Revue Britannique* for March 1840 reports 230,000 francs' worth of books sent from France to Brazil for 1838 (with 60,000 francs' worth sent to Cuba in the same year), while Belgian piracies amounted to 16,000 francs' worth of sales for Brazil and 112,000 francs for Mexico in 1837.[12]

Although beyond the scope of Franco Moretti's *Atlas of the European Novel* (1998), Latin America, if properly explored, would no doubt complete the literary routes that he draws for Europe in his discussion of narrative markets operating around the middle of the century. As in most European countries, so in Latin America, "the majority of novels are, quite simply, *foreign books*," that is, French and British novels, which "become models to be imitated."[13] Less clear, from the examination of individual collections, is what he defines as the "overpowering presence of the canon," an anachronistically problematic concept when used with reference to the nineteenth century, and one that can be applied only with the benefit of hindsight. In addition, the apparently peaceful coexistence of major and minor novelists on the shelves of Brazilian circulating libraries equally refutes any notion of the predominance of canonical works.

Nevertheless, this common literary repertoire seems to reinforce Moretti's argument in favor of the hegemonic role of what he calls the "Anglo-French core" over a literary world system.[14] Moretti contends that "in cultures that belong to the periphery of the literary system (which means: almost all cultures, inside and outside Europe), the modern novel first arises not as an autonomous development but as a compromise between a Western formal influence (usually French or English) and local materials."[15] There can be no doubt that, to a certain extent, this model applies to Brazil. Yet I would like to challenge Moretti's use of the term "compromise" to define the "encounter of Western forms and local reality" because it ignores the importance of particularities and contexts.[16] In fact, a very strong critical tradition in Brazil argues for treating texts individually, since artistic elaboration is always rooted in real processes, and their explanatory power is embedded in the literary form itself. As Schwarz insists, "there is no simple consequence to be drawn from such a dualism [between European model and Brazilian reality]; in a culturally dependent country like ours, its presence is inevitable, and its results can be either good or bad. Each case must be judged on an individual basis. Literature is not a matter of rational judgment; but of imaginative form."[17]

Crossing the Oceans

"Traduit de l'anglais": this is how most eighteenth-century British novels got to France, after having taken Britain by storm and become fashionable with common readers. Crossing the English Channel, however, was simply the first leg in a long journey to foreign lands and audiences. If *Pamela, or Virtue Rewarded*, published by Samuel Richardson in 1740, became a model imitated by countless British novelists, its impact on the European continent was certainly almost as considerable. Translated into French by the Abbé Prévost in 1742, this story of a heroine who resists all attempts at seduction by her master but who ends up marrying him and climbing socially as a reward for her chastity was enthusiastically received, thanks to Richardson's clever combination of realism and morally uplifting narrative. As he made clear, his main goal in his novels was to amuse and edify ("instruction without entertainment . . . would have but few readers"), and his work not only inspired many other novels of the period but also inculcated models of behavior for marriageable young ladies.[18] Pamela, then, becomes a kind of "civilizing" heroine, who would inhabit the pages of novels across the English Channel as well as in Britain, and leave indelible marks on the imaginary of novelists abroad. In its wake came hundreds of other novels that, in both Britain and France, filled the leisure hours of female readers, their privileged public, and helped consolidate the new genre.

From its birth, the novel had been described as a bastardized and popular genre, seen by many as disreputable reading, the pastime of the idle, or, even more dangerously, a corrupter of manners. Yet the positive reception that the works of the founding fathers of the British novel had in France, mainly between 1740 and 1760, was only the starting point for a dynamic process of exchange between the two countries, prompting a French critic and historian to define the eighteenth century as the century of the novel.[19] No matter how recalcitrant they were in relation to the British variety of social realism, which they judged to be "in bad taste," the French learned how to take advantage of the formal solutions proposed by their British counterparts and gradually substituted the demands of *vraisemblance* for the principle of *bienséance*, lending their stories a more realistic orientation to character composition, choice of setting, and introduction of new narrative methods.[20]

Never an especially affordable pastime, since sale prices were not particularly low, novels found an excellent source of publicity and dissemination in the circulating libraries, which became a crucial factor in the development of the habit of reading and in the genre's popularity. One of their main staples, the sentimental novel (greatly in vogue from 1750 onward), established a paradigm that transformed itself into a kind of formula through constant repetition by its producers. The heroines of popular novels were generally very beautiful, extremely delicate, sensitive, prone to frequent swoons and abundant tears. Models of virtue and perfection, they were innocent victims permanently threatened by callous villains or uncontrollable passions. If unlucky enough to be seduced, they were bound to perpetual imprisonment in a convent (reintroduced by the gothic novel). The blend of sentimentalism and gothic elements (present in the derelict old abbeys, dungeons, and castles that were frequently used as settings) was the main dish served to readers. In 1775, for example, William Lane founded one of the most famous British publishing houses of the period—the Minerva Press, which became a symbol of popular fiction for decades.[21] For almost fifty years, Minerva would be an important supplier of circulating library novels in Britain; most of these works were written by women who, protected by anonymity or pseudonyms, were often responsible for the period's best-sellers.[22]

Things were not much different in France. After the first *cabinet de lecture* opened in Paris in 1767, French readers' tastes for the novel were fed by the same stories of adventure, crime, and passion.[23] In fact, a comparison between the list of British novels translated into French and the catalogue of the publisher Pigoreau reveals an intriguing coincidence of titles and authors.[24] It is this same Pigoreau who provides clues to the parameters that may have guided the translation of these novels into French. After all, meeting public demand took precedence over fidelity to and respect for the original, since the modern concept of authorship, with strict controls over intellectual property, had yet to develop: "The lively and quick Frenchman does not read a novel but to amuse himself for a few minutes; he wants to be led to the conclusion by the shortest route. The phlegmatic Englishman loves to stop at the details, and does not want to reach the dénouement before strolling about the long circuits of a labyrinth."[25] It was therefore in the temperament of the reader that Pigoreau located the main differences between British and French novels, thus defining the guidelines that should govern the translator's process of adaptation. Pigoreau would have known what he was talking about, since he was one of the main publishers and booksellers in Paris and an important purveyor of novels to the circulating libraries.[26]

With their eyes always on the market, booksellers had already realized the great potential of the sale and rental of novels, which, like any other commodity, had to please the public and conquer new markets. The 1808 opening of Brazilian ports to foreign trade thus was most convenient. Throughout the colonial period, Brazil had confronted the structural impossibility of having books circulating in its territory. Without its own press, with works needing to pass censorship before distribution, and with a small number of booksellers, the country—even after the opening of its ports—depended on illegal trade, carried out by the British, the French, and the Dutch, and on a small publishing industry of books in Portuguese that supplied its small consumer market from London and Paris.[27] However, with the foundation of the Impressão Régia in 1808, the suspension of censorship in 1821, and the rise of French booksellers in Rio de Janeiro, this picture started to change. Little by little, ads began to appear announcing the sale of "novels" at the "Gazeta shops."

The booksellers and the circulating libraries were responsible, in Brazil as in Europe, for the diffusion and circulation of novels, playing as central a role as shapers and mediators of taste as their British and French counterparts.[28] If, in the 1820s, the shops adjacent to the daily newspapers sold and rented books, in the 1830s entrepreneurs founded libraries and circulating libraries similar to those in Britain and France as commercial ventures, making packages of novels sent from the metropolis available in the provinces. The "remainders," or the surplus editions for the French circulating libraries—as well as the "best-sellers" already translated into Portuguese—ended up in Lisbon and Rio de Janeiro.[29] The expression "translated from the French," which appears in a great number of novels that circulated in Brazil, is frequently a false clue, hiding the British origin of the novel, and may have given these books a kind of cachet, making them easier to sell and rent. According to Laurence Hallewell, there was in Brazil "an exceptional receptivity towards the ornaments of French culture," which was seen as modern and progressive, French being also the language of elite culture and society.[30] Moreover, the bitterness of Anglo-Brazilian relations, mainly over the slave trade and what was considered the British government's undue interference in local matters, may have contributed to this preference for things French. Symbols of civilization and refinement, French cultural products had the added advantage of being free of the taint of British imperialism and diplomatic imbroglios.

An examination of Pigoreau's *Petite bibliographie biographico-romancière* and Harold Streeter's *The Eighteenth-Century English Novel in French Translation* attests to the British origin of many of the novels "translated from the French" found in the catalogues of Rio de Janeiro's circulating libraries.[31] A comparison of the bibliographical information available, which includes the translator's name or initials, shows that the edition that came to Brazil, or served as the source text for the translation into Portuguese, was often identical to the editions that appeared in French circulating libraries—as for example with Ann Radcliffe's *L'Italien, ou Le confessional des pénitents noirs* (1830) and Mrs. Helme's *Alberto, ou O Deserto de Strathnavern* (1827).[32] Thus, as Marlyse Meyer has pointed out, the forms of the novel that came to Brazil were always British, though their mediation was French.[33]

Between 1808 and 1822, during the viceroyalty, the books published by the Impressão Régia show a predominance of works translated from French and a considerable number of sentimental stories and "moral tales." Likewise, the 1815 *Catalogue of Manuel Inácio da Silva Alvarenga's Books* includes *Gil Blas*, *Aventures de Télémaque*, Prosper Jolyot de Crébillon's *Oeuvres* (1802), and Denis Diderot's *Jacques le fataliste* (1778, 1796), all of them French works.

Similarly, the *Gazeta do Rio de Janeiro*, from its founding on 10 September 1808 until its demise on 22 June 1822, published in its Loja da Gazeta section lists of works available, for example, at the shop of Paulo Martin, Filho, a bookseller established at Rua da Quitanda, 34. While they give evidence of the regular supply of foreign works to the reading public in Rio de Janeiro, these ads announced several "very modern and entertaining novels." Some were of anonymous authorship; some were old and well-known books like Alain René Lesage's *Diabo Coxo*,[34] Jacques-Henri Bernardin de Saint-Pierre's *Paulo e Virgínia* and *A Choupana Índia*, *Mil e Huma [sic] Noites*, François-René de Chateaubriand's *Atala, ou Amores de Dois Selvagens*, and Jean-François Marmontel's *Belizario*. Most, however, were British fiction: Mrs. Helme's *Luiza, ou O Cazal [sic] no Bosque* (21 September 1816), Jonathan Swift's *Viagens de Guliver* (15 March 1817), Daniel Defoe's *Vida e Aventuras Admiráveis de Robinson Crusoe* (9 April 1817), Henry Fielding's *Tom Jones, ou O Engeitado [sic]* (10 May 1817), the anonymous *Vida de Arnaldo Zulig* (4 July 1818), and Samuel Richardson's *Historia da Infeliz Clarissa Harlowe* in eight volumes (8 March 1820).[35] Everything seems to indicate that these are the first British fictional works to circulate in Brazil.

It might also be worthwhile to note the ads for the arrival in 1809 of *Cartas de Maria Wollstonecraft, relativas à Suécia e Dinamarca, com uma notícia de sua vida por Francisco Xavier Baeta* and, in the year 1819, of *Carta escrita pela senhora de ***, residente em Constantinopla* [illegible] *em que trata das mulheres turcas, do seu modo de viver, divertimentos, vestidos, maneira de tratar os maridos, etc.*, which must certainly be one of Lady Mary Wortley Montagu's "Turkish Embassy Letters," which appeared in 1763. But it is Mary Wollstonescraft who merits a brief mention in one of Brazil's earliest novels, Joaquim Manuel de Macedo's *A Moreninha* (1844). In a lively dispute between two of the young male characters about courtship and women's hearts, the British writer is invoked as a champion of women's rights whose work the female protagonist may have read. The reference may not say much about women readers at the time, but it does inject a note of verisimilitude, as well as demonstrating that Macedo was well informed about what kind of writer Wollstonecraft had been.[36]

The *Jornal do Comércio*, founded by Pierre Plancher in Rio in 1827, also adopted the systematic practice of announcing the sales of its novels. British novels continued to figure in supply lists in the drugstores and bookshops that had now become part of the landscape of the city. But these works were found not only in the imperial capital; Gilberto Freyre notes that it was possible to find Portuguese translations of Defoe, Walter Scott, and Ann Radcliffe in the interior of the country as well.[37] Since reading habits and practices were rarely recorded in the nineteenth century, it is difficult to tell why these novelists were chosen and how their novels were used. But it is likely that what was offered to the tiny Brazilian reading public was what was in vogue or commercially successful in London and Paris.

British novels could also be found in Rio's British Subscription Library, which had a good supply of the latest European works. The British had established this venue in 1826 to serve the resident British community. This is where most of the novels could be found in their original English-language version, though editions in English also appear in the catalogues of the Gabinete Português de Leitura do Rio de Janeiro (founded in 1837) and the Biblioteca Fluminense (founded in 1847). Most novels in these catalogues, however, had already been translated into Portuguese from the French.

The French bookshops that clustered from the 1820s around the Rua do Ouvidor, the center of elegant life in the city, also ensured the sale and rental of novels to a tiny literate population, for whom reading novels became part of the pattern of good manners to be followed and imitated.[38] The truth is that the packages of British novels that did arrive in Rio de Janeiro in the first three decades of the nineteenth century almost always came from Paris or Lisbon, translated from the French. The flow may have been slow at first, owing to the two-month transatlantic voyage, but with the advent of the steamship after 1850 Liverpool was only twenty-eight days away from Rio, ensuring that the flow not only remained constant but intensified. As the century progressed, advances in the means of transport, changes in the economics of publishing and banking and, above all, changes in the interests of readers were crucial factors in guaranteeing that these novels were available not only in the collections of libraries and circulating libraries, but also on bookstore shelves.

The Burden of the Novel

Perceived as "light reading," in the words of the journalist Quirino dos Santos, owner of the *Gazeta de Campinas*, or "tenth-rate novels," in the words of another newspaperman, these books left strong marks on the imaginary of Brazilian novelists. José de Alencar was among those who believed that reading this type of novel had helped to "imprint on my spirit the moulds of this literary structure."[39] These were the novels that crossed the oceans, carrying within them the recurring themes of marriage, private and domestic life, and the usurpation of rights and inheritance, and imbued with strong and exaggerated emotions, usually expressed in ornate, high-sounding language. Similarly, the different genres of the novel current in eighteenth- and nineteenth-century Britain (domestic, sentimental, gothic, of manners, of doctrine, historical) circulated in Brazil, offering ideas to the country's first fiction writers. Following the useful distinction between *novel* and *romance* made by Clara Reeve in her *Progress of Romance* (1785), it can be said that the romance repertoire is undoubtedly present to a high degree in this initial period of novelistic production. Uncontrollable passion, seduction, kidnapping, betrayal, terrible villains, disrepute, last-minute revelations, absence of half tone, lack of causal links between events, and stereotypical characters characterize these works.

Some texts, however, began to lay more emphasis on verisimilitude and plausibility, presenting more lifelike language and scenes and bringing the story closer to the lives of common people, which is typically the novel's primary concern. It seems that because of the enbourgeoisement of manners and the changing role of women in Brazilian society, the novel began to flourish to the detriment of the romance, although the latter never completely disappeared from the work of romantic novelists. In its initial stages, Brazilian fiction also suffered from an overall lack of definition, with texts being referred to as novels, short stories, or novellas regardless of their length or formal characteristics. The use of the genre as "an instrument for the discovery and interpretation of the country," however, soon made realism predominate, with only a residual recourse to the romance.[40]

The formation and consolidation of the novel took about a hundred years in Britain, if *Robinson Crusoe* is taken as a point of departure and Walter Scott's works as its culmination. In Brazil, this timeline was compressed, since the nature of the country's cultural relations with Europe and the simultaneous availability of novels produced in Britain and France gave Brazilian novelists a much wider range of models. Thus works by the founders of the British novel in the previous century—Daniel Defoe, Samuel Richardson, Henry Fielding, Tobias Smollett, and Laurence Sterne—were on offer at the same time as the great nineteenth-century novelists.

Practically all subgenres current in Britain were available in Brazil: apart from Richardson's domestic and sentimental novel, Horace Walpole's and Ann Radcliffe's gothic fiction, Fanny Burney's novel of manners, William Godwin's novel of doctrine, Samuel Johnson's Oriental fantasy *Rasselas* (1759), and William Beckford's *Vathek* (1786), works by writers such as Edward Bulwer-Lytton and William Harrison Ainsworth could also be obtained. A survey of the British novels in circulation also attests to the presence of women novelists who had become well known and widely read in Britain throughout the eighteenth century: Fanny Burney, Elizabeth Inchbald, and Sophia Lee among them, together with those uncovered by Marlyse Meyer, including Elizabeth Helme, author of *Sinclair das Ilhas* (*St. Clair of the Isles, or The Outlaws of Barra*, 1803) and Regina Maria Roche, author of *Amanda e Oscar* (*The Children of the Abbey*, 1796).[41] There were also considerable numbers of anonymous works and of novelists generally associated with the "popular novel," that is, works of limited literary merit that were designed to feed the novel market and to meet the demands of the reading public in Britain and France.

The seclusion of Brazilian women, their limited education, and the circumscribed world in which they lived made them a privileged public as far as the consumption of *feuilletons* and popular novels was concerned, a situation very similar to that of British women in the eighteenth century. Confined to the domestic sphere and the patriarchal family, Brazilian women of status were denied access to the open world of the streets, where only prostitutes and slaves could roam unaccompanied. The paternal and social control over their lives also constrained their access to education and a professional life. Motherhood, home, and family were the only arenas in which they could engage, and marriage was the only means for them to ascend socially or maintain their status, and was always a matter of familial concern and interest. With the gradual introduction of bourgeois habits and values into Brazilian society, mainly during the second half of the nineteenth century, women became responsible for the family and the education of their children. Handed over from the authority of their fathers to that of their husbands, young women had very little room for intellectual development, and their main accomplishments included playing an instrument (usually the piano), embroidery and, if they were literate, reading.

Given the scarcity of available data, it is difficult to generalize about reading habits. However, judging from the number of circulating libraries established in several regions of the country during this period, it appears that reading novels became more widespread. Ana Luiza Martins has documented the presence of almost twenty circulating libraries scattered across the province of São Paulo alone.[42] Her survey confirms the predominance of the genre, especially *feuilletons*, and the massive presence of foreign authors in translation, among them Scott and Dickens. This expansion was certainly an object of concern, which may explain Júlia Lopes de Almeida's complaint at the end of the nineteenth century about the pernicious effects on women of reading novels. She warned ladies against "detrimental, unwholesome novels, filled with romantic adventures and dangerous heroes," while recommending works of a morally uplifting nature.[43] Almeida undoubtedly echoes the authoritative voices of the medical and psychological theorists, writers of advice manuals, reviewers, periodical journalists, and educators who had laboriously attempted to control women's reading throughout the nineteenth century in Britain, worried about the imaginative fulfillment of desire or the affective power that reading might entail. Rather than celebrate its beneficial potential, essayists and reviewers often speculated about the dangers of reading novels, their corrupting and morally debilitating influence, especially on women.[44]

To a certain extent, Horace's maxim *Omne tulit punctum qui miscuit utile dulci*, a touchstone of the eighteenth-century British novel, also crossed the Atlantic to Brazil.[45] Surprisingly, however, it appeared more in response to demand on the part of critics than as an essential component of Brazilian novels themselves. In some critical texts this demand is explicit, and fiction is expected to fulfill an edifying function, thus contributing to the building up of virtue and good habits. For the novelist Antonio Gonçalves Teixeira e Sousa, "the aim . . . of the novelist is (if the background of his work is fabulous) almost always to present the beauty of nature, to delight and moralize."[46] The "first manifestations of fiction in Bahia," according to David Salles, also had a moralizing goal.[47]

Published in periodicals designed to spread civilizing habits and introduce new European works, these short fictional exercises set in motion the usual romantic machinery (villainy, incest, coincidences, surprises, seduction, etc.) in order to tell a story that set a good example of moral behavior and condemned vice.

Fearful of the nefarious effects that reading novels could have on young ladies, the genre's first critics hastened to insist that writers pay attention to morality and virtue. We see this in Dutra e Mello's criticism of *A Moreninha* (1844), published in *Minerva Brasiliense* on 15 October 1844, and also in the article published in *Guanabara* in 1855 about *Vicentina* (1853), both novels by Joaquim Manuel de Macedo:

> The novel has a modern origin; it came as a substitute for the romances and stories that so delighted our parents. . . . Through it one can moralize and instruct the people. . . . If the theatre was justly called the school of manners, the novel is moral in action. But in order for it to bring the benefits we have just admired, it must follow the rules that belong to it; it must be like a beehive of tasty honey and not a cup of deleterious poison. The people in their candid simplicity seek through it to *instruct* while *entertaining* themselves.[48] (Emphasis added.)

In this comment, J. C. Fernandes Pinheiro simply echoes the opinion, common among British critics and reviewers, that the novel justified its existence only in its capacity for moral instruction, as an instrument of reform intended to instill appropriate patterns of behavior in a rising social class. In a new society like the Brazilian one, it is not difficult to understand why some also expected the novel to fulfill its mission as an instigator or reformer of customs. The gradual re-Europeanization of Rio de Janeiro during Dom João's reign, exemplifying the need to introduce more "refined" habits, brought about substantial changes in men's and women's ways of living. It altered customs dating from colonial times and made available to the emerging political, economic, and social elite better education, cultural products and equipment (theaters, libraries, books and bookshops, printing shops), and the latest improvements of European civilization. As mentioned above, with the establishment of the Portuguese Court in Rio de Janeiro and, later, with the city made into the seat of the first empire, there was an investment in urbanization and a campaign to polish manners and normalize conduct. The elite thus displayed a clear intent to "civilize" the people and build a national culture. Literature played a central role in this civilizing march and in building a national consciousness through literary periodicals, newspapers, and the prose fiction that was beginning to be produced locally. Novel writing became part of this cultural movement, though it was late in coming. (Teixeira e Sousa's 1843 *O Filho do Pescador* is considered the first Brazilian novel.) It is therefore easy to understand the interest that European novels generated among intellectuals, journalists, and writers of the time.

There was also a need to justify the new genre's lack of theoretical nobility, which, according to Antonio Candido, made seventeenth-century French novelists—and, I would add, eighteenth-century British novelists as well—avail themselves of the artifice of the "sweet remedy" (the *utile et dulci*) to overcome the perception that fiction was inferior to tragedy and epic. Because it arrived in Brazil as a genre that had already consolidated itself in Europe, the novel did not have to struggle so hard to gain acceptance, and Brazilian novelists could move on quickly to other materials and topics, such as the everyday lives of the common people. Indeed, when compared to its British counterpart, the Brazilian novel did not take long to get rid of its "state of ashamed shyness" and of the blemish of being a minor and bastardized form.[49] Likewise, the novel had fewer problems embracing the "validity in itself of mimesis" and the "free play of creative fantasy," since it was directly engaged in the tasks of mapping out the country—its history, geography, topography, and people—on the one hand, and of raising national consciousness, on the other, while still looking to British and French models for guidance.[50]

As Meyer comments, "the fictions imagined by eighteenth-century ladies and spinsters lulled Brazilian nineteenth-century imaginations"—an observation that seems valid for writers and readers alike.[51] In her exemplary study of the *feuilleton*, Meyer shows not only the remarkable penetration of the *romance-folhetim* (the counterpart of the popular British novel) in Brazil but also its later ramifications on melodrama and soap operas. The formula was much the same as that used in popular British fiction: kidnapping, treachery, dishonor, virtue in distress, terrible villains, seduced and abandoned heroines, all combined with realistic scenes of everyday life, the valorization of domestic space, and the new role of women in the bourgeois family.

In Brazil as in Britain, the interest in novels and romances may very well have been related to other types of changes also taking place in Brazilian society. As Nelson Werneck Sodré, writing about the 1860s, points out: "If the great majority of the public was constituted by marriageable young ladies and students, and the privileged literary theme must be, exactly because of that, marriage, a little blended with the old love motif, the press and literature, closely connected then, was bound to be led to meet this demand. Women began to free themselves, little by little, from colonial confinement and submitted themselves to the patterns of European fashion, appearing in the drawing rooms and a little on the streets."[52]

While novel and romance reading was part of this process, no less important were the periodicals created specifically for women. *A Mulher do Simplício, ou A Fluminense Exaltada*, launched by Paula Brito and printed by Plancher in 1832, is said to have been the first women's magazine in the country, but earlier in 1827 Plancher announced that his *Espelho Diamantino* had "the special aim of promoting the instruction and entertainment of the fair sex in this Court."[53] This was simply a repetition, on the other side of the Atlantic, of the same process Englishwomen had experienced almost a century before. It is not hard to explain why modernization was so delayed in the country, given the backward state in which the Portuguese had kept the colony, the low rates of literacy, the slow introduction of modern habits and improvements, the persistence of slavery until 1888, the presence of an an elite unconcerned with providing the great majority with education or civil rights, and the very violent nature of social relations.

Nonetheless, although schooling in Brazil was very deficient—the first official survey of literacy rates, made in 1872, reported that only one-fifth of the free population across Brazil could read—it is necessary to recall the habit of reading aloud at families' evening gatherings and to add the "circle of listeners" to the numbers of those who could, occasionally, take advantage of the circulation of books in the country; this included Brazilian women, whose lack of education was abundantly documented by foreign travelers. The testimony of the British traveler Maria Graham, however, presents an alternative viewpoint and suggests that at least a few women (albeit a small minority) were habitual readers, even of philosophy and politics; Graham cites the example of one Dona Maria Clara.[54] The publication of periodicals directed specifically at the "fair sex" likewise provides evidence of a female readership.

Scholars must therefore revise the myth of women's illiteracy and see its development as more relative; as early as 1813 the *Gazeta do Rio de Janeiro* published advertisements announcing the establishment of the first lay boarding schools for girls, such as that of Dona Catharina Jacob.[55] The frequency and regularity of ads heralding the opening of schools for young women—with sewing, embroidery, languages, dancing, and music on their curricula—presupposes a willing clientele. It is true that the standard of education was not very high, and it seems that many girls gave up their studies before their conclusion. Yet, as the warnings against the dangers of reading fiction clearly indicate, there was indeed a female reading public for the novels that regularly arrived on European vessels.

At the same time, the insistence on edifying or instructive reading points to an educational project that aimed to prepare Brazilian society for the future, as part of a civilizing mission that involved men of letters, the elite, and the government. A process of enlightenment ensued, similar to that which had taken place in Britain and France in the eighteenth century, and which in Brazil was embodied in the foundation of colleges, the development of the press, and an emphasis on the diffusion of knowledge. Thus periodicals proliferated, and they came to play an important role precisely because of their avowed role in educating men and women. *O Espelho Diamantino*, for example, made it very clear that it was interested in offering more than just entertainment to its female readers. These periodicals' claims to offer instructive and edifying material may be little more than an imitation of their European models, or even a marketing ploy to make such periodicals acceptable in respectable homes, but the intention to help women in their new roles seems to have been programmatic:

> Yes, we hope so, and God forbid we form such a frail idea of the talent and prudence they [the ladies] are endowed with that we endeavor simply to entertain them with novels or anecdotes. Of course, we wish to make the fair sex smile from time to time at some decent jokes and circumstantial stories; however, our main purpose is to provide mothers and wives with the necessary instruction (at least [encourage them to feel] the need for such instruction) to guide the education of their children and imagine the occupations, dangers, and duties of the careers their husbands and sons are called to follow and, as our readers belong mostly to the higher ranks of society, we must stimulate some readers to engage in the study of Politics: most certainly we could not give the ladies greater proof of our devotion and of the high consideration we have for their judgment than by beginning our work with the most abstract and judicious subject.[56]

Thus the press played a major role in the instruction of its readers. Newspapers and periodicals, with their sections of varieties, miscellanies, and *feuilletons*, seem to have constituted "a kind of local version of the *Encyclopédie*," thus decisively contributing to the process of formation of their public.[57] The decision to focus on edifying stories seems to have been the obvious course.

Side by side with the desire to create a national literature, represented by the experiments of early Brazilian fiction writers in various periodicals, there was also the long-lasting habit of including translations of foreign narratives, which filled the leisure hours of a public eager for European novelties. The periodical *O Beija-Flor* (1830–31) is emblematic of this dual purpose; in its very first numbers, it published both the anonymous *Olaya e Júlia, ou A Periquita*[58] and "O Colar de Pérolas ou Clorinda," a story attributed to Walter Scott, whose capacity for historical reconstruction and morality the translator praised highly. According to the translator's prologue in *O Beija-Flor*:

> One of Walter Scott's characteristics is the purity and decency with which he deals with love. There has never been a more chaste novelist. Even though they are in love according to the novelist's strict orders, his heroes, or heroines, do not generally appear but in the background. It is true that the lovers represent the first figures in the story that we have translated both because it is short—it takes up a mere two sheets—and because Walter Scott himself, giving himself a secondary role, depicts their physical and moral shape; however, the author veils their criminal passion with such delicacy and shows them so cruelly punished by the catastrophe, that the moral lesson which he wanted to teach cannot but deeply engrave itself in one's heart.[59]

The *Jornal do Comércio*, from the late 1830s onward, also profited from the formula of blending the first fictional experiments of Brazilian writers with the publication of well-known French novels. Opening the Folhetim section at the bottom of the page with *O Capitão Paulo*, a *feuilleton* by Alexandre Dumas, in 1838, Plancher adopted the practice of offering his readers fiction in installments, and gave Pereira da Silva, Justiniano José da Rocha, and Joaquim Norberto de Souza e Silva the opportunity to bring their work to the public.[60] These short Brazilian novels (a concept used very loosely among them) blend the ingredients, borrowed from their British and French counterparts, that would become their customary fare.

Borrowings

One of the most visible effects of what Candido calls the novel's "state of ashamed shyness"—that is, its permanent need for self-justification—also found practitioners among Brazilians. This explains the various artifices employed by the country's first writers of fiction, who aimed, on the one hand, to respond to the moralizing appeal and, on the other, to lend a certain air of truthfulness to their accounts. The assurance of authenticity was an efficient tool in the process of convincing readers that the hours they dedicated to reading fiction would not be wasted. The many attestations of veracity and the strategies used in the search for verisimilitude often seem formulaic (a mere imitation of similar claims in British novels), since by this time the suspicion against fiction had diminished considerably. In fact, there was not much condemnation of fiction in Brazil except from very conservative quarters and the church, and the novel there had the clear purpose of developing and stimulating patriotic spirit and spreading knowledge about the country. But early Brazilian novels did practice some of the tricks commonly found in eighteenth-century European novels, and even in nineteenth-century novels—for example, the recourse to old manuscripts, employed by Walpole, which we see in *Olaya e Júlia, ou A Periquita*: "As a matter of fact, at bedtime, my guest trusted me with a quite voluminous manuscript, which I devoured during the night and of which, with its owner's permission, I took a copy. I cannot publish it in its entirety, it being too long; but I presume that the summary I have made of it will be worthy of my readers' attention."[61]

In José de Alencar's *Lucíola* (1862), Paulo's letters are the raw material out of which the novel is composed, employing roughly the same device that Richardson used in *Pamela*. Richardson presents himself as the editor of a correspondence that has its "foundation both in *Truth* and *Nature*" and that was entrusted to him so that, once made public, it could become exemplary. The recurring references to the novel's commitment to truth cannot be overlooked; Joaquim Manuel de Macedo takes a similar approach in *Os Dois Amores* (1848):

> "[D]o you think novels are lies? . . ."
>
> "I am sure about that."
>
> "You are very misinformed in that matter, D. Celina; novels are always founded on truth; the novelist's hardest task consists in misrepresenting that truth in such a way that his contemporaries cannot give the characters acting in it their true names."[62]

Similarly, Manuel Antonio de Almeida's narrator apologizes to the reader for the repetition he is obliged to reproduce: "It is most unfortunate for those of us who write these lines to fall prey to the monotony of nearly always repeating the same scenes with minor changes: however, we are obliged to be faithful to the times whose customs we are attempting to depict."[63] In Alencar's *Senhora* (1875), the prologue claims that the "story is true; and the narrative comes from a person who was a confidant(e), in circumstances I am unaware of, to the main actors of this curious drama."

A common practice among these well-known novelists, these claims to narrative truth were also invoked in the works of their precursors, as they rehearsed their first steps in fiction writing. *A Perjura*, a novella published in 1838 in *O Gabinete de Leitura*, contains the epigraph "All is true" and employs as its strategy a letter to the narrator from a certain Eugênio. The letter contains the story that the narrator now retells, and it illustrates a discussion the two men had had about perjury and remorse. In it, Eugênio recounts a narrative he heard from an old woman while he was on his way to a trial in Cabo Frio. This story concerns the woman's granddaughter, Henriquetta, who has been punished for relinquishing Eduardo, the man she had promised to marry, and letting herself be seduced by the rakish Domingos, whose lover she becomes. Fate has it that Eduardo perishes while trying to save her from an accident with her carriage. Henriquetta, consumed by remorse, is overcome with hallucinations and madness and eventually dies. The moral implications are obvious, though not a word of condemnation is uttered.

In another story, "A Ressurreição de Amor (Crônica Rio-grandense)," published in four parts in the *Jornal do Comércio* between 23 and 27 February 1839, an atmosphere of mystery and terror predominates, conventions borrowed from the gothic novel, equally popular on both sides of the Atlantic. In the best tradition of the genre, its distraught protagonist, Francisco, violates the tomb of his beloved only to discover that she is still alive. The narrator wastes no opportunity to heap hyperbolic praise on the natural beauties of his province while telling this tale of horror and death. With long descriptions of the natural landscape, the anonymous author struggles to establish some causal relationship between setting and plot, producing a formal fracture between the Brazilian scenery and a story of thwarted love stemming from the social differences between the aristocratic Francisco, the governor's brother, and Amália, a rich but plebeian young lady—a narrative of love and madness very much in the fashion of European melodrama.

Early Brazilian writers of fiction not only capitalized on these artifices and devices to persuade their readers but also lavishly recycled the repertoire of situations, behavioral norms, and characters that defined European novelistic paradigms. The moralizing mission and the reform of manners, though not always explicitly proclaimed, reveal themselves in the choice of intrigue and dénouement, and with the punishment of vice and the reward of virtue, at the same time that extravagant plots, unhappy love, mystery and terror, revenge, and seduction constitute the dainty dish served in slices to readers, male and female.

However, a disjunction between form and content is nearly always evident. Attempts to provide "local color" through descriptions of Brazilian landscape end up putting these texts out of sync with their European-shaped plots. Brazilian authors of the period were not unaware of this contradiction and its implicit rejection of realism. Thus Paula Brito, in the preface to "O Enjeitado" (published in the Folhetim section of the *Jornal do Commércio* on 28 and 29 May 1839), claims that he wants to discard the conventions of gothic fiction, leaving aside castles, feudal lords, dungeons, and the supernatural in favor of "simple narratives" and contemporary stories. He is interested in recounting the lived experience of his era, he tells us, rather than fantastical stories rooted in the past:

> When the books sent us from old Europe are but remembrances of ancient ages; when, after the Goths, Vandals, and feudal lords have annoyed us, today we are only presented with Vandals, Goths, and feudal feats; when, after so many sermons against the crusades, Walter Scott and other pens, if not of the same stature at least of superior fame, had as many sermons in their favor; [when] our imaginations are heated with the heroes of Palestine, it will be hard to believe that we appear before the public with such naïve narratives; but we, whose life is recent, whose history is contemporary, whose annals are not yet concealed in the dust of old books buried at the bottom of libraries, we tell only what we see or hear, lending it only a few garments.[64]

Ironically, what follows is the narrative of the misfortunes of the lovers Emília and Júlio, both of them haunted by Júlio's mysterious origins. The bourgeois drawing room where they find themselves—like hundreds of European ones—is the stage for a conversation in lofty language in which the habitual sentimental and moral clichés can be distinctly heard, without anything that might betray the Brazilian character of the story.

However, the recourse to scene and the delineation of conflict, which sound very promising in comparison with other contemporary narratives, soon give way to a long narrative summary in which the narrator takes on the responsibility of uncovering his protagonists' past. The effort to explain to his readers his characters' motivation is evident, but the use of coincidences to propel the action seems inevitable, and it is Emília's mother who providentially unveils the secret of Júlio's birth. In a flashback, now reporting the mother's narrative, the narrator leaves behind the bourgeois drawing room for a prosperous sugar plantation populated by "hundreds of slaves" whose owner "was feared by all who approached him for any reason." Brazilians are at last on truly national ground; they will easily recognize the patriarch who "treats everybody as if they were his slaves," above all his daughters, "whose will is never consulted." If adultery and illegitimacy are common themes in European fiction of the era, the authoritarianism, tyranny, and violence here are genuinely Brazilian. This juxtaposition engages the interest of Brazilian writers and readers precisely because it exposes the author's difficulties in confronting his material. Nothing is satisfactorily tied together, from a formal point of view, although the effort to achieve some level of resolution is clear.

Narrative Paradigms

In the earliest examples of fiction in Bahia, Salles sees the coexistence of two patterns: the first, copied from outdated European models, emphasizes sound moral principles still active in the more conservative sectors of society. The second is characterized by the use of dialogue, the realistic description of scene, the relativism of the characters' behavior, and a certain social realism and is closer to the style of *A Moreninha*.[65] It is not possible to verify whether this observation applies to the whole of fiction produced across Brazil in its early stages, since a considerable part of the archive has been lost. However, with the consolidation of the genre after the 1840s, what came to predominate was verisimilitude in plot and a more satisfactory relationship between the depiction of setting and the situations enacted. If, in Macedo's sentimental novels, the edifying intent discussed above or the burden of romantic subliterature did not completely disappear, some of the qualities that made the writer a faithful chronicler of life in Rio de Janeiro, a "breath of fresh air," as he has been described, already stand out, secured by his search for plausibility and verisimilitude and by his investment in the depiction of local customs and social life.

In *Formação da Literatura Brasileira*, Candido points to two main narrative structures, thus establishing a fundamental distinction between novels that explore the subjective layers of characters' inner lives, in the manner of Fyodor Dostoyevsky and Joaquim Maria Machado de Assis, and those that deal with life as a series of related actions, where all the emphasis lies on the scene and event, and what matters is the "larger movement of social life," represented in Brazilian literature by Almeida.[66] Candido thus draws the two main paradigms that have structured plots since at least the time of Richardson and Fielding in 1740s Britain and that were closely imitated by their followers on both sides of the English Channel.

The clash between social and economic position, on one side, and virtue and the laws of love, on the other—which, according to Candido, is already delineated in Alencar's *A Viuvinha* (1857) and would become the central conflict in *Senhora*—is nothing but the transposition to a Brazilian social milieu of the pattern created by Richardson's *Pamela* and taken to extremes in *Clarissa*. It is no coincidence that Alencar, writing to D. Paula de Almeida, declares, "There are two ways of studying the soul: one is dramatic, similar to Shakespeare's; the other, philosophic, as in Balzac. The novelist has both at his disposal; but he should, whenever possible, choose the former, and make his characters reveal themselves in the course of action."[67] In his comments about this method of composition, Richardson employs exactly the same arguments, which Alencar may not have read directly but which he may have encountered in the novels he read in his youth and which had been made by Richardson's followers, as Alencar testifies in "Como e porque sou romancista."

Also fruitful are the relations that can be established between Fielding's novelistic method, expressed in his prefaces and introductory chapters, and Almeida's method in *Memórias de um Sargento de Milícias*, in spite of the two novelists' significant differences in perspective. Employing wit and humor, Fielding aims to set an example by advocating goodness and innocence, whereas Almeida's criticism of the "sad moral state of our society" (which is how his narrator describes his social milieu) is more adequately inscribed in the framework of the chronicle of manners. In both cases, however, what predominates is the logic of the event, the absence of soul-searching conflicts, and the narrator's distance from what he chronicles, characterized by a certain ironic—and at the same time playful—approach to the material.

From "Amélia," Emílio Adet's short treatise on virtue, to *A Moreninha*, fiction had come a long way, not so much in chronological terms as from the point of view of what had been learned and incorporated, thanks to the availability of foreign models. It would fall to Alencar and Machado de Assis, Brazil's first two great novelists, to resolve and overcome the impasses and formal mismatches that had characterized the work of their predecessors. Despite their limitations, these earlier writers were essential participants in a process of acclimatizing the European bourgeois novel to Brazilian soil. Their first attempts, though clumsy, paved the way for the more challenging and mature formal solutions found in Alencar and Machado. Of course, the acclimatization of the novel in Brazil took a very particular shape: it became a powerful instrument in the hands of these first fiction writers, deeply engaged in the mission to construct a nation and a national consciousness. In their inexperienced hands, this mission translated itself into blanket praise for what they conceived to be the most Brazilian of all subjects—the country's nature and its people. Later, with *O Guarani* (1875) and *Iracema* (1871), two of his Indianist novels, Alencar shaped his own imaginary version of a national literature and a hybrid cultural identity. As Doris Sommer puts it, "What could be more Brazilian and proclaim independence from the Old World more clearly than casting the nation's protagonists as Indians and as those first Portuguese who, turning their backs to Europe, chose to unite with the natives?"[68]

Inchoate Brazilian criticism, in its turn, found the opportunity to express itself in the various literary periodicals, however ephemeral, that proliferated across the land from the 1820s on. Although they exhibited deficiencies similar to those of the forerunners of fiction, these first critics also employed methodologies that they viewed as appropriate to evaluating the work of their contemporaries. These critics offer fundamental proof of the prevailing conceptions of the novel that were available in the period in which the genre was codified in Brazil. Although crude in form, it was a reflection of such important issues as the representation of reality and the social function of the novel—well-known and familiar questions in the critical debate that had been waged in Britain and France beginning in the eighteenth century.

As noted above, the aura of inferiority surrounding the novel in the face of classical forms like tragedy and epic meant that novelists were forced to defend themselves for choosing it as their means of expression. Criticism also seems to have been guided by its demand that novelists offer readers "the image of virtue . . . and the abhorrence of vice," as A. F. Dutra e Mello proclaims in his study of *A Moreninha* in *Minerva Brasiliense*, in which he actually quotes Horace's precept. Exemplifying that contrast would be the noble mission of a genre that came into the world a bastard, according to many of these critics.

Yet critics did not restrict themselves to the desire for edification, having remembered to address a few formal problems and to offer some pointers for new and inexperienced novelists. They demanded fidelity to the real because of the genre's investment in domestic settings and everyday life. Nonetheless, they failed to realize that, deep down, didactic moralizing and fidelity to the real might be incompatible. As Alencar remarks perceptively in his foreword to *Asas de um Anjo* (1858), written in response to accusations of immorality in his comic play:

> I do not consider reality, or rather, artlessness, the reproduction of nature and of social life in the novel or in comedy, a school, or a system; but the only element of literature: its soul. . . . I agree, as has been said, that at times repulsive scenes are copied from nature and from life that decency, taste, and delicacy cannot tolerate. But then the error lies not in the literature but in the writer; it is not art that renounces beauty; it is the artist who does not know how to give his picture those divine touches that gild the thickest darkness of corruption and destitution.[69]

Almost 150 years after Crusoe stepped forward in a short preface to address his readers and justify the story they were about to read, one can still hear echoes of similar conceptions, critiques, defenses, and arguments that were part and parcel of the history of the novel in Britain and France, and that made the period of its rise one of the richest in literary history, both in Brazil and on the other side of the Atlantic.

NOTES

The epigraph is from Roberto Schwarz, "The Importing of the Novel to Brazil and Its Contradictions in the Work of Alencar," in *Misplaced Ideas: Essays on Brazilian Culture*, trans. John Gledson (London: Verso, 1992), 50.

1. Antonio Candido, *Formação da Literatura Brasileira (Momentos Decisivos)*, 2 vols., 4th ed., (São Paulo: Livraria Martins Editora, 1971), 2:121–22. All translations from the Portuguese are my own unless otherwise noted.

2. With Napoleon's imminent invasion of Portugal, and the Portuguese monarchy under threat, Lord Strangford convinced Prince Regent Dom João to flee to his Brazilian colony in 1807. Soon after his arrival in January 1808, Dom João complied with the clauses in the treaties he had signed with the British government, not only by opening up trade between Brazil and Britain but also by ceding to Britain and her citizens advantages

and privileges granted to no other foreign country. Rio de Janeiro became the capital of the Portuguese empire at this time. Brazil broke from Portugal only in 1822.

3. Schwarz, "Importing of the Novel," 41.

4. The catalogues include books covering different subjects and novels in several languages, with the exception of that of the Rio de Janeiro Subscription Library, which lists only works in English; they include *Catálogo de Algumas Obras que Se Vendem na Loja de Paulo Martin (Vindas neste Último Navio de Lisboa)* (Rio de Janeiro: Tip. Nacional, 1822); *Catálogo da Biblioteca do Gabinete Português de Leitura do Maranhão* (Maranhão: Tip. do Frias, 1867); *Catálogo da Biblioteca Municipal do Rio de Janeiro* (Rio de Janeiro: Tip. Central de Brown A. Evaristo, 1878); *Catálogo da Livraria de B.J. Garnier* number 23 (Rio de Janeiro: Tip. de Pinheiro; Paris: Tip. de Simon e Cia., 1865); *Catálogo dos Livros da Biblioteca Fluminense* (Rio de Janeiro: Tip. Thevenet SC., 1866); *Catálogo dos Livros do Gabinete Português de Leitura do Rio de Janeiro* (Rio de Janeiro: Tip. Americana de L. P. da Costa, 1844); *Catálogo dos Livros do Gabinete de Leitura da Cidade do Rio Grande de São Pedro do Sul* (Rio Grande: Typographia do Cruzeiro do Sul de José Vieira Braga, 1864); *Catálogo de Livros Portugueses que Se Acham à Venda na Loja de Mongie* (Rio de Janeiro, n.d.); *Catálogo das Obras Existentes no Gabinete Português de Leitura da Bahia* (Bahia: Tip. de Tourinho SC., 1868); *Catálogo Supplementar dos Livros do Gabinete Português de Leitura do Rio de Janeiro* (Rio de Janeiro: Tip. Perseverança, 1868); *Catalogue of the Rio de Janeiro Subscription Library* (London: Smith, Elder & Co., 1842); *Primeiro Suplemento ao Catálogo dos Livros da Biblioteca Fluminense* (Rio de Janeiro: Tipografia do Arquivo Médico Brasileiro, 1849). See also B. F. Ramiz Galvão, *Catálogo do Gabinete Português de Leitura do Rio de Janeiro*, 2 vols. (Rio de Janeiro, 1906–7).

5. The collection comprises at least ninety-nine novelists and some five hundred titles, including works in English, French, and Portuguese. A considerable number of them can still be found in the Gabinete Português de Leitura in Rio de Janeiro.

6. See Márcia Abreu, *Os Caminhos dos Livros* (Campinas: ALB/Mercado de Letras; São Paulo: FAPESP, 2003). Luiz Carlos Villalta has examined private collections and postmortem inventories in his work. See his "O que se fala e o que se lê: Língua, instrução e leitura," in *História da Vida Privada no Brasil*, ed. Laura de Mello Souza, 3 vols. (São Paulo: Companhia das Letras, 1997), 1:331–85.

7. Irving A. Leonard, "*Don Quixote* and the Book Trade in Lima, 1606," *Hispanic Review* 8.4 (1940): 285–304, and also "*Guzmán de Alfarache* in the Lima Book Trade, 1613," *Hispanic Review* 11.3 (1943): 210–20.

8. José Mindlin, "The Book in Brazil," in *Literary Cultures of Latin America: A Comparative History*, ed. Mario J. Valdés and Djelal Kadir, 3 vols. (Oxford: Oxford University Press, 2004), 2:23.

9. Antonio Benitez-Rojo, "The Nineteenth-Century Spanish American Novel," in *The Cambridge History of Latin American Literature*, ed. Roberto González Echevarría and Enrique Pupo-Walker, 3 vols. (Cambridge: Cambridge University Press, 1996), 1:429.

10. See the entry in the Gabinete Português de Leitura do Rio de Janeiro catalogues for 1844, 1858, and 1868: "*Historia da virtuosa, e infeliz Clara Harlowe*. Escrita em inglês pelo célebre Richardson e traduzida em francês por M. Le Tourneur, e do francês em português pelo tradutor do *Viajante Universal*, em 12, Lisboa, Tip. Rollandiana, 1804–1818, 15 volumes." Paul Barde of Geneva was the publisher of the 1785–86 French edition.

11. See Eugenia Vera Roldán, *The British Book Trade and Spanish American Independence: Education and Knowledge Transmission in Transcontinental Perspective* (Aldershot: Ashgate, 2003), Appendix 2: "*Clara Harlowe*: Novela, trad. del inglés al francés por M. Le Tourneur, siguiendo en todo la edición original revista por su autor Richardson, y del francés al castellano por D. José Marcos Gutiérrez, 8 vols. Plates. Revised edition of: *Clarissa Harlowe* (Madrid, 1796). Transl. by José Marcos Gutiérrez from the French: *Clarisse Harlowe* (Geneva: Paul Barde, 1785), Transl. by Le Tourneur from the English: *Clarissa Harlowe* (1747–49). Ackermann's edition was a revised version of the one published in Madrid, 1796, with corrections derived from a comparison with the English original version."

12. "De la situation actuelle de la librairie et particulièrement des contrefaçons de la librairie française dans le nord de l'Europe," *Revue Britannique*, 4th ser., 26 (March 1840): 52–97. A table with comparative values can be found on p. 80.

13. Franco Moretti, *Atlas of the European Novel, 1800–1900* (London: Verso, 1998), 187. See especially chapter 3, "Narrative Markets, ca. 1850."

14. Franco Moretti, "Conjectures on World Literature," *New Left Review* 1 (January–February 2000): 54–68, and "More Conjectures," *New Left Review* 20 (March–April 2003): 73–81.

15. Moretti, "Conjectures on World Literature," 58.

16. Ibid., 62. "Compromise," in its correlated meanings of "mutual agreement," "arrangement," "adjustment," and "accommodation," hardly describes what resulted from this encounter.

17. Schwarz, "Importing of the Novel," 46.

18. Richardson to Lady Echlin, 22 September 1755, in *The Correspondence of Samuel Richardson*, ed. Anna Laetitia Barbauld, 6 vols. (London: Richard Phillips, 1804), 4:59–60. The full quotation reads, "but [I] am afraid instruction without entertainment (were I capable of giving the best) would have but few readers. Instruction, Madam, is the pill; amusement is the gilding."

19. See Georges May, *Le dilemme du roman du XVIIIe. siècle: Étude sur les rapports du roman et de la critique (1715–1767)* (Paris: PUF, 1963), 163.

20. Ibid., 162–63.

21. In fact, the name Minerva Press began to be used only after 1790. See Dorothy Blakey, *The Minerva Press, 1790–1820* (London: Oxford University Press, 1939), 106.

22. The Minerva Press catalogues, for instance, contain titles by Charlotte Smith and Ann Radcliffe. The list of 1798 best-sellers includes several female novelists who are

barely known today, such as Agnes Maria Bennett, Eliza Parsons, and Mary Meeke, but also Regina Maria Roche and Elizabeth Helme. Some Minerva novelists appear in the ads and catalogues in Brazil.

23. See Françoise Parent-Lardeur, *Lire à Paris au temps de Balzac: Les cabinets de lecture à Paris, 1815–1830*, 2nd ed. (Paris: Éditions de l'École des Hautes Études en Sciences Sociales, 1999), 10.

24. A. N. Pigoreau, *Petite bibliographie biographico-romancière, ou Dictionnaire des romanciers tans anciens que modernes, tant nationaux qu'étrangers; avec un mot sur chacun d'eux et la notice des romans qu'ils ont donné, soit comme auteurs, soit comme traducteurs, précedé d'un catalogue des meilleurs romans publiés depuis plusiers années, et suivi de tableaux propres à en faire connaître les différents genres et à diriger dans le choix des ouvrages qui doivent faire la base d'un cabinet de lecture* (Paris: Pigoreau Libraire, 1821–28, including supplements).

25. Ibid., 5th supplement, February 1823, 18.

26. Marlyse Meyer, *Folhetim: Uma História* (São Paulo: Companhia das Letras, 1996), 34. See also 49–50n28. Other French circulating library catalogues also confirm Pigoreau's prominent role in the business. Though Pigoreau is not directly mentioned in Balzac's *Illusions Perdues* (1835–43), critics generally agree that he is the model for Doguereau, the bookseller to whom Lucien de Rubempré offers his work for publication. See Pierre Citron's introduction to Honoré de Balzac, *La Comédie Humaine*, 12 vols. (Paris: Gallimard, 1979), 5:54–58.

27. Rubens Borba de Moraes points out that Jonathan Swift's *Gulliver's Travels* (1726) and Laurence Sterne's *Sentimental Journey* (1768) could only be read by special license because they had been included in the list of books forbidden by the Real Mesa Censória. See his *Livros e Bibliotecas no Brasil Colonial* (Rio de Janeiro: LTC, 1979), 56. See also Abreu, *Os Caminhos dos Livros*.

28. Nelson Schapochnik records the existence of Cremière's circulating library, on Rua da Alfândega, and those of Mongie, Dujardin, and Mad Breton, on Rua do Ouvidor. See his "Contextos de Leitura no Rio de Janeiro do século XIX: Salões, gabinetes literários e bibliotecas," in *Imagens da Cidade: Séculos XIX e XX*, ed. Stella Bresciani (São Paulo: ANPUH/Marco Zero/FAPESP, 1993), 147–62.

29. "Remainders" is a term used to refer to unsold stocks bought at reduced prices from the original publisher.

30. Laurence Hallewell, *O Livro no Brasil (Sua História)* (São Paulo: T.A. Queiroz/EDUSP, 1985), 117. France always served as a kind of role model as far as cultural artifacts and products were concerned.

31. See Harold Streeter, *The Eighteenth-Century English Novel in French Translation: A Bibliographical Study* (New York: Institute of French Studies, 1963).

32. Respectively, *The Italian, or The Confessional of the Black Penitents* (1797) and *Albert, or The Wilds of Strathnavern* (1799).

33. See Marlyse Meyer, "O que é, ou quem foi *Sinclair das Ilhas?*" in *Revista do Instituto de Estudos Brasileiros* (São Paulo: Universidade de São Paulo, 1973), 37–63.

34. Translation of *Le Diable Boiteux* (1707) and the first novel published by Impressão Régia, in 1810, according to Rubens Borba de Moraes, in *Livros e Bibliotecas no Brasil Colonial*, 120.

35. Respectively, *Paul et Virginie* (1788) and *La Chaumière Indienne* (1791); *A Thousand and One Nights*; *Atala* (1801); *Belisaire* (1767); *Louisa, or The Cottage on the Moor* (1789); *Gulliver's Travels* (1726); *The Life and Surprising Adventures of Robinson Crusoe* (1719); *The History of Tom Jones, a Foundling* (1749); *Life of Arnold Zulig* (1790); *Clarissa, or The History of a Young Lady* (1747–48). The dates in parentheses in the text above are the dates when the novels were first advertised in the newspaper. From 1801 there is evidence that license requests were made to the Portuguese board of censorship for the shipment of the French versions of Defoe's *Aventures de Robinson Crusoe* (Paris, 1799) and Richardson's *Histoire de Clarisse* (Venice, 1788) and *Histoire de Grandisson* (Amsterdam, 1777). For the circulation of books in the colonial period, see Abreu, *Os Caminhos dos Livros*, 95–97.

36. Joaquim Manuel de Macedo (1820–1882) was a doctor and man of letters. See *A Moreninha* (1844; São Paulo: Ática, 1995), 69.

37. Gilberto Freyre, *Ingleses no Brasil: Aspectos da Influência Britânica sobre a Vida, a Paisagem e a Cultura do Brasil*, 3rd ed. (Rio de Janeiro: Topbooks, 2000), 43. Both Freyre and Hallewell note that in 1832 the Tipografia Pinheiro, Faria e Cia. published, in Olinda, the novel *A Caverna da Morte*, but both wrongly attribute it to Ann Radcliffe. It must be the anonymous *The Cavern of Death: A Moral Tale* (1794).

38. Bookshops belonging to Villeneuve, Didot, Mongie, Crémière, Garnier, Plancher, and Dujardin were all situated in this area.

39. José de Alencar (1829–1877), novelist and politician, played a central role in the consolidation of the novel in Brazil. His testimony about the importance of foreign novels to his formation as a novelist can be found in "Como e porque sou romancista," in *Obra Completa*, 4 vols. (Rio de Janeiro: José Aguilar, 1965), vol. 1. Marlyse Meyer records references to Mrs. Helme's *Sinclair das Ilhas* not only in Alencar but also in Machado de Assis and Guimarães Rosa. See her "O que é, ou quem foi *Sinclair das Ilhas?*"

40. Candido, *Formação da Literatura Brasileira*, 2:109.

41. See the state-of-the-art listing of novels at www.unicamp.br/iel/memoria/Ensaios/index.htm. There was also the overwhelmingly popular Charles Dickens and the omnipresent Walter Scott, whose appeal has yet to be explained.

42. See Ana Luiza Martins, *Gabinetes de Leitura da Província de São Paulo: A Pluralidade de um Espaço Esquecido (1847–1890)* (São Paulo: FFLCH/USP, 1990). See also "As Leituras às Vésperas da República," in Suplemento de Cultura, *O Estado de São Paulo* 7 (no. 486), 18 November 1989, 4–6.

43. Júlia Lopes de Almeida, *Livro das Noivas*, 2nd ed. (Rio de Janeiro: Francisco Alves, 1896), 36.

44. For a discussion of reading during this period, see Kate Flint, *The Woman Reader, 1837–1914* (Oxford: Clarendon Press, 1995), and Patrick Brantingler, *The Reading Lesson: The Threat of Mass Literacy in Nineteenth-Century British Fiction* (Bloomington: Indiana University Press, 1998).

45. A. F. Dutra e Mello, "A Moreninha," in *Minerva Brasiliense* 1–2, 2.24 (15 October 1844): 747. The passage from Horace's *Ars Poetica* continues with the words *lectorem delectando pariterque monendo*. "He has won every vote who has blended profit and pleasure / at once delighting and instructing the reader." See Horace, *Satires, Epistles, and Ars Poetica*, trans. and ed. H. R. Fairclough (Cambridge: Harvard University Press, 1970), 479.

46. Antonio Gonçalves Teixeira e Sousa, Introduction to *Gonzaga, ou A Conjuração de Tiradentes*, 2 vols. (Rio de Janeiro: Typographia de Teixeira, 1848–51).

47. See David Salles, ed., *Primeiras Manifestações da Ficção na Bahia* (São Paulo: Cultrix-INL-MEC, 1979).

48. J. C. Fernandes Pinheiro, *Guanabara: Revista Mensal, Artistica, Scientifica e Litteraria* 3.1 (1 March 1855): 17–20.

49. See Antonio Candido, "Timidez do romance," in *Educação pela Noite e Outros Ensaios* (São Paulo: Ed. Ática, 1987), 82–99.

50. Ibid., 88.

51. Marlyse Meyer, "Mulheres Romancistas Inglesas do Século XVIII e Romance Brasileiro," in *Caminhos do Imaginário no Brasil* (São Paulo: EDUSP, 1993), 47–72.

52. Nelson Werneck Sodré, *História da Imprensa no Brasil* (Rio de Janeiro: Civilização Brasileira, 1966), 227–28.

53. *A Mulher do Simplício, ou A Fluminense Exaltada* was edited in Rio de Janeiro by Paula Brito and ran from 1832 to 1846.

54. Maria Graham, *Diário de uma Viagem ao Brasil*, trans. Américo Joacobina Lacombe (Belo Horizonte: Itatiaia; São Paulo: Editora da Universidade de São Paulo, 1990), 376.

55. Delso Renault, *O Rio Antigo nos Anúncios de Jornais (1808–1850)* (Rio de Janeiro: José Olympio, 1969), 19.

56. *O Espelho Diamantino: Periódico de Política, Literatura, Belas-Artes, Teatro e Moda* 3 (1827): 35–36. This journal carried the motto "Dedicado às senhoras brasileiras" (Dedicated to Brazilian women).

57. Flora Süssekind, *O Brasil Não É Longe Daqui: O Narrador; A Viagem* (São Paulo: Companhia das Letras, 1990), 79.

58. Marlyse Meyer calls this a "Franco-Brazilian" novel and attributes its authorship to Charles Auguste Taunay. See her essay "Uma Novela Franco-Brasileira de 1830," in *As Mil Faces de um Herói Canalha e Outros Ensaios* (Rio de Janeiro: Editora da UFRJ, 1998), 333–47.

59. Translator's prologue, *O Beija-Flor* 1 (1830): 32. There is no record of any work by Walter Scott under this title. According to the British Library's catalogue, this work is by

Constantine Henry Phipps and was published in the *Keepsake* in 1829. I am indebted to Ross Forman for this information.

60. Alexandre Dumas Père's *Le Capitaine Paul* appeared in 1838.

61. *O Beija-Flor* 4 (1830): 112–13.

62. Joaquim Manuel de Macedo, *Os Dois Amores* (São Paulo: W. M. Jackson, 1950), 12.

63. Manuel Antonio de Almeida (1830–1855) wrote only one novel, *Memórias de um Sargento de Milícias* (1854), which became one of the most important texts in the history of the Brazilian novel.

64. See *Os Precursores do Conto no Brasil*, ed. Barbosa Lima Sobrinho (Rio de Janeiro: Editora Civilização Brasileira, 1960), 197. It is interesting to note that the narrator indirectly shows that he is a reader of gothic novels.

65. See Salles, *Primeiras Manifestações*, 27.

66. Candido, *Formação da Literatura Brasileira*, 2:215–16.

67. Alencar, "Carta a D. Paula de Almeida," in *Obra Completa*, 1:1212.

68. Doris Sommer, "*O Guarani* and *Iracema*: Brazil's Two-faced Indigenism," in *Foundational Fictions: The National Romances of Latin America* (Berkeley and Los Angeles: University of California Press, 1991), 147. Sommer reads these two Alencar novels as national allegories that connect the love stories of their Indian and Portuguese protagonists to the foundation of the nation (and erase the violence and extermination that characterized this encounter).

69. Alencar, *Obra Completa*, 1:922.

WORKS CITED

Abreu, Márcia. *Os Caminhos dos Livros*. Campinas: ALB/Mercado de Letras; São Paulo: FAPESP, 2003.

Almeida, Júlia Lopes de. *Livro das Noivas*, 2nd ed. Rio de Janeiro: Francisco Alves, 1896.

Benitez-Rojo, Antonio. "The Nineteenth-century Spanish American Novel," in *The Cambridge History of Latin American Literature*, 3 vols., eds. Roberto González Echevarría and Enrique Pupo-Walker. Cambridge: Cambridge University Press, 1996.

Blakey, Dorothy *The Minerva Press: 1790–1820*. London: Oxford University Press, 1939.

Borba de Moraes, Rubens. *Livros e Bibliotecas no Brasil Colonial*. Rio de Janeiro: LTC, 1979.

Brantingler, Patrick. *The Reading Lesson: The Threat of Mass Literacy in Nineteenth-century British Fiction*. Bloomington: Indiana University Press, 1998.

Candido, Antonio. *Formação da Literatura Brasileira (Momentos Decisivos)*, 2 vols., 4th ed. São Paulo: Livraria Martins Editora, 1971.

———. "Timidez do romance," in *Educação pela Noite e Outros Ensaios*, 82–99. São Paulo: Ed. Ática, 1987.

Dutra e Mello, A. F. "A Moreninha," in *Minerva Brasiliense* 1–2, II.24 (15 October 1844).

Flint, Kate. *The Woman Reader, 1837–1914*. Oxford: Clarendon Press, 1995.

Freyre, Gilberto. *Ingleses no Brasil: Aspectos da Influência Britânica sobre a Vida, a Paisagem e a Cultura do Brasil*, 3rd ed. Rio de Janeiro: Topbooks, 2000.

Graham, Maria. *Diário de uma Viagem ao Brasil*, trans. Américo Joacobina Lacombe. Belo Horizonte: Itatiaia; São Paulo: Editora da Universidade de São Paulo, 1990.

Hallewell, Laurence. *O Livro no Brasil (Sua História)*. São Paulo: T.A. Queiroz/EDUSP, 1985.

Horace. *Satires, Epistles and Ars Poetica*, trans. and ed. H. R. Fairclough. Cambridge, Mass.: Harvard University Press, 1970.

Leonard, Irving A. "*Don Quixote* and the Book Trade in Lima, 1606." *Hispanic Review* 8.4 (October 1940): 285–304.

———. "*Guzmán de Alfarache* in the Lima Book Trade, 1613." *Hispanic Review* 11.3 (July 1943), 210–220.

Macedo, Joaquim Manuel de. *Os Dois Amores* [1848]. São Paulo: W. M. Jackson Inc., Editores, 1950.

Martins, Ana Luiza. *Gabinetes de Leitura da Província de São Paulo: A Pluralidade de um Espaço Esquecido (1847–1890)*. São Paulo: FFLCH/USP, 1990.

———. "As Leituras às Vésperas da República," in Suplemento de Cultura, *O Estado de São Paulo* 7 (no. 486), 18 November 1989, 4–6.

May, Georges. *Le Dilemme du roman du XVIIIe. siècle: Étude sur les rapports du roman et de la critique (1715–1767)*. Paris: PUF, 1963.

Meyer, Marlyse. "O que é, ou quem foi *Sinclair das Ilhas*?" in *Revista do Instituto de Estudos Brasileiros* 14, 37–63. São Paulo: Universidade de São Paulo, 1973.

———. "Mulheres Romancistas Inglesas do Século XVIII e Romance Brasileiro," in *Caminhos do Imaginário no Brasil*, 47–72. São Paulo: EDUSP, 1993.

———. *Folhetim: Uma História*. São Paulo: Companhia das Letras, 1996.

———. "Uma Novela Franco-brasileira de 1830," in *As Mil Faces de um Herói Canalha e Outros Ensaios*, 333–347. Rio de Janeiro: Editora da UFRJ, 1998.

Mindlin, José. "The Book in Brazil," in *Literary Cultures of Latin America: A Comparative History*, eds. Mario J. Valdés and Djelal Kadir, 3 vol. Oxford: Oxford University Press, 2004.

Moretti, Franco. *Atlas of the European Novel, 1800–1900*. London: Verso, 1998.

———. "Conjectures on World Literature." *New Left Review* 1 (January–February 2000): 54–68.

———. "More Conjectures." *New Left Review* 20 (March–April 2003): 73–81.

Parent-Lardeur, Françoise. *Lire à Paris au temps de Balzac. Les cabinets de lecture à Paris, 1815–1830*, 2nd ed. Paris: Éditions de l'École des Hautes Études en Sciences Sociales, 1999.

Renault, Delso. *O Rio Antigo nos Anúncios de Jornais (1808–1850)*. Rio de Janeiro: José Olympio, 1969.

Roldán, Eugenia Vera. *The British Book Trade and Spanish American Independence: Education and Knowledge Transmission in Transcontinental Perspective*. Aldershot: Ashgate, 2003.

Salles, David, ed. *Primeiras Manifestações da Ficção na Bahia*. São Paulo: Cultrix-INL-MEC, 1979.

Schapochnik, Nelson. "Contextos de Leitura no Rio de Janeiro do século XIX: Salões, gabinetes literários e bibliotecas," in *Imagens da Cidade: Séculos XIX e XX*, ed. Stella Bresciani, 147–162. São Paulo: ANPUH/Marco Zero/FAPESP, 1993.

Schwarz, Roberto. "The Importing of the Novel to Brazil and Its Contradictions in the Work of Alencar." In *Misplaced Ideas: Essays on Brazilian Culture*, trans. John Gledson. London: Verso, 1992.

Sobrinho, Barbosa Lima, ed. *Os Precursores do Conto no Brasil*. Rio de Janeiro: Editora Civilização Brasileira, 1960.

Sodré, Nelson Werneck. *História da Imprensa no Brasil*. Rio de Janeiro: Civilização Brasileira, 1966.

Sommer, Doris. *Foundational Fictions: The National Romances of Latin America*. Berkeley: University of California Press, 1991.

Streeter, Harold. *The Eighteenth-century English Novel in French Translation: A Bibliographical Study*. New York: Institute of French Studies, 1963.

Süssekind, Flora. *O Brasil Não É Longe Daqui: O Narrador. A Viagem*. São Paulo: Companhia das Letras, 1990.

Teixeira e Sousa, Antonio Gonçalves. Introduction to *Gonzaga, ou a Conjuração de Tiradentes*, 2 vol. Rio de Janeiro: Typographia de Teixeira & Co., 1848–1851.

Villalta, Luiz Carlos. "O que se fala e o que se lê: língua, instrução e leitura," in *História da Vida Privada no Brasil*, ed. Laura de Mello Souza, 3 vols., I:331–385. São Paulo: Companhia das Letras, 1997.

SANDRA GUARDINI TEIXEIRA VASCONCELOS is a full professor of English literature and comparative literature at the University of São Paulo, where she obtained her MA and PhD in literary theory and comparative literature. She did her postdoctoral studies at the University of Cambridge (1993–1994) and at the University of Manchester (2008), and was Visiting Research Associate at the Centre for Brazilian Studies at the University of Oxford (2005). Over the past years, she has been carrying out research on the presence and circulation of eighteenth- and nineteenth-century English novels in nineteenth-century Brazil. She has organized several books, has published articles and chapters both in Brazil and abroad, and is the author of *Puras Misturas: Estórias em Guimarães Rosa* (1997), *Dez Lições sobre o Romance Inglês do Século XVIII* (2002), and *A Formação do Romance Inglês: ensaios teóricos* (2007), for which she received the 2008 Jabuti Prize (Literary Theory and Criticism). She is curator of the João Guimarães Rosa Archive at the Instituto de Estudos Brasileiros (USP). She may be reached at sgtvasco@usp.br.

Reviews

JOÃO ALMINO.
The Book of Emotions.

Trans. Elizabeth Jackson. Champaign, Ill.:
Dalkey Archive Press, 2011.

João Almino's *Book of Emotions*, newly available in English thanks to a superb translation by Elizabeth Jackson, is narrated by a blind photographer. The trope of the blind prophet or poet is ancient, but a blind photographer is assuredly a very contemporary innovation. What truths might such a figure convey to a society that seems to have lost its way amid the tumult of images that through their superficiality and ephemerality distract our attention even from the social and political realities they purport to represent?

The Book of Emotions is Almino's fourth in a quintet of novels set in Brasilia, which together constitute a tender tribute to the flaws as well as the fortitude of the city's inhabitants. The septuagenarian Cadu narrates this installment of Almino's quintet, telling a story of the early twenty-first century from the vantage point of the year 2022. In his early fifties, when he still had his sight, Cadu was carried to Brasilia in the wake of the implosion of his relationship with Joanna, one of the great loves of his life. For a little more than a year he kept a photo diary; twenty years later he remembers those photographs so sharply that he is able to select from among them to assemble a "Book of Emotions," so named because each photograph represents an emotion he either experienced at the moment when he snapped the shutter, felt when he was photographed, or was overcome by when he viewed the developed image.

In Almino's novel we do not see these photographs but read Cadu's description of them. We thus inhabit a position contiguous with the blind photographer's. He works through memory; we work through imagination. The common ground upon which we meet is the territory of both emotion and interpretation. Cadu describes the composition and context of sixty-two photographs, on occasion pinning a specific emotion to an image but more typically allowing the emotional truth of the image to emerge circuitously. He is not a fully trustworthy narrator, and the legacy of Machado de Assis is in this sense persistent and influential. We may take his glosses with a grain of salt, for Cadu interprets his photographs and indeed his life choices in self-flattering ways, even when he feels remorse. He has devoted his life to art rather than commerce, to beauty rather than realism, to vengeance rather than justice, and to erotic passion rather than fidelity. His path is strewn with broken hearts, including, at times, his own. He considers the loss of his sight late in life a blessing in many respects, because it frees him from attachment to the beauty he sees when he looks in the mirror, as well as the beauty he finds in women.

A blind photographer is not as oxymoronic a figure as it at first appears. A photograph freezes a single instant in time, as particles of light reflect off objects and are captured by film or a CCD chip. Cadu's visual memories are also frozen in time: when he reencounters Joanna in old age, he imagines her forever youthful. Movement and change happen through time. The frozen moment defies movement and change and promises eternity. Crucially, for Cadu, beauty and sensuality operate under a similar temporality, for "Pleasure isn't measured by time but rather by intensity" (130). In this sense, Cadu is the perfect hedonist and the perfect photographer.

If Cadu is rendered comical by his romantic troubles and his bumbling efforts to derail the career of his nemesis, Eduardo Kaufman, the novel's playful engagement with temporality nonetheless offers a serious reflection on visual and textual art, memory, imagination, and social dislocation at the beginning of the twenty-first century. We learn that in 2022 Brasilia will have suffered even more from the social inequalities, poverty, violence, and crime common in Brazil's major cities today, that corruption will continue to flourish in government, and that social and political meaning will continue to be mediated by facile images that bounce across the screens of our virtual lives. In the face of all this, *The Book of Emotions* invites us into an interior and profound space in which the art of photography is celebrated, ironically, with the absence of photographs. Unlike W. G. Sebald, who unsettles our confidence in the inventions of fiction by including photographic reproductions in his novels, João Almino reinforces our confidence in our own visual imagination by not including photographs in this novel. As we come to understand the sixty-two photographs that make up *The Book of Emotions*, we find common cause with the blind photographer precisely in the capacity of narrative to plumb the depths of human experience and the ability of readers to think and feel their way up through those depths to solid ground. This extraordinary novel offers a lyrical homage not only to the art of photography but also to the art of living.

GREG A. MULLINS teaches comparative literature at the Evergreen State College in Olympia, Washington. He is the author of *Colonial Affairs*, a critical study of colonialism and sexuality, and is currently writing a book about the absorption of human rights law in the cultural practices of ordinary life. He may be reached at MullinsG@evergreen.edu.

PEDRO MEIRA MONTEIRO
Translated by Flora Thomson-DeVeaux

JOSÉ MIGUEL WISNIK.

Veneno remédio: O futebol e o Brasil.

São Paulo: Companhia das Letras, 2008.

Roots of the Twenty-first Century

Why does no one write works of national interpretation anymore?

Some will say that this kind of project has no place nowadays. Gilberto Freyre and Sérgio Buarque de Holanda, respectively, wrote *The Masters and the Slaves* and *The Roots of Brazil* nearly eighty years ago. We simply didn't know as much as we do today, thanks to decades of work by social scientists and historians. But if all this knowledge lets us write about Brazil with more nuance, it also stays our hand with the reminder that any attempt to set down national characteristics will be merely an impressionistic exercise, one that cannot stand up to rigorous historical analysis.

But the work of national interpretation is not and never was merely a record of accumulated facts. These works don't speak of Brazil *as it is*. Their horizon is radically different from that of purely scientific or historical studies; it is ethical, almost transcendent, and sounds out the nature of the collective. It asks not only how we arrived where we are but also where we're headed, and even where we should be going. Its field of vision encompasses the past, present, and future in a single continuum, taking an extremely long-term view of history, as if we were navigating on a current without knowing where it carries us. The true writer of national interpretation names our destination, making it into a fable in which the reader can recognize himself.

And so, after decades of development in social sciences and historical studies, is there still room for works that announce Brazil's purpose?

The answer came four years ago, in the form of a book that may become the *Roots of Brazil* of the twenty-first century: *Veneno remédio: O futebol e o Brasil*, by José Miguel Wisnik. It's lamentable that the book hasn't yet provoked much debate, especially in academic circles. Perhaps this shows some reticence regarding the book's subject material, since not all intellectuals are prepared to take football seriously. But perhaps the problem is that the book points to an unresolved question: miscegenation. Not simple miscegenation of genetic or phenotypic traits but miscegenation as the fundamental rupture of patterns associated with order and discipline. Miscegenation, in short, as the mixture of the structures and principles of civilization. Which would be, shall we say, a fertile mess.

For Wisnik, football isn't an escape valve for social tensions, or a banal form of entertainment, or the simple expression of economic and commercial interests. Rather, it's principally a symbolic system that brings wide sectors of society closer than they otherwise would be to real experiences of gain and loss—which, as such, should be felt and lived collectively. Either all lose, or all win. One can't overlook the political and identity-related ramifications of this shared adventure.

The temptation to see a populist drive behind the game of football, a possible manipulation of the masses, is powerful but misplaced. It's true that fans' devotion may be a form of eradicating respect for difference (hooliganism is a reality), but aside from fanaticism there is an immense gradation of associative possibilities, various ways of identifying with what's going on down on the field. The psychoanalytic framework of Wisnik's argument won't escape the reader: discussion of football turns into the analysis of complex mechanisms of transference. That is, what happens on the field has implications for the person watching the game, because history is coded therein—and, as it happens, the destiny of not just the observer, but of all, is involved.

A fundamental difference between the game of football and manipulative mass phenomena like fascism, Wisnik argues, is that its fans exist in the hypnotic state that moves them forward, avoiding anything that might give them a reality check (or an encounter with "the real," in psychoanalytic terms). The game, meanwhile, is a mesmerizing battle always on the edge of the real, and it will inescapably fall into the real. In fact, as mesmerizing as the game may be, when one plays for keeps the risk of defeat is both assumed and lived, as if loss formed part of the dialogue the subject holds with destiny. In playing, one learns how to lose. But the fascist model sustains itself through the negation of any and all loss, avoiding the shadow of frustration and always intent, irritably and brutally, upon sweeping from the map those who might contribute to an unacceptable defeat.

Why does Wisnik use the language of "poison" and "cure" to characterize Brazilian football? The formula recalls the *pharmakon*, which contains within itself the seeds of both healing and destruction. The book's argument is fairly simple, partly intuitive and unfailingly accurate: according to Wisnik, Brazil exists in an imaginary oscillating dualism of success and disaster. Either we're the best, or we're worthless. The country, Wisnik says, "is either the recipe for happiness or a dead-end failure." There is no compromise, no middle ground between the two poles. The most perfect satire of this state of the collective soul is the "Brás Cubas Poultice" that Machado de Assis puts into his protagonist's imagination; Brás Cubas dies just as he hits upon a providential solution that will alleviate "our melancholy humanity" once and for all. Against profound sadness, eternal happiness. Machado's lesson is that we'll die of this yet.

Veneno remédio is a book in which erudition on the subject of football is paired with cultural and philosophical analysis. If the argument that it proposes is closer to Sérgio Buarque de Holanda's radical uncertainty about Brazil's future, Wisnik's dense and elliptical prose puts him, at least stylistically, in the company of Gilberto Freyre. Or perhaps we can say that *Veneno remédio* plays midfielder between the two essayists, since the goalposts Wisnik uses come from their thinking. I shall limit myself to one question, a fundamental one even for those who don't follow football. It has to do with something that, in *Veneno remédio*, is termed "the nonlinear nature of Brazilian football."

Why are nonlinearity, ellipses, and sinuous curves called upon to say something that goes far beyond the football field? How can this resistance to the rectilinear help decipher the meaning of an entire social matrix and pose questions about collective destiny? The answer lies in a realization born of literature.

In addition to being a lover of football and a musician himself, Wisnik is a talented literary critic. Thus *Veneno remédio* takes its initial inspiration from the distinction made by the Italian filmmaker and poet Pier Paolo Pasolini, who, in the early 1970s, imagined the opposition between football played in *prose*, which he associated with European teams, and football played in *poetry*, a style identified with South American football, and Brazilian football in particular.

The provocation has profound consequences for understanding the game from within. But, at the same time, it points toward different ways of playing the social contract, different ways of exploring the spaces of society. On one side is the European style (capitalist, urbane, First World, etc.), "linear and goal-oriented," with "triangular passes, defensive emphasis, counter-attacks, crosses, and follow-through"; on the other is the Latin American mode (peripheral, rural, Third World, etc.), with its "creation of empty spaces, feints, autonomous dribbles, [and] a congenital tendency toward the attack." Two systems of playing and two proposed civilizations face off, even though the principles in question are present in each society.

Even with the proviso that the two methods aren't exclusive, this brings us to a delicate moment, when more irritable readers, suspicious of the "Freyrian" approach, which praises tropical civilization in all its malleability and ductility, will pin Wisnik with an apology of tropical *malemolência*—as if each effective dribble, in all its dazzling material beauty, were proof of the superiority of a society that sidesteps conflict, being unable to face it. Here one might see a superficial reading of the "cordial man" by Sérgio Buarque de Holanda, which the unwary tend to identify with the elimination of violence and the triumph of a "natural goodness" fully realized in this blessed homeland.

The reader in question is invited to swallow his irritation and put his lips back in their original position for a moment, before trying out his ironic smirk in the face of—just look!—one more thinker stepping into line behind Freyre. Discussing whether Wisnik is more or less Freyrian is, frankly, useless. Evidently, there is something quite modernist in the study of the consequences of these dribbles, something in these "irruptions" that end up short-circuiting the linear order of clear objectives defined by the logic of means and ends, which is perhaps closer to Mário and Oswald than to Freyre. Or perhaps that something is tropicalist, dreaming of a civilization that constructs itself against the threatening order of technique and predictability, valuing a Dionysian freedom born of the pleasure and joy of the body.

The football coach, in this sense, is an unwanted castrator. If necessary, he will ask the genius to put aside his creative outbursts in the name of efficiency, because results are what matter. This is a kind of Dunga or Parreira complex—men who, not by chance, ended up playing the paradigmatic role of the castrating coach. They were hated because they would have pruned back exactly what Brazil did best.

This is not to say that castration and technique are unnecessary. Any psychological organization (including the collective) develops in the space between the assumed and internalized rule, on the one hand, and the space normally identified with "freedom," on the other. This "free" space would not exist without the established order. Transgression can't exist without laws, just as freedom depends, after all, on the breaking of an internally fixed rule that functions on the subjective plane. To use the old psychoanalytic jargon: one doesn't play well when the superego dominates, but one can't let one's instincts run wild, either—the id, that is, the "this" that, when uncontrolled, would plunge all into a war against all, with no truces and no end.

Let us leave aside some of the book's internal mirages, such as Wisnik's enchantment with the unique character of football—which, unlike American football, supposedly lives on the edge of the imponderable, set against the cumulative and progressive strategies of the most popular American sports. There is something very interesting, in fact, about a sport in which the slightest and least expected details can decide the game. *Soccer* tends to give the sense that the best team isn't always the one that wins, as if in the end there were a certain poetic justice waiting to redeem even the weakest. Meanwhile, sports like basketball and American football function via the linear accumulation of points, making it practically inevitable that the best will win in the end—the team with the best strategy, preparation, and talent, that is—thereby eliminating, so to speak, the power of chance.

It is the power of chance (yes, Mallarmé is also central in *Veneno remédio*) that is at stake when the "superiority" of Brazilian football comes into play. But this is not chance as cosmic punishment, or as mythical determinant of history. The "chance" in question points toward the fertile power of uncertainty, that which opens into a myriad of possibilities, precisely because nothing can close off or control the environment when one is talking about a truly poetic play—and there are many, beautifully described in the book.

Poetry (and football as well, with its epiphanic moments) lives on the edge of uncertainty, testing and pushing the boundaries of the possible, in that "band of structural spontaneity" that Wisnik attributes to football. Technique, however, works with the boundaries of the possible, bending itself to them and respecting them in a kind of reverence for the given.

One can then imagine the range of the "nonlinearity" postulated as a national characteristic by *Veneno remédio*. Instead of constituting a fixed and inescapable character, it is simply *one more element in play*, which Brazilians should come to terms with and which might even benefit them. From a "rational" perspective (developed, controlling, technical, etc.), nonlinearity is a cardinal flaw. But it is from this drug that Brazil will extract its cure; rather, it is through this poison that Brazil can enter into dialogue with the masters of the world. In this sense football can be thought of as the "Brás Cubas Poultice that worked." The idea is tempting, and Wisnik calls another Buarque de Holanda to the field in the middle of the game—this time, the son of the author of *Roots of Brazil*.

Observing a scrimmage between European boys and the sons of immigrants in Paris in 1998, Chico Buarque noted that the rich boys played like "masters of the field," preferring "control of the ball as a way to occupy the field in an organized way," while the poor boys were merely "masters of the ball." The passage is worth reproducing for its striking conclusion: the immigrants' sons, says Wisnik, echoing Chico, "take advantage of the opportunity in football to instruct themselves as best they can in the art of intimacy with the ball (developing, within the game, the splendid and wasted expertise that we know so well from the fleeting spectacle of the 'stoplight jugglers'). Some people are *equilibrados* [well-balanced], others are *equilibristas* [acrobats]."

Between the well-balanced and the acrobat, the question begins to stir of the mastery of codes, and how much one can trust in the rules. The well-balanced rich boy plays as if the field were his natural plane, since every square millimeter of it can and should be occupied rationally. The exception, of course, is the exact, wandering point where we find the ball, because it is there that the "poor boy" shows up to even the game (the circuslike aspect of Ronaldinho Gaúcho leaps to mind). After all, nobody has told the poor boy that the field is his as well. This is why he should construct his marvels up and to the sides, always around himself, without losing the precious ball in its capacity as an unstable point of equilibrium.

Still in the fathers-and-sons bracket, José Miguel goes on with the observations of Guilherme Wisnik, reminding us that the occupation of space is revealing when it comes to American history and the nation's march to the west. In this, one can see "the imperialist proclivity for conquest," the tendency to advance point by point across the territory, which recalls not only the American football field but also a grand poetic lineage leading "from Walt Whitman to Herman Melville, including John Ford, Frank Lloyd Wright, and land art."

We, on the other side (an imaginary "we," naturally), find our balance wherever and however we can. However, in *Veneno remédio*, nonlinearity is called in not simply to speak to the truth of a "jeitinho" or a "bossa"—"our things," as Noel Rosa called them. It would be no use to gild these "things" and hang them on the wall of our illusions like trophies, telling ourselves that we are the best even if the rest of the world doesn't know it. In short, this is neither self-deprecation nor self-glorification. *Veneno remédio* poses the urgent question of what to do with what we have: how to evolve, given the state of things?

At one point in the book, when various authors are pulled in to say something about football, Wisnik recalls Mário de Andrade, who, writing about Brazil's defeat by Argentina in 1939, imagined the Brazilians as "eleven hummingbirds," defenseless before the oiled platinum machine, as if a "Minerva-Argentina" had delivered a masterful slap to the face of an "adolescent, completely drunk Dionysius," who, in his divine stubbornness, still invented "a few subtle trips, a few samba-like ways of deceiving," and "a few lightning-swift volleys, a radiant, Pan-like thing, full of the most sublime promises."

Here is the secret of *Veneno remédio*: it depicts a sublime and unrealized promise, a spasm of beauty and genius that consumes itself in the same instant, that empties itself without becoming productive—a fleeting and useless spectacle, like the boys juggling at the stoplight. But how to turn this unproductive productivity, this glorious moment without consequences, into a project, a chain of clear and stable consequences for society? How, out of the incessant pleasure that drives Macunaíma throughout his antihero's saga, to construct something? Must Macunaíma be sent to school to learn the technique that he ignores and scorns on principle?

Garrincha is Macunaíma; Macunaíma is Garrincha. Beyond the "biographical" similarities with this *saci-curupira* with the crooked legs—exceptional birth, abnormal growth, simultaneous precocity and retardation—Garrincha is the master of the dribble, and he takes it to unimaginable extremes of grace and curvature. And the Macunaímian dribble of Mané Garrincha is, for Wisnik, the fortuitous conjunction of three terms: *ellipse* (a flight from linearity that produces a poetic effect on the rhetorical plane); *slip* (a flash of the unconscious, in Freud's vision), and *syncopation* (a contrametrical accent found in the intersection of European and African rhythms). All three are dribbles, in their own way: the ellipse is a way of getting around the next logical step, creating a suspension and an unexpected swerve in the discourse; the slip (*Witz* in the original; *ato falho* in Portuguese; *mot d'esprit* in French) is the shift that gets around the censorship of the conscience and lets loose that which was guarded in the unconscious; syncopation makes it possible for the body to slide between the beat and the backbeat, doubling over to fit into a space that resists the military step of the march and then expanding in those swaying *requebros* of capoeira that, in the eyes of more traditional writers at the turn of the twentieth century, seemed like a simple, regressive element, dangerously Africanized—and that in the modernist view was justly regarded as a treasure, something closer to our purest essence (or, perhaps, in Mário de Andrade's words, our most "sublime promises").

But nations aren't made with Garrinchas alone, and we may ask to what point a stubborn and premodern amateurism can still exist in an advancing society that is starting seriously to test the waters of its future. *Veneno remédio* has appeared, and not by chance, at a moment when Brazil is testing out the strange feeling that, just maybe, there might be a place for it at the table of developed nations. Evidently, the tension between technique and freedom, predictability and spontaneity, virtual and real, becomes an agonizing question for the country and explains, at least in part, why the "essay of national interpretation" has been reborn exactly now, in the midst of the thrust of the past decade (God only knows where it will carry us). When the transcendent question about the collective's fate starts making sense and increasing its volume, the essay becomes urgent and lets critical imagination loose the ties of strict objectivity, just as necessary as it is limiting.

Best not to get into Pelé, leaving football lovers with the task of looking for the dialogue that Wisnik strikes up with Tostão and Décio Pignatari in order to understand the utterly exceptional player who seems to have "brought the virtual into the present." Let us remain with the unresolved (and unresolvable) pendulum between technique and freedom, the well-balanced and the acrobat, which throws us into a sort of tunnel in the history of ideas, at the end of which are the luminous debates of Brazilian modernism, which in turn become relevant in the discussion that, in the midst of the dictatorship, the critic Antonio Candido made of the constant swing between "order" and "disorder"—a restless, provocative swing, which Candido would famously name, and not without irony, the "dialectic of malandroism."

When he published his essay in 1970, Candido analyzed Leonardo, the protagonist of *Memoirs of a Police Sergeant*, by Manuel Antônio de Almeida. Here, we can see precisely the problem that Wisnik tackles in his essay. In the nineteenth-century novel, according to Candido, "we can say that there is a positive hemisphere of order and a negative hemisphere of disorder, functioning like two magnets that attract first Leonardo's parents and then Leonardo. The dynamic of the book supposes a seesaw between the two poles as Leonardo grows up and participates in one, then the other, until finally being absorbed by the conventionally positive side."

It so happens that, in a critical reading of a clearly modernist bent, Antonio Candido made (according to Wisnik) "a surprisingly positive reading" when he concluded that the novel produced, in its atmosphere of negotiations, "an enchanting 'world without blame' with a democratic and tolerant spirit, against all stigmatization and witch-hunts." But Wisnik sees a discreet preference for the paradoxically positive value of disorder. It's as if Garrincha had won the battle, if perhaps not the war.

For pointing out the ways in which social structures permeate novels, Antonio Candido's arguments would be fundamental for Roberto Schwarz, who criticized Candido's flirtation with disorder—affirmed precisely when Brazil needed some order to face off against the arbitrary will of the dictatorship—in an essay titled "Assumptions, Unless I'm Mistaken, About the Dialectic of Malandroism." But before we lose ourselves in this thicket of interesting issues, we must note that the "dialectic of malandroism" refers to a balance, a "see-saw," between two poles, without necessarily indicating that either will prevail. Neither poetry nor prose, neither technique nor epiphany, neither football nor *futebol*—what we have is first and foremost radical irresolution.

The productive reading of *Veneno remédio* demands not only that the reader take the title's provocation seriously but also that he or she pay attention to the fact that its argument is carefully set up in successive oppositions, rich in their irresolution and tension: "prose and poetry," "leather ball and capital," "ritual and game," "mud and grass," etc. One need only note how the essay is constructed to see that Wisnik is writing about an *indivisible* (and not by chance; *indivisível* is the title of his recent album) unit of contradictory forces, a perpetual pendulum that proclaims itself the deepest truth about Brazil. This is not an essential truth, frozen in space and time and buried in the geological depths of "being," but a truth of tension and irresolution. And the impression remains that, whenever they can, Brazilians will fall toward the pole of disorder, because it is there that clashes are "softened" and the world is potentially made more "open."

Here we return to the bone of contention, because this supposedly malleable and porous side of things indicates precisely the bloodless confrontation, cordiality in its most generous aspect—opening the curtains of the past to reveal the thorny question of the legacy of slavery and how it was established and developed in Brazil.

One can't accuse Wisnik of avoiding the problem. On the contrary, he tries to take the bull by the horns when, taking up the dialogue between the exiled critic Anatol Rosenfeld and Mário Filho about the presence of blacks in football, he suggests a sort of "racial democracy on the field." In the wake of the first debates about affirmative action in the country, it's worth reproducing the passage in full: "We can say that racial democracy in Brazilian football prescribes (in the medical sense, of recommending a cure), but does not describe, Brazil. Or perhaps that it describes realized and significant possibilities that do not form a complete system. In other words, the country does not align with itself; racial democracy has to be thought of as something which both is and is not. This paradox is the crux of the problem."

The question is how to leave the football field and realize what is only realized as a fleeting and spectacular moment—how to spread this promise and turn it into reality or a "system," allowing society to dribble through the harsh opposition between classes and races. The problem becomes even more glaring when class and race overlap and mingle as much and as often as they do in Brazil.

Miscegenation is not, however, the simple promise of mixture. Wisnik sees no "cosmic race" on the horizon of this civilization, nor is there any intention to deny racism in Brazil (racism "à brasileira," as Roberto DaMatta would say), or to negate the importance of the *negro* movements. What we have in *Veneno remédio* is a vote for the plurality of a composite formula, as if a new, more "porous" model of civilization could spring from it, one with a healthy disregard for the straight lines that clarify, with no margin of error, who is on which side.

The path is treacherous, and Wisnik is well aware of its traps. The biggest is Gilberto Freyre's "Lusotropicalism," which, in its most unfortunate and reactionary moment, flirted with Salazarist Portugal and advocated the exceptionality and the gentleness of Portuguese dominion over the tropics (back when Portugal still had its African colonies, that is). One could argue that the political solutions of a Lusotropicalist Freyre weren't fully revealed back in 1933, in *The Masters and the Slaves*. But let us stop walking on coals and return to the horizons of *Veneno remédio*.

The ungovernable principle—which Wisnik calls, with entertaining and ironic precision, "anthropological π" suggests that we will always be approaching some undefinable quantity in this laboratory, which would be, essentially, football. Something in the sport, like a reigning uncertainty, recalls Caetano Veloso's diagnosis when he, looking in the North American mirror, reminds us that "down here, uncertainty is the rule."

The tropicalist wave, which others besides Caetano and Wisnik have joined (Hermano Vianna, for one), is carried on the belief in this threshold space, a place where order slips and ultimately fails, permitting the entrance of an unexpected, unclassifiable element. From here are born racial theorems, or post-racial ones, which not a few critics identify with a perverse form of self-negation by a country that never quite settled its scores with blacks. But this would be a way of putting authors like Wisnik, Caetano, and Hermano (different as they are) into a bubble where they are made to become representatives of a revived and poorly understood Freyrianism. This violent, reductive interpretation is a way of *not hearing* what they're saying.

Reflections on the limits of order are a vital way of thinking about the limits of classification, not to mention the limits of social spaces—which doesn't mean, of course, that the playful (dis)order on the field can break down the real, cruel barriers off the field. The problem is that this problem doesn't exist solely on the plane of ideas, and as such it forces us to face historical and sociological questions. After all, the "alchemy" of the poison/cure—Brazilian football—has yet to produce the formula to bring democracy into the plane of the real, to provoke that "reality check/fall into the real" that Wisnik proposes, and that may be the only effective way of breaking the enchantment of any magical formula. But once the spell is broken, what will become of Brazil?

PEDRO MEIRA MONTEIRO is an associate professor in the Department of Spanish and Portuguese Languages and Cultures at Princeton University. He is also associated with the Program in Latin American Studies, the Princeton Institute for International and Regional Studies, and the Department of French and Italian. Dr. Monteiro's research focuses on literary studies and intellectual and cultural history. His books include *A queda do aventureiro*, *Um moralista nos trópicos*, *Andrés Di Tella: cine documental y archivo personal* (co-edited with Paul Firbas), *Sérgio Buarque de Holanda: perspectivas* (co-edited with João Kennedy Eugênio), and *Mário de Andrade e Sérgio Buarque de Holanda: correspondência*. He may be reached at pmeira@princeton.edu.

RICHARD SIMAS

Gonçalo M. Tavares

"The Inside of Things"

> Mister Valéry earned a living by selling the inside of things. Mister Valéry did not sell the object so to speak, but only the inside of the object. The buyer would take a dish, for example, but in truth he only owned the inside of the dish. . . . Problems, however, arose when the owner of the inside of something happened to meet the owner of the outside of the same object.
> —Gonçalo M. Tavares, *Mister Valéry*

Contemporary Portuguese writer Gonçalo M. Tavares is a literary figure of international prominence as well as a professor of scientific theory at the University of Lisbon. His radical, unpretentious work, still relatively unknown in North America, offers microscopic examinations of human nature in which he tests the materials of logic and language with each sentence, reducing the world to magnified parts only to recompose it for the reader in extended literary forms. Logic and language play abound in witty texts that converse as freely with contemporary subjects as they do with world literature and Western philosophy. In a little more than a decade, Tavares has established his unique voice in contemporary Portuguese and European circles by publishing more than thirty books, translated into numerous languages, ranging from poetry, novels, and short fiction to theater pieces and unclassifiable "investigative works" such as his 2001 *Livro da dança* (Book of Dance). Internationally, his texts have inspired installations, theater, visual art, and operas. Portugal's Nobel laureate José Saramago declared of him, "Gonçalo M. Tavares has no right to be writing so well at the age of 35! One feels like punching him!" His 2004 novel *Jerusalem* and the more recent epic and singularly lyrical narrative in poetic form, *Uma viagem na India* (A Voyage to India), have been acclaimed as contemporary masterpieces.

Each Tavares book is part of an evolving, extensive oeuvre divided into such categories as "O Bairro" (The Neighborhood), a series of books loosely inspired by his view of illustrious creators: Mister Eliot, Mister Brecht, Mister Calvino, Mister Walser, and Mister Valéry. "Encyclopedia" offers three works filled with puzzlelike miniatures, on the subjects of science, connections, and fear. The quartet "O Reino" (The Kingdom) contains four novels, including his recent *Aprender a rezar na Era da Técnica* (*Learning to Pray in the Age of Technique*). Fortunately for English readers, a portion of his oeuvre is available in high-quality translations, and more are in progress.

Promotional photos and video interviews with the dark-haired, intense Tavares suggest a brooding Mephistopheles seized abruptly by the camera. Such appearances, however, disguise the uncomplicated elegance of an amiable, generous, and attentive conversationalist. He is a question mark of a writer who carves fictions in the same manner in which he thinks, probing systematically with a surgical scalpel. Too relentless and close to the bone to allow for nostalgia, Tavares's work lacks the characteristics often identified as Portuguese and contrasts sharply with the work of other writers of his generation.

In the opening lines of *Jerusalem*, Ernest Spengler is about to throw himself from his window when he receives a call from the schizophrenic Mylia. Mylia leaves her apartment at 3:00 A.M. to go to a church. Wandering the streets at the same moment, in search of a prostitute, is Theodor Busbeck, Mylia's ex-husband and the doctor who attempted to cure her schizophrenia years earlier. In the same vicinity is Hinnerek Obst, a war veteran so traumatized by fear that he is taken for a murderer. These are the disturbing figures Tavares winds up tightly and then sets in motion on darkened, anonymous city streets.

In his ominously titled *Learning to Pray in the Age of Technique*, the reputable surgeon Lenz Buchmann is a domineering figure whose days are filled with cold, unwavering decisions about life and death on the operating table. Obsessed with his superiority and believing himself destined to work on greater projects than ailing human bodies, he becomes involved in politics. He succeeds as brilliantly in the public arena as in his medical profession, advancing toward the summit of political power, until he is diagnosed with a brain tumor.

Tavares treats the body as an intimate and political figure in *Learning to Pray*, as he explores raw human impulses in varying contexts, contrasting them in wide-angle and close-up views. His novels afford the space required to create tension between the poles of systematic logic, in which a yes-or-no response is inevitable, and the less predictable decisions of fictional humans for whom no clear solution to conflict is evident. Tavares is a master at depicting this fertile confrontation. *Jerusalem* concludes with a question that exemplifies this duality, when Mylia says to the person who answers her knocking at the church door, "I killed a man. Will you let me enter?"

Born in Portugal's colonial Angola a few years before the 1974 Carnation Revolution, Tavares is uncomfortable with identifying himself with a specific generation of contemporary writers. He claims that what you write has more to do with what you read than with when you were born. "Each person has a 'library' of references," he says, "and two people from the same generation can have very different libraries. A text is the result of many influences, and the idea of generation is an exclusion." Further, he believes that personal culture is more determining for a writer than external causes, and finds cross-generational links from the past to his own writing. However, he acknowledges that although he grew up with access to his father's books and space to roam freely outside, his parents' Portugal was an isolated country where only the elite had access to contemporary culture. It wasn't so much that things were prohibited as that they simply weren't accessible.

"I don't want to be free of the past," Tavares responds to the suggestion that he grew up in a liberated environment after the Salazar dictatorship. "It's incorporated in my experience, my cultural heritage."

Most of Tavares's texts have nothing specifically Portuguese about them with respect to cultural references or locations. His literary purpose is much broader. As evidenced in his characters' names, if there is filiation in his work, it is closest to the German and central European traditions of Kafka, Musil, and Walser. He also expresses affinities with the literature of Latin America.

His work is free of any trace of quaintness or notion of a grander past, such as Portugal's folk motif of the sleeping king, known as Sebastianism, which inspired such writers as Fernando Pessoa. Rather, Tavares probes the contemporary and seemingly nonbiographical themes that link all humans: their animality as expressed in desire, violence, agitation, and fear. "Culture is what surrounds that," he notes; "the decor . . . it's not essential." The objects that people employ (a rock, a knife, a pencil, a cup) serve as extensions of emotional dimensions, and he zooms in, narrating how his characters relate to them.

"Cups and Hands"

> Mister Juarroz was always loath to pick up his coffee cup because he couldn't help but think that it wasn't one's hands that picked up objects but rather the

> objects that picked up one's hands. And this fact displeased him, since he couldn't accept that a simple cup could grab his hand.
> —Gonçalo M. Tavares, *Mister Juarroz*

"How you look at things determines how you interpret them," Tavares observes. His *métissage* of analytical thought and fictional narrative is distinctive in contemporary literature and unprecedented in the Portuguese canon, amounting to a mixing of blood that is uncannily entertaining, revealing, and savvy. His comment about viewing and interpreting is a key to reading his work. As in his books *Mister Juarroz* and *Mister Valéry*, reversing the apparent evidence of ordinary things makes for playful images and unexpected observations.

Critical of the Cartesian tradition inherent in Western scientific theory, which he confronts candidly in his fiction, Tavares comments, "In Western tradition we take things apart when we don't understand them. Understanding means to comprehend the parts rather than seeing the similarities in things. It is rich in detailed knowledge, but the cost has been great in sacrificing other perspectives." The interweaving of holistic and reductionist views is a philosophical, artistic issue for Tavares, one that he manipulates constantly to dynamic effect.

Suggestive rather than didactic, Tavares's novels are still unmistakably systematic and filled with clear intention. In *Learning to Pray in the Age of Technique*, Lenz Buchmann watches people from the window of his upper-level apartment. In the operating room, he performs surgery with microscopic precision. In his move toward political power, he imagines the same processes operating on the body politic as on an infirm human body. The longer, more spacious fiction of the Kingdom collection allows his metaphors to gain dimension and force.

"The Ingenuous Country"

> Sadness was so prevalent that people were paid to smile. Amid the city crowds, plainclothes men watched for the few smiling citizens that happened to pass by and, discreetly, ordered them to stop.
> —Gonçalo Tavares, *Six Tales*

Much of Tavares's work reads like a puzzle with echoes of a cosmic joke. There is a fertile zone between yes and no, between perfection and imperfection, between beauty and ugliness. This is the sensitive flesh that Tavares probes with words. "A book is done when I have corrected the error I made in the first sentence," he says. The notion of error is essential to his relentless analysis of reality, humans, and the material world. Particularly in his short fiction, he systematically challenges the idea of success and error, as if performing a literary laboratory test. Perhaps each writing project begins with a flaw because that is the only way to start, and it provides an irresistible stimulus for an exacting writer to work his way through the creative labyrinth and back to the beginning. His notions of truth and error are as metaphorical as they are technical.

So far, there are no professors of science theory in Tavares's oeuvre, but one senses the control of a "technical age" Lenz Buchmann in Tavares. It is revealing that at age twenty-one, with finished manuscripts already in hand, he decided to wait ten years before publishing, all the while elaborating an oeuvre that since then has allowed him to present an average of three new works per year and vault to the forefront of contemporary Portuguese literature.

Tavares is a keen observer of humans' relationship to technology, commenting in particular on its omnipresent role in contemporary life. "The new thing in our age, and what the Greeks couldn't anticipate, is technology, for example, in relation to the body. It's not what's around us but what is inside us that is different now. Traditionally, the flesh was sacred. A bullet or a blade was fatal. The natural and artificial worlds were different. Now we are artificial and natural at the same time. A factory can make a body part." For Tavares, this is the subject of ongoing speculation and ripe material for his texts.

He is fascinated by a journalist's excited report that a computer program had been created that could write news stories. The journalist marveled at a machine that could render him useless and unemployed. Tavares ponders such behavior and our blind faith in the superiority of technology. The marvel lies in how a human could be so apt at inventing a means of making him useless and admire it at the same time. "It's a kind of happy suicide. . . . One problem of our economic crisis is that we believe technical progress is equated with human progress. We have to figure out whether it makes sense that a machine replaces a human or not. It is an illusion that technology allows everyone to be more creative. Many people don't want to be poets."

It's exciting to wonder where the pace and scope of Tavares's literary production will lead, and such anticipation adds to the pleasure of reading his work. Technology could never invent the world he depicts. He retains the childhood memory of viewing the construction sites where his father worked, and how they were transformed from a hole in the ground into buildings with windows and doors. There is no doubt that in his expanding, multilevel literary oeuvre, Tavares is erecting a world that it is imperative for English readers to discover. As they do, they will discover the mutually inclusive forces of a sensitive human observer and furiously productive writing machine.

NOTES

This essay is part of a series of portraits of four contemporary Portuguese writers, written with support from Portugal's Institute Camões and the Québec Arts Council.

For more on Gonçalo M. Tavares, visit http://goncalomtavares.blogspot.ca/ or www.mertin-litag.de/authors_htm/Tavares-G.htm.

WORKS IN ENGLISH

The following titles are available from Dalkey Archive Press:

Jerusalem
Joseph Walser's Machine
Learning to Pray in the Technical Age

The following titles are available from Transbooks:

Mister Valéry
Mister Henri
Mister Brecht
Mister Juarroz
Mister Calvino

RICHARD SIMAS is a freelance writer living in Montreal with a background in literature and the contemporary performing arts, particularly contemporary music. His fiction and arts journalism has been published widely in Europe and in North America, including in the Journey Prize anthology. He also was winner of a Fiddlehead Fiction Prize. The interview with Gonçalo M. Tavares is part of a recently completed project on "A New Wave of Portuguese Writing: Four Contemporary Portuguese Writers." He may be reached at richardsimas@netaxis.ca.

LÍDIA JORGE.
A noite das mulheres cantoras.
Lisbon: Dom Quixote, 2011.

Cities recapture what they once were. Oblivion, the dissimulated manifestation of any loss, is an unresolved ever-present "endless cycle" (227). *A noite das mulheres cantoras*, the latest book by Lídia Jorge, is set in Lisbon in the late 1980s and represents the stage of a society saturated with "presentism" (Hartog). This extraordinary tale of five female singers against the ephemerality of the "minute empire" (the term Jorge uses to describe the dizzying speed of the roaring '80s) is an exercise in "acknowledging the singularities" (Traverso 2008)—"I go back to the trivialities of the past and tie myself to their use" (30)—of the collective history of the "realm of the ephemeral" (18) into which postrevolutionary Portugal and postwar Europe in general were transformed. On the one hand, these are the singularities of a group of women who are "joyful because they are so sad" (152). On the other hand, they are also the singularities of a time without "any visible order" (312), a time of both celebration and mourning. They are described from the perspective of Solange de Matos, the protagonist. Although at first sight the scenes show no causal relation to one another, they interweave the thread of the narrative as they are bound by remembrance, the absurd, and the art of improvisation when faced with memory gaps. In short, the narrative focuses on a woman's body—the narrator's and simultaneously the archetypal female—looking for a stage while straining against the transcendence of the "limitless abundance" (310) and its underlying oblivion: "If I insist on the oblivion issue, it is because maybe no other issue has been this important" (229). The stage is also the text, and the act of writing memory is a way of simultaneously celebrating and putting on the show.

The setting is the 1980s and a mysterious halo of forbidden uncertainties, the beginning of "the society of the spectacle" in Portugal, shortly after it entered the European Union. Solange, the main character and first-person narrator, is a nineteen-year-old student who has started the music group ApósCalipso with Gisela Batista, the Unstoppable Maestro, the Alcides sisters, Maria Luísa and Nani, and Madalena Micaia, a black jazz singer. They intend to change the world with their pop swing music: "We want to forget everything that is behind us and to determine everything that is before us" (198). The story focuses on the recording of their debut album, and more specifically on their rehearsals in a garage somewhere near the Tagus. In fact, a series of uncommon adventures unfold, where behind the curtain laughter goes hand in hand with naked bodies on stage—and catastrophe. Being quickly forgotten is another feature of the "minute empire," but behind a curtain there is always an old looking glass—the other side of the illusion—which is also where the world begins and ends.

This tale is told twenty-one years after the "minute night," or "Perfect Night," which is the title of the first section of the book and refers to the night on which the main characters meet again on a live TV summer game show. It has been exactly two decades since the end of the adventures described. The real threat is the past—"Anyone who would try to reproduce it would be a fool" (24)—and this dictates the need to tell the story. This is also a tale about what is left of that ghostly realm of comfort and abundance, which is buried and resurfaces over and over, because, as Jorge tells us early on, "the history of a group always reflects the history of a people" (9). The well-kept secret of this group of women mingles with the secret of this "suspended world" (14), namely, Portugal in the '80s, and it is impossible to disentangle one from the other. In fact, the tragicomic history of this secret is described as an "unstoppable mass of air" (202) of which, as it passes, only dust remains.

To a certain extent, the '80s were the time when art took over the stage; "I believe we are on a stage and all improvisation is allowed," says Solange (245). Jorge describes the memory of several bodies in ecstasy taking on several stages: time, which is volatile, reconstructed and extended, and facing oblivion; space, namely, the city, here representing the large stage of the profound social and cultural changes Portugal was undergoing in that decade. These bodies are also transformed into spectacle, "dancer[s]" (281) of memory and of the surrounding scenery, the "bright" city (150), "full of junk and drifting papers" (197), as it slowly falls asleep. However, a body vanishes. Narrative is also a way of bringing that empty space into the scene, filled by the silence of practically all that is mute in history and in memory. In a body brought back on stage, its disappearance stands out. Celebration or mourning? There is no definite premise. Meanwhile, both coexist peacefully in this "small minute world which Earth has become"

(299). What is certain is that irony is also a state of exhilaration and that the text is the balance, or the art of (un)tidying up and making everything fall into place.

SANDRA GUERREIRO DIAS is a PhD Fellow at the Center for Social Studies and the Faculty of Humanities of the University of Coimbra. As a specialist on cultural and social change and poetic arts post–25 April, she has published articles on Lídia Jorge, Eduarda Dionísio, Alexandre O'Neill, and Olga Gonçalves. She has been granted a research scholarship by the Fundação para a Ciência e Tecnologia (Foundation for Science and Technology) since 2010 and is currently at work on her doctoral dissertation, "Poetics of the Body: Performance and Citizenship in the Eighties." E-mail: sandra.cgd@gmail.com.

MÁRCIA VALÉRIA ZAMBONI GOBBI.
A ficcionalização da história—Mito e paródia na narrativa portuguesa contemporânea.

São Paulo: Editora UNESP, 2011.

A ficcionalização da história is much more than an impressive work proposing to analyze an extensive corpus of Portuguese contemporary fiction. It is also an erudite study that highlights a key theme in the country's literature, beginning with Camões and continuing to this day. Márcia Valéria Zamboni Gobbi's work becomes even more interesting if one places Portugal in the context of the European Union, taking into consideration its social, political, economic, and cultural issues. Gobbi sets out to validate the mechanisms that turn history into myth (and parody) in our times, as the title suggests, even though her perspective cannot benefit from the distance of time. This is a task that requires not only careful analysis but also detachment. Writing from Brazil, however, Gobbi does take advantage of her *geographical* distance, enabling her to follow the Portuguese historical and literary path, which, as she notes, is still "under construction." She realizes the difficult goal of promoting an "insider's" viewpoint while remaining on the "outside" through her clever use of the concept of otherness. In this way she is able to insert Portugal into the broader context of the European Union by using its differentiating characteristics: "a identidade não é o oposto da diferença: a identidade depende da diferença" (identity is not the opposite of difference: identity depends on difference; 22).

The book is divided into three long chapters that together showcase the perpetuation of myth, which can be seen as the process of transforming history into culture, and the subsequent formation of Portuguese identity. There is a theoretical and methodological introduction, in which the author crafts an argument so strong that the reader marvels at the impossibility of forming a counterargument. She begins with the evolution of the concept of history in philosophical studies, continues by delineating Roland Barthes's idea of myth, and finally discusses the concept of parody as defined by Linda Hutcheon. Gobbi does not forget, however, to revisit other authors relevant to contemporary studies, such as Foucault, Jameson, Benjamin, Gadamer, and also Nietzsche, as opposed to Carlo Guinzburg. She also develops a study of the imaginary and the real in which she makes use of historical, anthropological, and philosophical texts. This addition not only broadens the scope of her study of literature and linguistics but also cultivates an interdisciplinary viewpoint.

The second chapter deals with Portuguese myths found in contemporary literature—for instance, Afonso Henriques, Inês de Castro, and Dom Pedro, the Portuguese sea, Dom Sebastião, and some elements originating in the colonial war. Gobbi persuasively analyzes the presence of these myths in novels by Agustina Bessa-Luís, Almeida Faria, Helder Macedo, João de Melo, Jorge de Sena, Lídia Jorge, Lobo Antunes, Mário Cláudio, and Saramago, and also in two short stories, Mário de Carvalho's "A inaudita guerra da Avenida Gago Coutinho" and Herberto Helder's "Teorema." Finally, in the last chapter, she focuses on the formation of a Portuguese national identity, using Eduardo Lourenço's works as a basis for her conclusions. Gobbi also revisits Camões, the first Portuguese translator of history into fiction.

A ficcionalização da história is revealing not only in its manner of exposing the presence of historical myths in Portuguese literature today but also in its proposing a path by which a Portuguese cultural identity based on these myths can be affirmed. This is an exceedingly important contribution, especially when Portugal is contextualized in a rather vast European Union, requiring "um reposicionamento histórico, geográfico, político e ideológico que confronta as bases míticas da identidade portuguesa e a própria soberania e autonomia dessa imagem de si, sustentada por séculos" (a historic, geographical, political, and ideological repositioning that addresses the mythical basis of Portuguese identity as well as its own image of a sovereignty and autonomy that has been sustained for centuries; 246). It is worth reading.

TANIA MARTUSCELLI is an assistant professor of Luso-Brazilian studies at the University of Colorado at Boulder. Her work has appeared in *Portuguese Studies*, *Colóquio/Letras*, and *Brasil/Brazil*. She is currently working on a book manuscript entitled "Livro de linhagem do surrealismo português," which addresses the uniqueness of surrealism in Portugal when compared to its French counterpart. She may be reached at Tania.Martuscelli@Colorado.edu.

Fiction & Interviews

EVANDO NASCIMENTO
Translated by Anthony Lennard

A Portrait of the Author as a Reader

My sketch is of an author who I already am or try to be.[1] It is a portrait that is at once natural and (to quote the beautiful title of the Brazilian poet Cecilia Meirelles), denatural and denatured, whereupon the question arises: how not to talk about oneself or how, moreover, to talk about oneself?

From the outset I define the author as a reading animal, as the title suggests, hence his lack of essence, existing first and foremost as an interbook writer, the perfect example of which today would be the Catalan Enrique Vila-Matas and his portable literature. Other examples are Borges, Joyce, Thomas Mann, Machado, Rosa, Proust, and many other encyclopedic writers, who seem to carry a library on their backs, so numerous are their implicit and explicit references.

I start from the assumption that authorship is a matter of transdisciplinary reception and production. It is an instance of passage, in which several discourses are articulated and transmitted: those of literature, philosophy, arts, media, sociology, anthropology, etc., precisely because authorship is based on reading and is not a biographical essence. The biography that interests me is less factual than bibliographical, a biobibliography, if you will. The author is a device, both personal and impersonal, at the limit of anonymity. He is initially the author in the first person—"I write"—but then he must transform himself into several other persons, both discursive and empirical: he, she, them, you, we, and even the former thou. A fully self-identified author is stillborn, since he is incapable of putting on the different masks without which there is no authorship: narrative voices, characters, poetic subjects, dramatic voices, *dramatis personae*, essayistic, biographical, and social personas—in short, all sorts of masks. To paraphrase Nietzsche, I would say that the author is a composite of all the characters at a great masquerade. Without these frankly mimetic heterographical records (and heteronomic ones, according to Fernando Pessoa), he falls into the expressivism of an "I" who can only say I, never him/her, you, us, them.

This dispersed method of enunciation is what constitutes the wealth of authorship, and as much as its death has been staged, for good reasons, in recent decades, it survives its own ruin. I would say, following Derrida in *Mémoires d'aveugle: L'autoportrait et autres ruines*, that the ruin, rather than an external evil that befalls it over time, constitutes the portrait and the self-portrait. The author survives as a ruin, not in spite of it, precisely because he has metamorphosed into the reader, as Barthes announced at the end of his notorious essay "The Death of the Author": "the birth of the reader must be paid for with the death of the Author."[2]

On the other hand, in his equally famous "What Is an Author?" Michel Foucault states that "the theory of a work does not exist."[3] The same can perhaps be said about the "theory of the author," that it does not exist. Not because of an empirical contingency, that is, for lack of a theoretician fit to develop it, but for one essential reason: the question of authorship has gone through so many changes over the centuries that it is impossible to gather them into a single concept. The category of "author" comprises an extremely scattered set of factual and transcendental notions, values, and methods.

In 1978, in his course La Préparation du Roman (The Preparation of the Novel) at the Collège de France, Roland Barthes summarized his position regarding the authorship issue.[4] Exactly ten years after the publication of his little-understood essay, "The Death of the Author," Barthes explained the about-face that he underwent after the publication of *The Pleasure of the Text*. In the watershed year 1968, when he published the essay on authorship, it had been crucial to suppress the omnipresence of the author in literary studies so as to avoid the biographism inherited from the critical positivism of the nineteenth century. In traditional biographical studies, the empirical life of the author, as it were, overpowered the work, but in the 1960s, still at the zenith of the structuralist movement that Barthes had helped to start and that was soon to go into decline, it became necessary to release the literalness of the text. Barthes thereby avoided suffocating the text with any empiricism that might compromise the independence of fictional literature.

The entire power of literature was therefore taken away from the author and attributed to the reader ("the birth of the reader must be paid for with the death of the Author"). So the flesh-and-blood author died, and the author-reader was born, the Borges archivist, whom Barthes called the *scriptor* of a text made up of multiple quotations. In this sense, the only biography that really mattered was the literary one, consisting of pieces of texts that together registered the private intellectual history of each writer. But this biography was inscribed and made available above all in the fabric of the work, interwoven with the multiple threads of culture, requiring a transdisciplinary approach.

I do not think that the Barthes of the 1970s, the one of *The Light Room* and *The Preparation of the Novel*, fully broke with this conception of the author-reader, since quotability continues to be a driving force in his refined writing. We have only to check the index of names in his works during this so-called poststructuralist period to see how much Barthes the reader inseminates the author figure. There was only a displacement of interest and a rescaling of values. As I see it, there is a correspondence between the reading power and an interest in the biography (in the strict sense) of the great authors, so much so that Barthes revealed, in one of his classes, his interest in writing a biography of the composer Schumann but ended up giving up the project because he could not read German.

The facts of the life of a great author gained importance for Barthes, who was preparing to write a novel himself, marking a turning point in his career as a critic and theorist of literature and writing, although this novel, because of Barthes's death, remained forever in limbo.[5] It is as if Barthes, at the end of his life, sought in the great artists the creative power to help him carry out his own project of inventive writing, a departure from the kind of writing he had done until then. Proust presents the absolute paradigm of that *search* or *research* (*recherche*). It is not at all a question of being limited to the plain facts of a great life, but rather of understanding the relationship of tension between the world and literary creation. For example, we have to live, to waste time, in order to then rediscover time, as in Proust's case. We waste enough time to gain it back before we die via literary fiction. But if the loss of time is excessive, the work can remain forever unfinished, or worse, unwritten, because it is too late. There is thus competition between worldly experience and literary experience. The latter depends on the former for its existence, but if the former takes up too much time and space, it ends up sacrificing the invention, the ultimate justification for the life of a writer. We are therefore faced with an almost insoluble quandary, as if Barthes researched the lives of the writers he loved—Tolstoy, Stendhal, Proust, Kafka, Flaubert—for help, if not in resolving then at least in settling the tension between everyday life and literary invention. Without experience, there can be no literary work (the Work, as he calls it). But an excess of experience also prevents the achievement of the Work. Barthes asks: "How can the writer (the one I'm talking about: the one who wants to write a Work) protect himself against the encroachments [*empiètements*], the aggressions of Administration (in the broad sense of the term, broader than exclusively professional administration), the demands of life?"[6] This question has no simple answer:

everything in the world and the so-called practical life is done against the Work, but without the world or daily life, there is no Work, either. And each author must reach a balance between worldly experience and literary writing, there being no formula to solve this impasse. The biographical drama of the writer starts there, but it also ends there. One of the keys to fictional imagination, those that allow the opening and the pursuit of literary invention, is to solve this difficult problem.

Literature as Nonreading

One of the most curious books translated in recent years is Pierre Bayard's controversial *How to Talk About Books You Haven't Read*.[7] The thesis of the essay is bold, but also somewhat naïve, and can be summed up as follows: the real reader is a nonreader. The only person who really reads is the reader who gives up reading completely, working his way through the volume, so as to find himself at the end of his journey. Reading, and indeed literature, becomes a mere narcissistic projection of what we supposedly read. Developed over the course of more than two hundred pages and endorsed by such authors as Umberto Eco, Montaigne, and Valéry, all great readers, Bayard has recourse to a text by Oscar Wilde to help explain his thesis. Distorting Wilde somewhat to serve his purposes, Bayard argues that reading is really only useful when it enables the reader to discover himself and become creative. All criticism and all creation are actually autobiographical. We read another in order to talk about ourselves. The work, Bayard says,

> fades anyway within the discourse, giving way to an ephemeral hallucinatory object, a ghost-work capable of attracting all projections, which never stops transforming as a result of the interventions. It is therefore preferable to bolster it up with a work on ourselves and try to write fragments of our internal book from the few elements available, attentive to what these elements tell us that is intimate and irreplaceable. *It is ourselves that we try to listen to, and not to the "real" book—even if it can possibly serve as a reason—and it is to the writing of ourselves that we must devote ourselves, making sure not to allow ourselves to deviate from that task.*[8]

This is a fascinating argument, and one with which I would agree were it not for two basic misconceptions. First, Bayard the academic forgets that the critical conception of Wilde is dated and has a history, which is quite complex but easily summarized. It is impressionist criticism, concerned with the moods (positive and negative) that a work causes in its reader, who is potentially a writer. To reduce any or all reading to this practice, disregarding the value of others, seems to me an unacceptable blindness in a lecturer in literature, however provocative it may be. Second, the reduction of reading to "me" is as harmful as the reduction of writing to "me." Although the "writing of me" or of "oneself" is in fashion, what fascinates me in these various practices of self is the opposite of what Bayard argues, i.e., the encounter with others and not with oneself. My thesis, if I had one, would be almost the antithesis of his: I write not to find myself as a demiurge or creator, much less to aestheticize my life (a narcissistic and tedious task) but to find the other. What fascinates me in literature and philosophy is the discovery not of oneself or myself but of the he or she whom I do not know. It is these precarious and *tiny lives* (to quote Pierre Michon) that give me new life, invading the realm in which I am no longer myself. So I see myself as another, away from myself, Sá de Miranda's famous "I have fallen out with myself," populated by ghosts and fantasies of the other that I soon also become. I quote this beautiful sixteenth-century poem, a precursor of an entire genre of poetry of the twentieth century and beyond:

I HAVE FALLEN OUT WITH MYSELF

I have fallen out with myself,
I am set in all danger;
I cannot live with myself
Nor can I flee from me.

In pain, I fled from people,
Before this one became so great:
Now I would flee
From myself, if from myself I could.

What means can I expect, or what end
To the vain work that I carry out,
Since I bring myself with me
Such a great enemy of myself?[9]

Rimbaud's "I is someone else" (*Je est un autre*), little read in its original context of two letters to Georges Izambard and Paul Demeny, also means this:

the authorial device's infinite capacity to dress up as someone else.[10] This is the reason for the theme of literary and artistic transvestism, which appears in artists as varied as Vila-Matas, Duchamp, Warhol, Flávio de Carvalho, Oiticica, Almodóvar, and (more recently) the cartoonist Laertes, among others. I cannot resist quoting a small passage from Rimbaud's famous letter to Izambard about the clairvoyant: "It is false to say: I think [*je pense*]. We should say: I am thought [*on me pense*]."[11] More anti-Cartesian than this it is impossible to be. Clarice Lispector elaborates on the idea: "The shortcut with refreshing shade and reflection of light among the trees, the shortcut where I am finally me, I have not found it. But one thing I know: my path is not me, it is another, it is other people. When I can fully feel the other I will be safe and I will think: this is my port of arrival."[12]

The main examples that Bayard puts forward to defend his thesis that we read to discover ourselves and to be able, finally, to create are all men who spent a large part of their lives in libraries. Their relationship with reading and not reading is completely different from that of a young man who is graduating (Bayard's preferred public), still immersed in the natural ignorance of beginners. If Valéry, for reasons opposed to those of Bayard, defended with great irony the right not to read Proust or Anatole France, it was because he spent his life immersed in books. Like Montaigne, he selected what interested him, learning from others the discovery of self through the encounter with otherness. This is the literary journey, via reading, without which no author can be fulfilled. It was only in this sense that Barthes announced that the birth of the reader must be paid for by the death of the author. From then on (but it has always been like this, I think), every great writer has been above all a great reader. Ignorance, or the reading of the flyleaf, which Bayard advocates in favor of narcissistic writing, serves only for books without any use at all—useless books. But the reader decides what is useful, leafing through and reading one chapter or another, effectively acquainting himself with the work.

The only chapter of Bayard that excited me, despite the imposture of the author, was one in which he addresses forgetfulness as a creative factor for Montaigne. Lack of memory as a condition of writing has not yet been dealt with sufficiently. I can testify here that I am an author with a short memory. Mine always fails me when I need it. I never dare to quote a sentence or particularly a verse from memory; it never works—my mind goes blank or things come out all garbled. I can refer to an idea or notion, or summarize a concept, but memorize each word of a long passage—never. I simply remember very little of the books I have read and the movies I have seen, just as Montaigne complained many times of picking up an unknown book from the shelf and discovering that he had already read it and annotated it, without being able to recall a single line! He thus began to write the date of his reading on the last sheet of each volume, giving a brief impression of the work, so as not to have to pick it up again needlessly, especially when the book was bad. His trouble remembering was so serious that the author of the *Essays* often did not recognize the sentences people quoted from his own works; he even forgot the books he himself had written![13]

(Something similar happens with the famous report that Clarice Lispector gives us, in *The Discovery of the World*, of an encounter with Guimarães Rosa. Rosa told her, she says—if this is not just one more of Clarice's fictions—that he read her "not for literature but for life." He then went on to quote many passages from the book. She claims that she did not recognize any of them.)[14]

Nothing distressing about that. For me, real memory is a function of this great ability to forget. We remember so that later we can forget. But the opposite may also be true, as in Drummond's beautiful title, *Forgetting in Order to Remember*. In any case, remembering and forgetfulness are not mutually exclusive but feed each other. Freud's "magic notepad" has great retentive capacity because it erases, deleting what was written on the translucent sheet and marking the block of wax.[15] That many authors have forgotten what they've read, and even what they've written, does not imply that the texts have disappeared forever. They have just been displaced to another dimension, which was once called the unconscious but today might better be called the "virtual" (a question I will defer to future reflection).

I often feel embarrassed because I cannot summarize a novel I read or a film I saw a month ago, or even last week. Never ask me the exact title, the names of characters, much less the actors' names—I never know for sure. But I would never say, like Bayard, that I read these books or watched these films in search of myself. When I saw them and loved them, that experience was so intense that a real and virtual mark was made somewhere in my body. And the intensity of this mark will certainly emerge, consciously or unconsciously, at a future time of creation, because virtually it remains there, or rather *here*, like an inscription in my body. If I wish to check some information later, I can simply look up the book or see the film again—thanks to the proliferation of interactive media, there is always a record of the work in question, whether in a physical library or in a file in cyberspace. Google makes things easier, although it is also a very dangerous instrument; no aid to memory is innocent. The Internet has real value only when combined with a good book culture; otherwise we are exposed to a great deal of misinformation.

I would never say that forgetting details of a book or film amounts to ignorance, negligence, or simply nonreading. Rather, this is a case of what Nietzsche calls *active forgetting*, a function as important as, or more important than, memory. Such forgetting is decisive for our mental and physical health:

> To temporarily close the doors and windows of consciousness; to remain undisturbed by the noise and struggle of our underworld of helpful organs cooperating and diverging; a little peace and quiet, a little tabula rasa of consciousness, so that there is room again for the new, especially for the more noble functions and employees, for governing, foreseeing, predetermining (for our organism is arranged hierarchically)—this is the usefulness of active forgetting, as I said, a kind of doorkeeper, a caretaker of psychic order, peace, etiquette: from which we can see that there could be no happiness, joviality, hope, pride, *present*, without forgetfulness.[16]

It is therefore crucial to erase memories, freeing the mind for new ones—to remember one minute to forget for all eternity, perhaps, and only to recover what was actually important, bringing it to the fore and to the corps de ballet of the new writing. Active forgetting is what enables true memory, memory that reinvents the world through writing, by preparing the novel. This might be the difference between the writer who is just cultured and a rather erudite critic. Both read a lot, but the former reads intensively (referring to Deleuze, a reader of Nietzsche) to exercise the inalienable right of deletion. The scholar, by contrast, reads to have a vivid memory of books and of authors, places, and characters, which he loves to quote, preferably by heart. Bayard is right about this: too much information functions as a block to invention, but the converse is also true: he who misreads literally as a discovery of himself will spend the rest of time traveling around his navel and reading one and the same text, that of his autobiography. I remember in passing that *Inscription and Erasure* is the title of a beautiful book by Roger Chartier.[17] The title could be paraphrased as *Type and Delete*. As is well known, the word "delete" came into the English language in the sixteenth century, meaning to "remove, suppress, deliberately omit," derived from the Latin root *deletum*, supine of the verb *delere*, to "destroy, annihilate, efface, blot out."

What we call conscious memory is a delaying tactic: the facts and the meanings attributed to them are reconstructed retrospectively, only after the original inscription, often already forgotten.[18] To remember is to recover something from oblivion and then forget it again. Between two forgettings there emerges a memory, until it disappears forever in the waters of the river Lethe, a powerful tributary of unmindfulness. Writing, creating, and inventing are also, or especially, an art of "de-leting," of making inscriptions and experiences go to sleep so that later an active reader can reactivate them, bringing them to the precarious space of our memory. This process is always in vain, but it is worth the effort of the delayed recovery. This is the monumental event that in the West and elsewhere is called writing: this game of life and death between inscribing and deleting, survival and annihilation, recording and consummating, recalling and forgetting, etc. Nonreading, or what Harold Bloom called (but meaning something else) misreading, becomes a powerful category of reading.[19] We unread not out of ignorance but because of an active desire to forget, to continue to read, that is, to write-read as Barthes defines the erotic category of reading in "Writing Reading."[20] The best readings are difficult because they force me to lift my head, in a continuous and polyphonic movement of reverberation with the other's text. The true and carnivalizing polyphony is that of reading, not that of the text itself. The erection of reading eroticizes the body that delights in the text of the other, reinscribing it in his body as spilling and spilled subject matter in his own bibliographic corpus.

Was this then what Derrida once called dissemination, potent reading, erect, spilling the semen of knowledge, spilled and converted onto previously blank pages—the seminal and disseminating blank of Mallarmé too, where everything begins, the abyss to which everything goes, as in a Throw of Dice: "Can be / only / the Abyss / raging / whitened / stalled / beneath the desperately sloping incline / of its own wing through / an advance falling back from ill to take flight / and veiling the gushers / restraining the surges," and later, "that rigid whiteness / derisory / in opposition to the heavens"?[21]

This is the immeasurable contemporary event that digital media only spread; if the Web is not the only model of the virtual (other models have existed and will continue to emerge), it is where we have plunged for at least a decade, or, to use another, more appropriate metaphor, it is where we have surfed as active reader-writers.

If digital democracy does not always promise high-quality writing, the wealth of digital data is undeniable, in principle within the reach of anyone who has mastered the language of the writing assignment. The literary archive is irrevocably connected to this large collection, not only because many works can be read, consulted, or downloaded from the Web but because today's writers are formed more and more by the global network of computers. The virtual or real book is, and will increasingly be, one of the modalities of what Barthes and Derrida called philosophically *text* and *writing*, precursors of hypertext. When *Grammatology* announced in 1967 the end of books and the beginning of writing, its purpose was not physically to destroy books but to demonstrate their historical limits, to be not exactly overcome but subsumed within a broader, less codified, and less standardized notion of writing. I quote Derrida in one of the essays from *Paper Machine*:

> Now what is happening today, which is announced as the very form of the future of the book, still as a book, is, *on the one hand*, beyond the closing of the book, the irruption, the displacement, the disjunction, the dissemination without any possible meeting, the irreversible dispersion of this complete codex (not its disappearance, but its marginalization or its being put aside, according to ways that we would need to return to), but simultaneously, *on the other hand*, the constant reinvestment of the book project of the book of the world or the world book of the absolute book (that is why I also described that end of the book as interminable, endless), the new space of writing and reading of electronic writing, which travels at full speed from one point to another in the world, and which links, beyond the boundaries and rights, not only citizens of the world in the universal network of a potential *universitas*, of a mobile and transparent encyclopaedia, but any reader as a possible or virtual writer, etc. This reawakens a desire, the same desire. This re-induces the temptation to consider that whose figure is the global network of the www as the ubiquitous book finally reconstituted, the book of God, the great book of Nature, or World-Book in its onto-theological dream finally fulfilled, even though it repeats the end as future.[22]

Reading Schemes

The literal defense, with or without irony, of nonreading also results in great ingenuity because deep down it ignores what I call *reading schemes*. This general category is actually personal and nontransferable; otherwise it becomes dogma (or *paideuma*, as it was called previously). Each author-reader invents his system of reading. The typology that I suggest here should never be generalized in itself; each of us can certainly invent his own, according to the taste (and the knowledge) of the pleasure of the text. For me, there are at least five types of text available for reading. I emphasize, however, that this typology is interchangeable; the same work and the same author may appear in more than one classification, moving from one sphere to another and complicating their own taxonomy. Everything depends on the community of readers. The examples are also brief, but they could be multiplied to infinity; many authors and works important to my formation are not included here.

First, there are the authors and works that are read or heard in childhood and adolescence: the fairy tales of the Brothers Grimm or Perrault, the Monteiro Lobato stories, children's and teenagers' stories, legends and folk tales. But we must also consider the authors who started me on more adult reading, which in fact took place only from the age of twelve or thirteen. The following list of names is purely arbitrary, according to my memory, which often, as I said, fails: the romantic and Parnassian poets Álvares de Azevedo Fagundes Varella, Casimiro de Abreu, Gonçalves Dias, Castro Alves, and Olavo Bilac; the novelists Érico Verissimo, Jorge Amado, and Hermann Hesse (the fundamental *Steppenwolf*); and the poet and lyricist Vinicius de Moraes. These are authors whom I loved and emulated in my tender years. They constitute what Barthes beautifully called *Ursuppe*, the original soup, with which I began to nourish myself, especially the rich work of Jorge Amado, which I read passionately while still attending elementary school in the Camacã multifunctional school in Bahia. Certainly, what my schoolteachers, my family, and my friends put into my hands was also significant, in addition to the abundant bibliography of cartoons and comic strips (all my love of pop culture comes from those; I will never be able to ignore it). I feel no need to go back to those authors, unless a biobibliographical incident occurs. So there they are, like a seminal and inseminating milestone of the literary field.

A second type are the authors who sealed my taste and my desire to write—who sharpened in me what I would call the *imitative impulse*, already aroused by the first group of authors. I remember in particular Dalton Trevisan, whom I first read when I was about fourteen or fifteen and continued to read, then stopped reading for decades, recently went back to, and still love. Another great initiation was the Abril Cultural edition of *Don Quixote*, which also had such a great impact on Milan Kundera and his *Book of Laughter and Forgetting*. In the same collection by Abril I read Dostoyevsky and Kafka, as well as Sartre, among many other classics. Then came the discovery of Thomas Mann and his gigantic *Magic Mountain*, *Death in Venice*, and even the magnificent *Doctor Faustus*, at different times of my life. In school I read Machado de Assis and José de Alencar (the former remained lifelong reading), Carlos Drummond de Andrade, and João Cabral de Melo Neto, first in their beautiful poetic anthologies and later in their so-called complete works. A great shock came with *First Stories*, then *Grande sertão veredas (The Devil to Pay in the Backlands)*, by Guimarães Rosa; by this time I was at university at the age of eighteen, thanks to the influence of Evelina Hoisel, the great professor of literary theory. Rosa's *Grande sertão* is one of those books that I have read and reread throughout my life, one of maybe ten such books (I am keen on lists, like the filmmaker Peter Greenaway). They are essential rereadings, although today at some distance. I reread *Grande sertão* especially for the musicality, at once refined and barbaric, of the speech of the ruffian-poet-philosopher Riobaldo. An even bigger shock was the discovery of *The Hour of the Star*. Clarice Lispector became a river that never failed to pass through my life; in fact, I have just completed a work of critical readings from her texts for the collection I am editing for Record Publishing. I could go on listing titles and authors, but that is not my intention here, and it would just be a synthesis.

The third category of authors includes those for whom I developed a passion at some point but to whom, for reasons of time, I seldom return. I am thinking of Gregório de Matos, whose work I only occasionally reread in bits and pieces; much of what I think and dream of doing in poetry comes from him. Also Jorge de Lima and his oceanic *Invention of Orpheus*, as well as several other poems, which I began to read in a course with Judith Grossmann; at a certain point his texts were for me poetry par excellence. I have always read Cecilia Meirelles and continue to reread her, but sparingly, so as to be moved by life as it is. Marguerite Duras is an author whom I would like to reread in her entirety, and in the original—but will there be time?

The fourth category, the *hors concours*, so to speak, would include authors who are read out of compulsion and the desire to understand their achievement: Proust (I recommend, for those who do not have time, reading the first and the last volume of *Remembrance of Things Past*: the first to learn about his writing, the last because it is perhaps the most revealing book I have ever read—Marcel's *Thousand and One Nights*, as he himself reveals in the end. All the other volumes are research on how to become a writer, and when he finally learns the secret, it is too late; his work and his life come to an end. Art was too long for such a short existence. Hence the paradoxical impossibility of time rediscovered: the secret of the narrator-character, that is, the true principle of all writing, will die with his silence. Literature is just a great *rehearsal* for the book that is forever to come, as Maurice Blanchot understood very well). The Greek tragedies, especially those of Sophocles, the tragedies, comedies, and sonnets of Shakespeare, and the tragedies and comedies of Nelson Rodrigues are rivers flowing through a lifetime, without a starting point or an end. Everything flows into these fluent and confluent writings. That would be my way of reinterpreting and shifting the notion of influence, by replacing it with that of *confluence*. The most important authors and works for a particular writer are confluents of a small, new stream, which may one day take on another dimension; that is certainly the bet. Decisive poets like Pessoa, Whitman, and Kavafis also inhabit this fourth category.

There is, finally, a fifth category of rare books, for me impossible to read, not because of some shortcoming but for structural reasons. How could I have read *Finnegans Wake*, by Joyce, for example? Anyone who tells me that they read it in the traditional sense is lying. It is a true hypertext, written in several languages. It would be necessary to know Greek, Latin, Irish, and many other languages in order to decipher all the codes of this nonbook. The work resists any simple deciphering, and every translation is always approximate because of the plethora of voices. Moreover, as I have already said, the true polyphony is that of the reader: each of us is more or less able to hear the voices of a text, so as to, as it were, repitch them. All of us are potentially writers. We bring the real sound boxes with which we multiply the virtual polyphony of any text, generating gibberish. Another text that is unreadable for me is the Bible. I've read several of its books, at different times in my life and with multiple purposes, not feeling the need to go through it completely but always in bits and pieces according to specific interests, religious ones being the least of them. Also some texts by Guimarães Rosa—I am thinking particularly of *Tutaméia*—would be in this category of books *that don't allow themselves to be read* (as Poe says in the beautiful "Man of the Crowd," itself a story that does not allow itself to be read completely, as we shall see below). Some tragedies by Shakespeare, such as *Hamlet*, fall into this category.

This would be, briefly, my personal list of books. It is a nondogmatic list by a reader who has long dreamed of being an author through an imitative instinct, strictly instinctual, almost an animal thing. An instinct that always makes you want to be the other, to expropriate yourself in a continuous movement of alteration, becoming another, and de-identification.

Before finally closing the typology of this personal list, however, I would like to pay tribute in part to Bayard's thesis. There would be, then, factual nonreadings. There are a host of these. Like Clarice Lispector, I have not read many masterpieces of Western humanity, much less Eastern, if such boundaries still remain. I have read scarcely anything of the great Russian novelists: one or another Tolstoy, one or another Dostoyevsky, besides the Russian poets in the wonderful translation by the Brothers Campos and by Boris Schneidermann. I note that there is no longer any excuse for not reading them, because there have been many good translations directly from the Russian in recent decades in Brazil. I have not read Balzac as I would like to, but I am proud to have dedicated myself from an early age to Stendhal and then Montaigne. I have never read José Lins do Rego properly, but I plunged deeply into Graciliano Ramos, whom I read to this day with great pleasure. Et cetera. The list is huge, by definition, and I could go on quoting names, read and unread, venerated and forgotten. I must declare, however, that I read with great joy a French translation of the four volumes of the *Thousand and One Nights*, before they had been translated directly from Arabic into Brazilian Portuguese.

There are also books that I have heard of: some I intend to read when I have time, such as the Anglo-German Sebald and the South African Coetzee, both of whom I have actually started to read. Others I definitely have no intention of even browsing through, such as certain writers who are in fashion. I prefer not to name them, leaving it to the imagination of the reader to guess who they are (after all, it is very easy; many of them are always in the public eye). Factual nonreading—Bayard is right—should be an active category, just like forgetfulness, in no way a fault or an original sin. But neither should it become a way to defend ignorance in the name of creativity as self-assertion. The risk is to fall into the void of no invention, neither one's own nor the other's. In this case, the nonreader is always converted to a nonauthor—or, what is worse, a mediocre author.

There were also the many theoretical readings to which I dedicated myself, especially after I went to study in France in the 1990s. Works of literary theory and philosophy have been crucial to enhancing my appreciation of ideas in fiction that writers like Thomas Mann, Lispector, and Machado, among others, awakened. Right now I find myself involved in contemplating the questions and themes of Descartes, Foucault, and Derrida, as I develop an essay on the history of madness. This all contributes greatly to the way I conceive and elaborate the difficult and pleasurable literary invention.

Baudelaire: The Artist and the Man of the World

In "The Painter of Modern Life," an essay on Constantin Guys originally published in the daily newspaper *Le Figaro*, Charles Baudelaire makes a distinction between the artist and the man of the world. Without scorning the former, the poet prefers the latter because it is broader. Instead of simply "mundane" in the negative sense, the man of the world has, so to speak, the *feeling of the world* (to quote Drummond again). He is therefore *worldly*, rather than a cosmopolitan bourgeois who has the money to travel. He would not even necessarily travel around (at least this is my interpretation), and his knowledge of animals, plants, and humans would be of such a vast scope that the mere category of artist would not be broad enough to encompass it. For the artist, says Baudelaire, is a specialist, and therefore has a rich but limited view of the world. Basically, he does not reject the world; in my view, he only judges it insufficient to be a man of the world. I infer, therefore, that one must be a man of the world as well as an artist. Someone who could fully achieve this near perfection would have the sensitivity of the artist and the magnitude of view of the man of the world. He would be the true painter of modern life, epitomized, for Baudelaire, by Constantin Guys and Eugène Delacroix. This is how the author of *The Flowers of Evil* defines the two kinds of men: the man of the world "is interested in the whole world, wants to know, understand, appreciate everything that happens on the surface of our globe. The artist lives very little or even not at all, in the moral and political world."[23] Baudelaire himself combined both types: the great artist who does not give up the rest of the world, thus uniting, in his view (and who would contradict him?), the three most valuable categories of human existence: the ethical, the political, and the aesthetic.

Baudelaire later praised artifice to the detriment of nature.[24] Showing himself to be especially anti-Rousseauean (he does not mention Rousseau, but he depicts the eighteenth century as the rival to be crushed), he demonstrates how nature is brutal and barbaric. Art should not embellish nature, making more complex what in its natural state is simple. The artist's work aims to surpass the natural world, creating the world of true beauty. The author of *The Flowers of Evil* is not afraid to praise makeup, because adornment expresses the sophistication of a people. The so-called savages are quite civilized, because they cultivate a great love of colors and ornaments of every kind. What distinguishes the human animal is reason, which enables him to invent artifices in every way imaginable. Makeup is not used to hide ugliness or age but to enhance what is already beautiful. Artificiality is second nature, the more useful because it reveals the talent (not natural) of human labor. In short, art, *mimesis*, does not examine the natural world in order to copy it but invents its own world, with unique rules, to achieve the perfection of what is good and beautiful. Therefore, unlike Rousseau, Baudelaire sees man in nature as insufficient, inadequate. Only art, used in the service of reason, can improve the natural man. In this sense, women's makeup, which is totally artificial, is the paradigm of the artistic. Baudelaire thus has a very different view from that of Prince Hamlet, who condemns outright the masks that beautify women as evidence of the malignancy of females—the "chaotic cosmetic" (to quote a dense verse by the composer and singer Caetano Veloso).

The Impossible Reading and the Rereading

In closing I would like to refer to a text that I reread recently for the umpteenth time, though I found it more enchanting this time than ever before. It is the short, magnificent story by Edgar Allan Poe, "The Man of the Crowd," which I reread in a trilingual edition of 1993 that includes, in this order, Baudelaire's wonderful French translation, the English original, and the good translation by Dorothée de Brouchard into Portuguese, with excerpts by Benjamin. I think that if I have read this short text so many times, it is precisely because it does not allow itself to be read. I am paraphrasing a comment already referred to, by the first-person narrator of the story, who in turn is quoting what the Germans used to say about the booklet *Horticulus animae*, a prayer book that was very popular in the sixteenth century, in Latin and Germanic editions: "Er lasst sich nicht lesen" (literally, it does not let itself be read), the narrator declares at the beginning of the story, and he repeats this statement at the end. Surely this applies to Poe's own remarkable story and perhaps to great literary texts in general. The best literature is that which cannot be read, and when we have finished reading we are assailed by so many doubts left by obscure passages that all we can do is look forward to rereading it. This was well understood by Guimarães Rosa, who proposed two indexes for his *Tutaméia*, one for reading, another for rereading. I quote one of two epigraphs by Schopenhauer in *Tutaméia*, both advocating the need to reread: "Hence, therefore, as I have already stated, the first reading requires patience, founded on the certainty that, in the second, much or all will be understood in an entirely new light." Again, Bayard was right, but for very different reasons than he argues in his book: there is always a trail of nonreading in reading; that is why we need to reread, for the discovery of the other to take place more fully, though never completely. And so we close the pages of the best books thinking of reopening them as soon as a new opportunity arises. Like when they invite the reader-author to speak at the opening of an exciting symposium.

NOTES

1. This is the modified text of a lecture given in the graduate program in literature at the Federal University of Espírito Santo on 6 October 2011, the Academy of Literature of Bahia on 18 November 2011, and the graduate program in literature at the State University of Rio de Janeiro on 28 November 2011.

2. "La naissance du lecteur devra se payer de la mort de l'auteur." Roland Barthes, "La mort de l'auteur," in *Oeuvres complètes* (Paris: Seuil, 1994), 2:491–95.

3. Michel Foucault, "Qu'est-ce qu'un auteur?" in *Dits et écrits I: 1954–1969*, ed. Daniel Defert and François Ewald (Paris: Gallimard, 1994), 794.

4. Roland Barthes, *La préparation du roman I et II: Cours et séminaires au Collège de France (1978–1979 et 1979–1980)*, ed. Nathalie Léger (Paris: Seuil/IMEC, 2003).

5. Entitled *Vita Nova* in homage to Dante, this novel remained unfinished owing to Barthes's tragic death—he was run over by a van—on 26 March 1980.

6. Barthes, *La préparation du roman I et II*, 289.

7. Pierre Bayard, *Como falar dos livros que não lemos? [How to Talk About Books You Haven't Read]*, trans. Rejane Janowitzer (Rio de Janeiro: Objetiva, 2007).

8. Ibid., 199, emphasis added.

9. In Sá de Miranda, *Poesias Escolhidas* [Selected Poems], ed. José V. de Pina Martins (Lisbon: Editorial Verbo, 1969).

10. Arthur Rimbaud, *Lettres de la vie littéraire: 1870–1875*, comp. and ed. Jean-Marie Carré (Paris: Gallimard, 1990), 37–53.

11. Ibid., 39.

12. Clarice Lispector, "Em busca do outro" [In Search of the Other], in *A descoberta do mundo* [The Discovery of the World], ed. Paulo Gurgel Valente (Rio de Janeiro: Nova Fronteira, 1984), 166.

13. Cf. Michel de Montaigne, "Des livres—Chapitre X," in *Essais*, ed. Albert Thibaudet and Maurice Rat (Paris: Gallimard, 2002), 387–400.

14. Lispector, "Conversas" [Conversations], in *Descoberta do mundo*, 193–94.

15. Sigmund Freud, "Uma nota sobre o 'bloco mágico'" [A Note on the "Magic Notepad"], in *Edição standard das obras psicológicas completas de Freud* [Standard Edition of the Complete Psychological Works of Freud] (Rio de Janeiro: Imago, 1976), 19:283–90.

16. Friedrich Nietzsche, *Genealogia da moral: Um escrito polêmico* [*The Genealogy of Morals: A Polemic*], trans. Paulo Cesar Souza (São Paulo: Brasilense, 1987), 58.

17. Roger Chartier, *Inscrever e apagar: Cultura escrita e literatura (séculos XI–XVIII)* [*Inscribe and Erase: Written Culture and Literature (11th–18th Centuries)*], trans. Luzmara Curcino Ferreira (São Paulo: Ed. Unesp, 2007).

18. I address the relationship between memory and forgetfulness in Nascimento, *Derrida e a literatura* [Derrida and Literature], 2nd ed. (Niterói: EdUFF, 2001), 165–270.

19. Harold Bloom, *Um mapa da desleitura* [*A Map of Misreading*], trans. Thelma Médici Nóbrega (Rio de Janeiro: Imago, 1995).

20. Roland Barthes, "Écrire la lecture," in Barthes, *Oeuvres complètes*, 2:961–63.

21. Cf. Stéphane Mallarmé, "Um lance de dados jamais abolirá o acaso" [A Throw of the Dice Will Never Abolish Chance], trans. Haroldo de Campos, in *Mallarmé*, 3rd ed., ed. Augusto de Campos, Décio Pignatari, and Haroldo de Campos (São Paulo: Perspectiva, 2006), 156–57, 165; cf. Mallarmé, "Un coup de dés jamais n'abolira le hasard," in *Oeuvres complètes*, ed. Bertrand Marchal (Paris: Gallimard, 2004), 1:362–87.

22. Jacques Derrida, *Papel-máquina* [*Paper Machine*], trans. Evando Nascimento (São Paulo: Estação Liberdade, 2004), 30–31.

23. Charles Baudelaire, "Le peintre de la vie moderne," in *Critique d'art*, ed. Claude Pichois and Claire Brunet (Paris: Gallimard, 1992), 343–84.

24. Ibid., 374–78.

EVANDO NASCIMENTO is an associate professor at the Universidade Federal de Juiz de Fora. He concluded postdoctoral research at the Freie Universität–Berlin on the contribution of Walter Benjamin's work to deconstruction. He is internationally acknowledged as a leading specialist on the work of Jacques Derrida. He also specializes in the interactions among literature, philosophy, and the arts. As a scholar he has published and edited several books, among them *Derrida e a literature* and *Pensar a Desconstrução: Jacques Derrida*. He also is the author of *Retrato desnatural*, and his book of short stories, *Cantos do Mundo*, was a finalist for the prestigious literary award Portugal Telecom de Literatura. He may be reached at evandobn@uol.com.br.

MILLICENT BORGES ACCARDI

The Story as Question Mark
An Interview with Portuguese Writer Jacinto Lucas Pires

Jacinto Lucas Pires, born in Oporto in 1971, currently lives in Lisbon. He is the author of three novels written in Portuguese, *Do sol* (2004), *Perfeitos milagres* (2007), and *O verdadeiro ator* (2011); a short story collection, *Assobiar em público*; the novella *Azul-turquesa*, and *Livro usado*, a travel book about Japan. He has also written plays (*Writing, Speaking*; *Extras*; and *Sagrada família*) and film scripts. He is part of a new wave of younger Portuguese writers gaining international recognition. His story "L" (included in this issue) is thus far the only work that has been translated into English, anthologized in *From the Edge*, a bilingual edition of Portuguese short stories (Lisbon: Ulices/Ceaul, 101 Noites, 2006).

In June 2011 Pires gave a public reading of "L" (translated into English by Patricia Odber de Baubeta) at the Center for English and Anglo-Portuguese Studies at Universidad Nova de Lisboa for the first annual Disquiet conference, sponsored by Dzanc Books. Disquiet brought together Luso writers from all over the world for workshops and discussions with prominent Portuguese writers, including Richard Zenith, Fernando Pinto do Amaral, and António Lobo Antunes.

The name Disquiet was adopted from the poet Fernando Pessoa's *Book of Disquiet*, in which Pessoa writes:

> Once more I see you—Lisbon, the Tagus, and the rest—
> A useless onlooker of you and of myself,
> A foreigner here like everywhere else,
> Incidental in life as in my soul

Pires is an animated performer. His boyish charm mixes with a dark brooding aspect and his reading is punctuated with exuberant childlike gestures. As the protagonist in his story "L" walks the city streets, for example, Pires raises his hands and demonstrates playfully how the left and right hands flail about. "I take pains to move all of me. Not just my legs and one arm swinging at a time, no, I don't like that, that's ugly, no, whenever I walk, it's so strange, I make the most of each inch and move all of me. A kind of walk that begins in the pelvis and spreads out, upward and downward, like a kind of dance."

Pires wears a light blue long-sleeve shirt that matches his eyes. There is a mischievous glint like a smile when he talks, as if life itself is a joy to him.

A Renaissance man, Pires is a writer, musician, actor, and filmmaker. He even sings with the band Os Quais and jokes with the audience that until that morning he wrote a column about soccer for a Portuguese newspaper.

During his talk, Pires discusses the craft of writing, explaining that there is a hidden danger in writing in Portuguese: "When you read and when you write it is almost too easy to make it sound beautiful. And this is a problem. . . . It has an extra difficulty because Portuguese is also a poetic-sounding language." And writing that is easily beautiful runs the risk of being precious and of calling attention to itself in a way that distracts the reader and takes away from the story.

"The great decision is what not to write," he says. What to leave out to make for a more powerful story is one of the most important tasks a writer can take on.

He feels that in writing, as in acting, one takes on a role and inhabits the characters: "Writing is to tell a story with people being there." Comparing his work to the film *Being John Malkovich*, Pires claims that "the only way to understand is being this guy. Being this guy waiting in this story." It is not enough merely to describe him. "I'm not talking about or commenting about a character but being him for eight pages," Pires says. He follows where the work takes him, because "the writing knows more than you do," and "good intentions do not make good literature." Writing, for Pires, is "imagining the truth," and a part of that truth is where you live. "Lisbon inspires me to be strange people."

Discussing how change is often difficult in writing and other arts, particularly fado music (a melancholy Portuguese style of folk song, often sung by peasants), Pires jokes about traditional fado being transformed slowly through the addition of new instruments and melodies. "Fado is a little like the Vatican. You cannot change it all at once—it's a religion. Fado, I mean."

"Ideas and images are the same thing," according to Pires. His tales often begin with an image or a place, rather than a plot. Pires got the idea for "L" from a house. "In Campolide there is a single house right in the middle of large buildings," he explains, "as if it does not fit in; and on the other side of the house is nothing—around it there's really just the waste ground that isn't really anything; that's why I say it's a house, like, in the middle of nowhere."

Pires's stories are often derived from a lyrical impulse rather than from the requirements of narrative, as in this description of the boy's journey in "L": "I carry on along the shoulder of the road to the big avenue with tall buildings. I want to see if I can find something to eat or drink but all I can see are pages from magazines with photographs of famous people."

With respect to Portuguese being read globally, Pires believes that Portuguese and Portuguese-American writers should "put big ideas in small places, small stories," rather than promote a political agenda or write for a particular cause. He's seen many great writers get lost in the web of writing for the government or to push a particular opinion or agenda, a wrong turn, in his view, that undermines the writing, making it uninteresting and artificial. "It's very political, how a society takes care of their dead," Pires observes, explaining that each culture is responsible for the living and the dead, and that how the dead are cared for is a political choice.

When asked to comment on the inherent challenges of translation, Pires admits, "Translations are the shadow of the original"; they follow the story around very closely but they are not the original. They are connected; they mirror it, but they cannot by definition be the same thing.

Asked where he gets ideas for his fiction, Pires talks about the boys he sees on the streets and in the metro stations of Lisbon, who hand out business cards for Professor Mamadu, an alleged psychic and astrologer. "Do they believe in this shaman or are they just doing it for a living?" he wonders. The place, the motivation of people—that is what fascinates Pires and informs his work.

Q: When I heard you read your story "L," the reading was more of a performance, with gestures, and your delivery was animated, with even some physical comedy. How has your experience with theater affected your public readings and your writing? Has it informed it or enhanced it?

A: Yes, theater—writing plays but also participating in rehearsals, discussing scenes, and dialogue with actors and directors—is a great school for writers of any genre, I think. Because, on one hand, it forces you to be in the character's shoes, to *be* the character in order to really get his point of view, his specific voice, and on the other hand because theater is the territory of clarity and stylization. It's a paradox, maybe, but a true one: if you want to write complex, nuanced, even ambiguous novels or short stories, you have to know the lesson of clarity and stylization.

Q: You mentioned that your work has not been translated into English. Yet you speak English very well. Is there a reason why you do not translate your own work?

A: English is not my first language, and that makes a difference. Also, I think that what is great about translation is the idea of an encounter. Like traveling or playing. Someone who comes from a different language, a different culture, arrives at a text, and this *distance* is actually a good thing, it's what makes it possible to really *see* all the things written in the text, to see it through the fresh eyes of a new language.

Q: Both Portuguese and Portuguese-American writers seem to suffer from a lack of exposure or popularity in the United States. Perhaps an identity crisis? There are great writers, but very few people know about them in America. Do you think this is true, and what can we do to spread the word?

A: It is true. And yes, we've been living in an identity crisis for ages now, since we "came back" from the "whole world" to our little Atlantic, European rectangle. . . . But, honestly, I think this "lack of exposure" says more about the United States than about Portugal. I love America, don't get me wrong, but I'm afraid there are no magical solutions. The only way would be to show some of these stories (translated versions, of course, and that costs money) to American editors. I'm sure that if some of these writers were published in the U.S., they would find an audience.

Q: Does language affect your stories?

A: It doesn't only "affect"—language becomes the story. When I think about a story, I don't think of it in a neutral, blank, synopsis way; I think of it more as a "charged mass," where what you tell and how you tell it are really the same thing.

Q: If your stories were written in English, would they be different? If so, in what ways?

A: Definitely. Because of what I just tried to explain above. The world in Portuguese just happens differently. In English I would be a different person and a different writer. In Portuguese, I try to write "against" the tics of "poetic" Portuguese. I try to cut the load of adjectives and adverbs that sound "beautiful" but tend to cliché-zise (is this an actual word?) your vision. I try to be honest and to write all these mysteries that surround us in day-to-day life in the most transparent possible way. But one never knows, that's part of the joy. I guess in English I would write lyrical, hard, comic, sci-fi stuff.

Q: Is Portuguese an inspiration to you? What do you like about the language?

A: It's much more than that. I feel, I think, I dream in Portuguese. When I write, Portuguese is the place I'm in—there's the famous saying by Fernando Pessoa: "my homeland is my language." When I write, Portuguese is the tool and the matter, it's the air I breathe. In that sense, yes, I guess you can say it is an inspiration. What do I like about it? Portugal's Portuguese is a very elegant language on paper that becomes very shy out in the world. When it is spoken, its vowels shut down and suddenly it's like a beautiful young nun trying to dance at a worldly party. It is the language of "fado" in a time when "fate" is so out of fashion.

Q: Do you have a favorite Portuguese saying? And what is it? Like "only the good die young" or "all's well that ends well."

A: A good one is "Mais depressa se apanha um mentiroso do que um coxo" (literally: it's easier to catch a liar than a limping man). It's a good thing for fiction writers to remember.

Q: Describe your writing routine (or nonroutine). Do you write in the morning, for example? Do you write at a desk or outside? Do you play music or prefer silence?

A: I prefer to write in the afternoon and through the night. I like mornings to read what I've been writing—and cut, cut. I need silence, but I'm getting used to having children going around asking, "Dad, do you know this Beatles song?"

Q: What other writers do you admire?

A: I'll name three: DeLillo, Bolaño, Chekhov.

Q: What ability would you like to steal from another writer?

A: DeLillo's precision, Bolaño's boldness, Chekhov's wisdom.

Q: Does writing matter? Do you feel that writing makes a difference in the world?

A: It's a good question. That's the difference writing makes in the world: asking questions.

Q: What are you working on now?

A: I've just published my third novel and I am reading it across the country (next stop, Coimbra). I'm also working on a nonfiction book collaboration with a photographer, Tiago Cunha Ferreira, sponsored by the Gulbenkian Foundation, about young, talented Afro-Portuguese men and women.

Q: What books or stories of yours have been published in English?

A: None. Well, there's that story, "L," in the anthology *From the Edge*, a bilingual edition of Portuguese short stories (a showcase for Portuguese writers, really).

Q: Some of your images are dreamlike. What role, if any, do dreams play in your work?

A: You're right, but I'm not sure I know the answer to that question! My last novel, called *O verdadeiro ator* (The True Actor, in a literal translation), is actually full of dreams. I tend to write dreams as actual scenes, as "facts," and sometimes "factual" scenes become dreamlike. As if dreams and reality weren't exactly different countries. A Fellini-type of hyperrealism?

Q: You play in a band. How does music inform or affect your writing? Do you listen to music when you write?

A: No, not at all. I need silence to write, though I'm getting used to have my kids interrupting me with questions about soccer or whatever. I wonder if that's changing my work in some way. I like to play music in between my writing. Music as a kind of refresh button; it empties my head in a wonderful way. After music, I can go back to my work and read what I'm doing with new, *clean* eyes.

Q: What was the first story you remember writing?

A: It was about a man on a bus that went around Lisbon. I don't remember what happened, I just remember this idea of movement and my will to characterize the man through what he saw in the glass (the city, his reflection, the passing of things, et cetera).

Q: How do you revise? What is your revision process?

A: I revise as I am writing and then I revise the whole thing when I get to the end. After that, I get away from it for a time—weeks, months, it depends—and then I go back to rewriting it. It's a coming and going process.

Q: Do you consider your stories fables or tales that teach a lesson?

A: No. I think of them as question marks.

MILLICENT BORGES ACCARDI is the author of three books: *Injuring Eternity*, *Woman on a Shaky Bridge*, and *Only More So* (forthcoming from Salmon Press Ireland). Accardi is the recipient of fellowships from the National Endowment for the Arts, CantoMundo, the California Arts Council, Barbara Deming Foundation, and Formby at the Special Collections Library at Texas Tech. Research interests include Portuguese fairy tales, Kay Boyle. She is an independent scholar with a BA in English from California State University, Long Beach, an MA in literature (ABT) from CSULB, and a Master's in Professional Writing from the University of Southern California. She may be reached at millb@aol.com.

JACINTO LUCAS PIRES
Translated by Patricia Odber de Baubeta

L

It's been two days and two nights since my father stopped opening his eyes and closing them and winking just one of them with, like, a strange smile as if he were sharing some joke with me that didn't need words, for example if a very fat woman was going past outside or if the wind came and turned the men-in-suits-and-ties' umbrellas inside out, and he's stopped smoking, and putting on and taking off his sturdy boots, and he's also stopped getting up out of bed and going and standing next to the window looking out with his light-colored eyes, I've never known if they're blue or green, at the road, the cars, the people, the rubbish blowing about, well, he's stopped doing a lot of things, just about everything, to tell the truth, all he does now is stay lying down in his room, facing the ceiling but with his eyelids closed, a skinny father naked on the rather old bedspread, just making a silence and a smell of intestines and sweat or maybe not exactly that but not so very different from that. I, of course, didn't really know how to react to this change, but in the middle of all my confusion I did manage to decide that after two days and two nights had passed I would go out at nine o'clock in the morning, no matter what happened I would go out. It's nine o'clock in the morning, that's why I'm going out. I've got a watch that tells the time very clearly, it was my father who gave it to me, I don't know how he got hold of it, one day he turned up and he was wearing it. He wore it on his wrist for two years, then he got fed up and gave it to me. It's a digital watch, with straight numbers. The zero is an upright rectangle, the nine is a square with just one leg. It was made in Taiwan.

Our house, mine and my father's, is a little house, in ruins, but even so it has a roof, and its very own color that I haven't seen anywhere else. Not exactly a color, more a tone, a grayish-brown with patches of damp and dirt. It's, like, in the middle of nowhere, on waste ground that turns to mud when it rains, where the worst cars of the people who work in the buildings are parked, the biggest and the best cars go inside the buildings. It's a house, like, which just has tall blocks around it and a kind of expressway that passes close by. Everything, the buildings, the road, even a shopping center, everything is fairly close to the house, but not exactly on top of it, because around it there's really just the waste ground that isn't really anything, that's why I say it's a house, like, in the middle of nowhere.

I carry on along the shoulder of the road to the big avenue with tall buildings. I want to see if I can find something to eat or drink but all I can see are pages from magazines with photographs of famous people. I'm not that desperate. I feel as if I have a drill in my stomach that's twisting and turning, but when I move, when I walk, it's better, as if the slow movement of the drill in my belly is hindered by my general movement. When I walk I take pains to move all of me. Not just my legs and one arm swinging at a time, no, I don't like that, that's ugly, no, whenever I walk, it's so strange, I make the most of each inch and move all of me. A kind of walk that begins in the pelvis and spreads out, upward and downward, like a kind of dance or almost, I don't know how this would look from a distance, how someone passing on the other side of the street would see me, would it look artistic, like dancing, or not really, not really? But the important thing is that this somehow helps me, it's a way to get about but also to clear my head, take exercise, although that doesn't interest me that much, and a way of not having to think about my body. That's what really matters. Now I stop.

On top of a pylon a mess of electrical things. All sorts of cables and whirling things that look as if they're some kind of sign. Behind, on high, a very blue sky and that thing so real, like, full of flashing and complicated mechanical stuff, human complications, objects mixed up together without rhyme or reason, objects I don't know what they're called but they might be called turbines, poles, wires, switchboards, like something worthwhile in its own right, like a sign. I look at that thing for fourteen minutes, I time it on my watch, and then I carry on. My belly hurts. Let's see if walking, like, I feel a bit better.

Cars go past, the colors almost always the same, white, black, dark blue, and red, and they make a noise but it's a noise that doesn't bother me at all because I am so used to it, so very used to it, I think I'd feel poorly and get a headache if it disappeared, a noise that is like a kind of noisy silence, something there right in the background that goes vroom without stopping, nonstop, without stopping. And the buildings have people who come out and go into them, and they're as high as the sky, and there are pictures reflected in them, for example other buildings or sky with clouds or flashes of brightness like little suns.

On the pavement people look at me when they're far away, but then they avert their gaze and when they come close they pretend they can't even see me, they pretend I'm not even there, but the way they look down at the ground or in the other direction leaves no room for doubt about their lying. I try very hard to look at them, but it doesn't work. I try to look at them just for a laugh, because it doesn't actually help at all. Anyway, I have to say I don't know what I'm going to do or what I ought to do. That's one reason why I waited at home for two days and two nights before going out. My father's the one who left the house and went and sorted out things for us to eat or else things that could be exchanged or even money, which was quite unusual, almost completely impossible even, maybe it happened once, if at all. Once or twice, no more, certainly. But, anyway, I don't know how he did it. Probably, he was out there just waiting for the right moment, a lucky break, I don't know.

I have a white shirt and a purple jacket, one of those [ones] with big shoulders, oversized. Of course, the shirt is already a bit on the grubby side, with some stains, earth, like, or whatever, and the jacket is far too big on me and has two stains on the back, it already had them when my father brought it for me, but apart from that it's a nice outfit and even if I say so myself it actually suits me quite well. It's the trousers I have a problem with. The hems are coming down and so at times I tread on them and lose my balance a bit.

Which means I fell face down in the street.

And then to my great surprise who should I see when I get up but Marlena.

Marlena's a pretty woman, a bit fat and she doesn't have many teeth left now, but pretty, with her hair dyed blond and she always wears short, tight skirts. I know her because one day, on my twentieth birthday, my father turned up with her at home and said for the two of us to go to his room. In the bed where he's now lying down, like, making a silence and a strange smell she showed me how to take off all my clothes and put them back on again. When I'm on my own I never take them all off, because I get cold. Not even in the summer.

"What are you doing here, London?" she asks me. That's what she calls me, London.

"Well, I was walking along and . . . er . . . er."

"You went arse over tip," she says, and smiles a toothless smile with her eyes suddenly very wide open, and her eyebrows a single stroke sketching an arch across her forehead, and this embarrasses me a bit.

"Yes . . . huh."

"Your father, how is he? I haven't seen him for . . ."

"He's having a lie down."

"Fine. You don't have any money, do you? Do you want to come with me, wander about a bit, take a turn, eh?"

"I don't have any money," I say. "I don't have any money, but I would thank . . . think me . . . it would please me . . . yes, it would please me very much to take a turn with you, Marlena."

"Oh, I can't after all, I forgot I have to go to the shopping center, sorry."

"No, it doesn't matter, Marlena. Goodbye."

I stand and watch her as she moves off, her legs fat but with the slenderest ankles, very slender, her fat backside inside the tight-fitting skirt, then I work up my courage and turn back to my path. As I watch her walk, like, in the distance my face has suddenly become slacker and longer, I feel my cheeks sagging inside, as if there is too much of them, loose flesh, and that this, whatever it is, immediately spreads through my arms, reaches my shoulders and hurls itself back down and when it reaches my hands it makes them heavy, with the weight of blood, full of blood, full of a desire for red blood under the skin and the nails, and at the same time there is a kind of slowed-down explosion in my chest, oh! in the hole of my chest, and my whole body is a broken body, fragmented, something like that.

Between the tower blocks and low houses, I walk for I don't know how many miles for an hour and three minutes, I time it on my watch. The three is a capital E facing left. The façades have that good light when the day is nearly over but this changes into shadow and darkness and I look up and there are dark clouds closing in. Big clouds, very dark, very close to each other covering the blue color.

An old badly shaved man is watching me from the door of a tall building covered in scaffolding. He watches me even when I walk up, unlike all the others. When I go right up close to him, on the pavement, he shouts at me, "Hey! Hey! You're Lopes's boy, aren't you?"

"Eh? . . ." Some people call my father Lopes. " . . . Yes, yes, actually."

"What?" asks the old man.

"Yes, I'm the son."

"Ah, I thought as much, I certainly thought as much! . . . You know, I'm a great friend of your father's. A great friend. That is, we sometimes get together to play cards there in the park, up there, see?"

"Yes."

"Right then, one day he showed me a photo of you. Did you know that? Yes, yes . . . one of those instant photos you take in a booth, you know? One of those instant photos, you know? That was before your time, you probably don't know, right? But you're just the same, it's incredible, just the same as the devil in the photo. Those photographs, you know the ones? Instant photos, that's what they're called: instant photos, those photos normally completely ruin people's faces or at least, I don't know, they change them, the people in them almost never look the way they really are, do you understand? But not you, I can say that about you, Christ, not you, you look, you're just the same, it's the spitting image of you. Well, look here, your father showed me that photo of you, an instant photo, I don't know if you know what they are, probably not, now they almost don't exist anymore, now there are new techniques an' all, but anyway, I was saying, your father showed me that photo of you . . . now, when was it . . . it was, well anyway, today is Wednesday . . . we usually meet on Mondays . . . but not last Monday . . . nor the Monday before that . . . look, that makes it more than a fortnight . . . it must be more than a fortnight . . . perhaps more and, don't you see? I still recognized you, eh?"

"Right," I say.

"Did I or didn't I recognize you?"

"You did."

"Did I or didn't I recognize you? Eh?"

"Yes."

"Yes indeed," says the old man, and he falls silent looking at my face. In the direction of my face but through it, it seems. For a moment no one speaks. It's a bit embarrassing being, like, in the street with that old man looking me in the face without speaking.

"A coincidence . . ." I say.

He seems to wake up. "And your father, how is he?"

"He's . . . having a lie down."

"Great, great," he says, still half-absent, as if separated from the words, as if through me he had seen something terrible or important, and he turns to go back into the building. I watch him move away, closing the door of black glass behind him. I think, I didn't know my father had a photo of me, and I'd like to see myself in an instant photo.

Further ahead, I'm crossing a huge, deserted square, which is enormously unlucky, when it begins to rain, pelting down, hard and heavy, persistent, rain, rain, I repeat. I see a kiosk with a little roof which might help perhaps if I huddle beneath it, but I don't run. A man has a certain pride. No. I carry on with my usual walk, without thinking, an artistic movement that goes downward and upward from the pelvis, etc. I don't know what anyone watching from a distance will make of me, but this is how I get about and there's nothing more to be said about it.

Now sheltered from the rain, underneath that little roof, looking at the square which is very white because of the water falling and also because it's so big and empty, like, at the same time, everything at the same time, I have contradictory feelings. I'm happy because I've got away from that awful rain but I also imagine Marlena and think about being with her so that she can show me again how to take off all my clothes and put them on again and then I have an urge to go out naked into the square and walk calmly, in my own way, to suffer the consequences beneath the rain that, well, let's say it doesn't stop and it goes thud, thud, thud on the cobblestones, on the houses, on absolutely everything there is, hard and heavy rain, persistent, rain, rain, I repeat.

But then again, it's obvious that I'm not going to do that.

My stomach hurts, that thing like a drill in my stomach twisting and turning, so I set off walking to see if I can shrug off that kind of image. I think about things that have nothing to do with it. And I walk along close to the buildings, under the balconies, the overhang of the entrances, the shop awnings to avoid the rain. I thought I loved the rain, but that was when I was inside the house and I had the window, the glass of the window, separating me from the water so to speak. I liked to see the almost invisible little lines that sometimes can only be seen if you squint your eyes like a Japanese, just a tiny little bit open, looking, like, or else against dark colors, dark things, I liked to see them bend and unbend with the wind and I liked the people with umbrellas, I really really like umbrellas, I don't know why, I think they're cheerful and mad and funny, then there's a gust of wind and they all turn inside out well I never, it's really, how do you say it, it makes you split your sides, you fall about laughing, you die laughing. When he saw something like that, that kind of thing, umbrellas blown inside out or dogs looking to both sides before crossing the road or fat women prancing along, my father would wink an eye and smile, like, he'd tilt his head ever so slightly and he'd look at me like someone saying "Did you get a load of that?" without actually saying a word.

Silence.

Suddenly it's nighttime and I'm standing, my stomach all twisted and burning, under the last awning before the waste land. I look up at the black sky and see a light falling. A shooting star? An airplane? I don't give any importance to the thing in itself, so to speak, but rather to what it might, so to speak, represent, as a materialization, a conclusion, a closing, of whatever, no matter what it might be, had been opened, launched, because of the electrical mess on top of the pylon against the blue sky which I looked at for fourteen measured minutes appearing before me like some kind of sign, so to speak.

A sign, I think, and I break into a run, now, yes, no longer moving myself in that loose-jointed way, more than loose, incredibly free, but running, spot on, the way it's meant to be, like top athletes in a competition, head slightly down and my body thrusting forward, further and further forward, yes, I'm running as much as I can, my legs feel empty inside, sprinting in between the rain, I run and run and there's nothing to eat, I think, I'm giving up eating, I think, and I don't stop until I get inside the door of the house.

In the room my naked father, now a slightly different shade, no longer so characteristic, patches of damp and dirt that come from inside, lying on the bed on top of the bedspread. It doesn't smell too good. Even more original and difficult to explain than in the morning.

I begin to poke around his old bits and pieces, dropped in a corner, clothes, objects, bits of objects, an impeccable Panama hat. In a pocket I find: an instant photo. I look at the photograph and to begin with I don't like it, then I do. I put it in the window, propped against the glass, looking out at the rain falling in the night. From this side it's just a white rectangle with the letter L written on it.

Then I push my father a bit further toward the edge of the bed and I lie down beside him. I look at the ceiling and listen to the sounds in the street and in my head and the worms eating the woodwork and whatever else there is and, inside that terribly dense smell which was never, but never, my father's smell, I fall asleep.

Tomorrow I'll do exactly the same.

JACINTO LUCAS PIRES was born in Oporto in 1971; he currently lives in Lisbon. He is the author of three novels written in Portuguese, *Do sol*, *Perfeitos milagres*, and *O verdadeiro ator*; a collection of short stories, *Assobiar em público*; a novella, *Azul-turquesa*; and a travel book about Japan, *Livro usado*. He has also written plays (*Writing, speaking*; *Extras*; and *Sagrada família*) and film scripts. In 2008, he was awarded the Prémio Europa—David Mourão-Ferreira. He keeps a blog at: http://oqueeugostodebombasdegasolina.blogspot.com.br/.

MARIO ARAUJO
Translated by Alison Entrekin

The Extreme Hour

The boy is sitting on the sofa in the living room watching TV. But he knows that in just a few minutes he won't be anymore. At nine thirty on the dot, although this is a nebulous idea for him, his mother comes to whisk him off to his bedroom. A kiss on his cheek, sweet dreams darling, and darkness.

He lies there motionless under the blanket listening to the sounds that escape from the TV over the frontiers of the living room. When it finally silences, he presses his ear to the darkness. In the room next door, the baby deserves full attention; in the garden, the inaudible slowness of the snails; in the street, not a single car. And like this, keeping watch without seeing palpable things, the boy finally drifts off to sleep. When he wakes up the day will be in full swing, and that is all he knows of the moods of light, of the brightness-darkness of the world.

The most impressive spectacle he has access to is twilight, which he finds daily in the vacant block next door. It is a slow, sad thing, like a kind of multicolored shipwreck, and reminds him of the image of one beast eating another beast. His musings on the nature of twilight are always cut short by his mother's nonnegotiable call and the aromas of dinner.

But the boy's dream, the biggest of all, his heart's deepest desire, is to one day see midnight. He nurtures a veiled admiration for it, as it is the most famous of all nocturnal hours and because it only offers itself occasionally to human eyes—to his, for example, never. He imagines it to be pitch black, the tarry heart of the nocturnal body whose color fades at its extremities. He imagines that it is a narrow path between two abysses. Or the moment when all creatures hold their breath, only to, immediately afterward, continue on as if nothing has happened. He dreams so much of midnight, and it may well be that it has already brushed past his window outside, unnoticed, while dreamed by him.

Back in bed again, sweet-smelling sheets, nice blanket. The baby cries a little through the thin wall, but his mother and father are listening out. There is also a cousin of his mother's who is spending some time with the family until she finds a job. Crumbs of TV sounds reach his bed in the form of indistinct dialogues interspersed with music. Suddenly, his bladder full, his foot touches the floor. He opens the door slowly, without turning on the light, and disintegrates into the corridor to reintegrate only ten meters later, already in the bathroom.

On his way back, relieved, he dares to take a detour and peeks into the living room: deserted, the TV is keeping up the only dialogue in the house on its own. His father, mother, and cousin must be getting ready for bed. He hears the bathroom door close. Curiosity; a desire to raid the kitchen and steal the hours on the clock over the china cabinet. But he decides to avoid the risky maneuver and jumps back into the corridor. He opens and closes his door in a second, without waking up the room that remained sleeping without him, leaving behind the lit, palpitating rooms. He hides his desires under the sheet and lies there resigned until sleep comes. It is quick because, in spite of all his restlessness, the boy isn't used to the infinite waits of the night, its hours loose and without reference, like an invertebrate. Perhaps, wandering about lost in these marshmallowy hours, he would become nostalgic for the day, with its precise skeleton, its well-defined architecture, and then begin to miss himself.

During the night, his desires tucked under the sheet become a plan, the first plot woven out of the hitherto loose threads of his spirit. Thus, when he breaks his fast before the plastic bowl prepared and served by his mother, the boy is no longer so innocent.

As the day goes on, he secretly rests between the beats of his skipping heart, saving his energy. He snoozes for two seconds while his mother soaps up his back, snores covered by the sound of the cutlery, makes use of commercial breaks to get on with the dreams that he won't have time to dream later.

At nine-thirty, his mother flips the switch and the shadows in his room race to hide under the furniture. His mother smoothes the sheet and blanket over his chest and leaves. The cousin clears her throat in the living room. Why does the TV volume go up in commercials? His own dry cough shakes his abdomen and, seeking to relieve his bladder, he heads into the corridor again.

All the lights in the house are on; he feels as if life is going on behind his back. At midnight there must be a big celebration, with people hugging one another and talking in loud voices and the digital clocks blinking a peculiar 0:00. On his way back from the bathroom, relieved, he quickens his step to the kitchen, where a kettle is boiling alone, and steals the old alarm clock with noisy hands, which tread on each second as if in high heels. He returns to his room without messing up the dark and holds the alarm clock to the window so that the light coming in from outside, from the lampposts and half moon, helps him follow the work of the hands. It is ten twenty-eight.

In one eye, the descent of the big hand, in the other, the surprise of the garden clothed in shadow, as he has never seen it before. The rose bushes almost unrecognizable, confused with the fence. This, in turn, mixed with the walls of the neighboring houses. The houses transfigured by the streetlamps. And everything dissolving into the black air. All of the contours memorized during a lifetime—nine years!—are lost.

The wind shakes everything, but the dark shadows don't fall, they appear to be nailed to objects. The boy is left agape, obliged to rest his gaze on branch after branch until he relearns each color and shape. Suddenly, he gets a fright like a pinch, the sort his mother gives him: he brushes his pajama sleeve on the clock and it topples from the window ledge! But the sound of it meeting the ground coincides with the boy's cough. An ugly cough, like a dog behind a closed door. His mother tends to him, already back in bed, with honey and watercress cough syrup, a hand on his forehead, smoothes the blanket on his chest once again and leaves. The cough crosses the night, scattered through the wee hours.

It was ten forty-six the last time he saw the clock, which now rests broken under the blanket with him. Sensing that the danger of his mother is already distant, he takes it to the light of the window for assessment. There is the big hand, inert, while the small one still struggles, trying in vain to continue its barely begun climb. The hand pulses, advances in the space of one minute to then return to where it was before, bogged in.

The boy doesn't know how much time has passed since the fall, but he borrows the school material that was holidaying in his backpack and sets out scribbling a careful operation in multiplication in a notebook. Talent in mathematics. Struggling against the seconds that now pass in absolute silence, and in the small light from the window, he concludes that he will have to count almost until five thousand!

Back under the covers with the old alarm clock. Eyes closed. 331, 332, 495, 517 . . . Proudly: I am faster than the seconds! Little by little, however, the quick march of time that he invented himself begins to stumble and lose itself along the dark path. In the darkness reality strays. He imagines his body outside the walls of his room. He imagines the plants in the garden inside the room. What was the distance between his bed and the wardrobe again? What if a filthy rat were about to brush past his pure cheek? He rolls onto his side, accommodating his two long arms together between his knees, as if seeking shelter in himself. Comfort on the fat pillow, the smell of fabric softener on the blanket, his father's familiar snore. And thus the same process as almost every night takes place, when his arms slide from his chest and his slack fingers let the thread of his Ave Maria slip. A little fear of hell. But what nice darkness, what delightful night, and how the rumbling of a car engine in the street below caresses him.

He wakes up with the high light of the morning, the kitchen already awake for hours, the murmuring of the pressure cooker, the sound of water in the sink. With his eyes closed, he gazes through the curtains at the garden he knows, with the rose bushes bathed in sunlight and the clothes drying on the line. In his school backpack, slumped as it waits for the books yet to be bought for the new school year, he hides the broken clock. But how to explain its absence in the kitchen? His mother must have noticed already, since all of the morning's tasks are authorized by the hands of the clock.

To his surprise, however, his mother says nothing over breakfast, although the empty space over the china cabinet is evident. The radio supplies the measurement of time necessary for the organization of the domestic tasks. The boy is not sure whether to put the clock back in its place or not. He mulls the matter over for a few minutes, in silence, as he watches the mixture of milk and cereal flakes disappear from the bottom of the plastic bowl. He finally decides to decide nothing, getting up from the chair in an impulse and racing out to the yard, with the sound of a motor car on his lips.

The boy takes advantage of the day to prepare: a fifteen-minute nap on the foosball table during halftime; a minute longer lying in the grass after being fouled by his invisible opponent in a simulated soccer game; a couple of hours of meditation in the attic, among dust and old magazines, where he also finds refuge from any investigating his mother might want to do.

At night, at the end of the second soap opera, realizing that the moment to leave the living room is nigh, and trusting that his mother is entertained with the baby, he turns to his father and asks what time it is. He wants to know what to do. Nine twenty-five, says his father in a loud, clear voice. Is his mother, in silence, an accomplice? At this exact moment, the baby quiets down and his mother takes him into their bedroom and nestles him in the cot next to the double bed, where he will sleep as long as he wants, until he feels hunger, thirst, a fright or the discomfort of a wet diaper. He will wake up whenever he wants, reflects the boy about his little brother, and this can even mean at midnight, he thinks, feeling relegated to an exiguous limbo, squeezed between the free world of babies and the permissive universe of adults.

The creaking of the wooden floor announces that his mother is coming and he asks his father again: it is nine thirty-three.

He brushes his teeth counting, good night to his cousin, his mother's kiss in the bedroom, the blanket, but the counting doesn't stop. He is alone in the dark, juggling numbers and the holy words of his prayer. Religious obligation fulfilled, and having counted to 867, he goes over to the window, the sill at nose height, leaving his mouth submerged. He stretches his body then, in an effort to commit all of his senses, and there he stays, among numbers that are increasingly grand, stratospheric, and the mesmerizing sight of the shapes in the garden, modified by the night.

The day is always on the move, the sun winks without stopping, putting in appearances, then leaving, restless, fickle, and colors transform constantly. But nothing compares to the night, with its unmoving, or almost unmoving, tones that only change very subtly, and it is precisely this variation in texture, as a counterpoint to the passing minutes, that the boy seeks, with his two hands resting on the windowsill and his chin resting on top of them.

He sniffs the air carefully, looking for signs of the midnight that approaches. Will it be blacker, whiter, colder? Will the outrider that announces its arrival be a big din or a solemn pause? Or a siren heard from afar? Will the animals and plants in the garden hold a big demonstration, a march past the now unused, ownerless clothesline, or will they merely observe it in respectful silence? There is also the possibility of a ghost parade, as they say usually takes place at midnight, and with this thought goose pimples kiss the back of his neck. Ghosts, hauntings, lost souls, what color will they be? Some say a dense white like milk, others that they are transparent and, in this case, they must take on the background color, meaning black. Or they are like gases and smoke, which are a rarefied color, and tend to become thinner as they drift into the air. He should be prepared, should souls appear, in the event that the soul of his dog, buried in a corner of the garden, at the foot of the wall, accompanies the procession.

He has so much going on: the counting, now at a height hitherto never dared; the goose pimples that clung to the back of his neck and stayed there; the martyrdom of his elongated body; his breath fogging up the glass; but, above all, there is the sleepiness that is insinuating itself through the cracks in his concentration. And, at the vertiginous number of 3,976, against all odds, he falls asleep.

He awakes with a start. He dreamed that the morning was coming through the window and that he could do nothing to stanch it, and soon the murmuring coming from things going on in the kitchen began, the water, pots and pans, his mother clearing her throat. But now he realizes that the night is still there. The hard part is figuring out which night it is that parades motionlessly in front of him. A night without a clock is like a creek without a paddle.

There is no point resuming his count now. It is evident, however, that the landscape on the other side of the glass hasn't presented any apparent change. Branches and leaves lulled by the wind, points of yellow light on the lampposts, the half-closed white eye of the moon. There is no reason to believe that midnight has passed while he nodded off, because he couldn't have tolerated that uncomfortable position for so long. He is thus possibly on the outskirts of midnight, mindful of the texture of the sky and the composition of the air, which soon, soon will begin to transform until they are unrecognizable.

Time passes.

More time passes and nothing happens. The day has its own production of moods and states of mind, while the night is a monolith.

The boy leaves the bedroom, taking care not to make the wooden floor growl under his footsteps, groping the furniture, controlling the tickle in his throat. On tiptoes, he goes into the kitchen and finds the radio, which he turns on at a low volume. The radio is an old model, the kind that doesn't show what time it is, but only reveals it in words, in the breaks between one song and the next. At the moment there is no music playing, but an endless yackety-yacking, a long dialogue whose content he can't discern at that volume, and so he must wait. What he hears appears to be a question-and-answer game. Then comes the nightly news.

Then the radio finally says what time it is: eleven forty-eight. He immediately starts a new count, like in boxing rounds and basketball games. This time, the pulsing of the numbers in his head is accompanied by the beating of his distressed heart. He heads for his room slowly, forced to be careful, the rhythm of his footsteps in disharmony with the rest of him. He reaches the window and contemplates the night that remains blank, making him doubt what the radio just said and what any clock would say. Then, kneeling on a chair, he starts to open the window, impatiently but slowly owing to his lack of strength, softly sliding the windowpane up until it clicks, while the night begins to light up his room, with its cool wind, its aromas and firefly lights. There is only one minute left. He feels a shiver, no doubt explained by his innate fondness for nature, because he too counts branches, dew, leaves, and stones. He starts counting more slowly now, drunk on the smells from the garden, and sixty long seconds later, he understands that midnight is the secret hour in which snails and jasmines get together to exhale. Somber colors explode in a vibration not perceptible to diurnal creatures. The silence outside superimposes the silence inside, being a cooler silence, disturbed by sounds that are always unpredictable, while the silence inside is stagnant, oppressed between his father's roars and the baby's sighs—only his mother has learned the art of sublimation even when unconscious. Invaded by the silence, by the fragrance and the blackness of the night, the boy's room no longer belongs to the house; it has been annexed by the world. Midnight is, in fact, the hour of extreme night.

But midnight only lasts a second, or a minute, and he needn't wait for the small hours to unravel their yarn. Then, with his face caressed by the cordial wind of the deciphered enigma, he slides down the windowpane and returns his body to immobility under the warm covers. Deep down, he knows that night really is a statue, unchanging from eight until five. He sleeps peacefully.

MÁRIO ARAÚJO was born in Curitiba, the capital of the Brazilian state of Paraná. He has published two books of short stories: *Restos* and *A Hora Extrema*, which received the prestigious Prêmio Jabuti 2005. He is currently finishing his first novel. He may be reached at marioaraujo63@yahoo.com.br.